Nuts, Bolts and Magnetrons
A Practical Guide for Industrial Marketers

Paul Millier and Roger Palmer

JOHN WILEY & SONS, LTD
Chichester · New York · Weinheim · Brisbane · Singapore · Toronto

Other Wiley Editorial Offices

John Wiley & Sons, Inc., 605 Third Avenue,
New York, NY 10158-0012, USA

WILEY-VCH Verlag GmbH, Pappelallee 3,
D-69469 Weinheim, Germany

Jacaranda Wiley Ltd, 33 Park Road, Milton,
Queensland 4064, Australia

John Wiley & Sons (Canada) Ltd, 22 Worcester Road,
Rexdale, Ontario M9W 1L1, Canada

John Wiley & Sons (Asia) Pte Ltd, 2 Clementi Loop #02-01,
Jin Xing Distripark, Singapore 129809

British Library Cataloguing in Publication Data
A catalogue record for this book is available from the British Library

ISBN 0-471-853259

Typeset in 10/12pt Palatino by MHL Typesetting Ltd, Coventry
Printed and bound in Great Britain by Bookcraft (Bath) Ltd, Midsomer Norton, Somerset
This book is printed on acid-free paper responsibly manufactured from sustainable forestry,
in which at least two trees are planted for each one used for paper production.

P.M.

To Pascale, Clement, Renaud, Maxence and Arthur
let this book be the proof that this wonderful year in England was not just a dream.

R.A.P.

To Ginnie who makes everything possible
and to Sophie and Anna who make it necessary.

Contents

PART VI DEALING WITH YOUR INTERNAL ENVIRONMENT 207

PART VII THE MARKETING EXPERT'S TOOLBOX   243

Acknowledgements

Paul Millier would like to thank the people and institutions that supported the writing of this book. In particular he would like to thank Patrick Molle, Director of EM LYON, and Daniel Michel, formerly Head of the Marketing Group of EM LYON, for allowing him the opportunity to spend one year abroad to conduct his research. Sincere thanks also to Professor Leo Murray, Director of the Cranfield School of Management, and Professor Martin Christopher, Deputy Director and Head of the Marketing Group, who welcomed him with so much kindness and support during an unforgettable sabbatical year in 1999.

Gratitude is also expressed to the FNEGE (*Fondation Nationale pour l'Enseignement de la Gestion*) who supported this work. This allowed Paul Millier to carry out the research that preceded this book.

He also recognises and acknowledges his immense debt to his fellow researchers, Robert Salle and Jean-Paul Valla, who developed some of the principles of industrial marketing that underpin this book. Lastly Paul Millier would like to express his warmest thanks to Roger Palmer, his close colleague in this unique experience of coauthoring a Franco-English book.

Roger Palmer, on behalf of both himself and Paul Millier, gratefully acknowledges the contribution made by the managers and MBA students who have attended our various industrial marketing programmes and became involved in subsequent discussions and focus groups. Their interest and involvement in our work provided both raw material and the incentive to progress. We also thank the dozens of practising managers throughout Scandinavia and Europe who were interviewed or completed questionnaires as part of the background research. In particular we would like to express our grateful thanks to Jean-Robert Passemard, Executive Vice-President, Product and Marketing, Renault Automation and Dr Graeme Clark who read various drafts of the book and provided us with valuable comments and feedback. We also express our sincere thanks to our editor at John Wiley and Sons, Claire Plimmer, whose enthusiasm for our work supported us from the beginning and throughout the project.

Roger Palmer would particularly like to express his thanks and acknowledge the contribution made by Hayley Tedder whose ability to turn chaos into order has proved both remarkable and essential. Finally he would also like to express his deep appreciation to his friend and colleague Paul Millier whose academic skills and experience contributed to a rich collaboration and learning experience on this book and other projects during his sabbatical year at Cranfield.

The book's route maps

The success spiral in Figure 1 describes the core elements of marketing success. This is described in more detail in the two different types of route map illustrated in the Figures II and III on page x: the 'spiral' and the 'ladder'. These describe the framework of the book, provide a tool to help you to understand how the book is constructed and to navigate your way through the text. The numbers in the figures refer to parts of the book, each part being composed of several chapters.

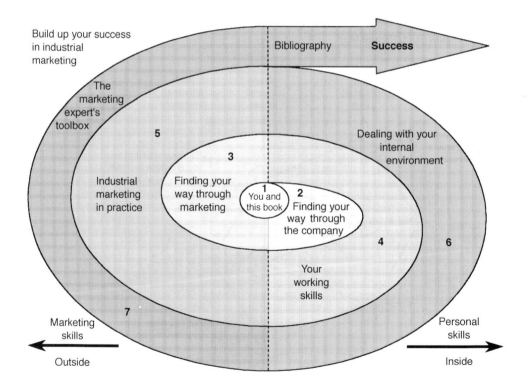

Figure I   The Success Spiral

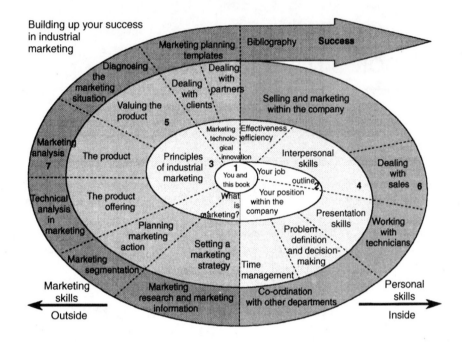

Figure II   The Spiral Route Map

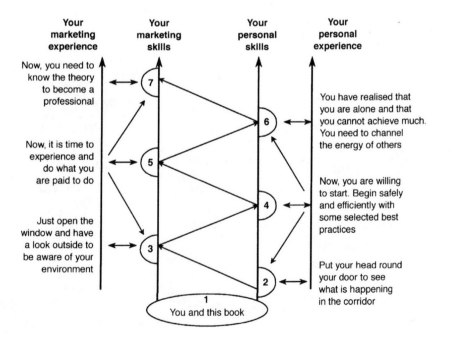

Figure III   The Ladder Route Map

PART I

You and this book

You and this book

1

KEY POINTS

- *If you have recently been appointed to a marketing position in an industrial company then this book is for you.*
- *This book does not contain theory; it is practical and down to earth.*
- *It has been written after listening to the interests and needs of dozens of managers in order to understand the problems that they encounter in their day-to-day jobs.*
- *This book gives some practical solutions to these problems.*
- *It contains short, easily read chapters organised around a clear outline or route map.*
- *The book does not just discuss marketing issues but also some essential skills that will help you to be more efficient and effective in your job.*

TARGET MARKET

Who is this book for? If you have recently been appointed as a marketing manager in an industrial company then you are our primary target. We hope that if you are considering a career in industrial marketing, or indeed have been wrestling with the problems of the job for some time, you will also find this book to be of value. Briefly this book has been written for people who typically

- have recently been appointed to a marketing position in an industrial company, perhaps from a field sales or technical background
- have a technical or scientific orientation but with an interest in marketing and management issues
- are thinking of a career move into marketing, but are not quite sure what to expect from a job in this area
- have made the move into marketing but find that their expectations have not been matched by the reality
- have perhaps read some of the other marketing books that are available but still do not feel that they answer their questions and help them to do the actual job of marketing

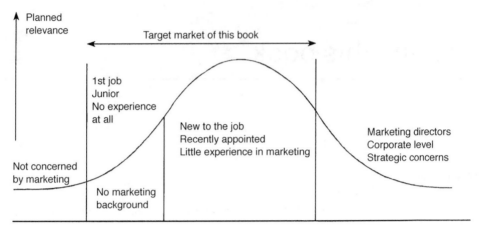

Figure 1.1 Different levels of experience in marketing

- want to develop their marketing skills and grow into the job or would like a suitable day-to-day reference

- have bought one of the venerable tomes on the subject of marketing but have yet to remove it from the shelf. (The people who write these books have tremendous reputations, but then again, they do not have to read them.)

- want to get to grips with the job of marketing and understand some of the realities that other managers come up against.

On the other hand, this book has not been primarily designed for marketing directors who think through the corporate strategy for large international corporations. Their concerns are more strategic and are not ones that we specifically aim to address in this book. Instead we have in mind less experienced marketers who may have little marketing background or indeed not very much industrial experience at all. The book assumes that the reader has at least some work experience that will allow him or her to recognise the situations and challenges we shall describe.

In any event we hope that both the inexperienced marketer and the marketing director will find something of interest for them; perhaps it will help the director to gain more insights to the problems of his team, and for the less experienced marketer to discover the reality of the job. We can summarise the target market for this book in Figure 1.1.

WHAT IS THE PURPOSE OF THIS BOOK?

This book aims to present simply, clearly and in a revealing way some of the basic and fundamental principles of industrial marketing. It will help you to understand not only the principles but also to develop your understanding of how to implement these ideas and actually do the job of marketing. We will also provide you with many examples to illustrate the points we make and to give you some dos and don'ts, although of course it is a foolish person who would suggest that there are rules that apply with a subject like marketing.

As two marketing situations are never alike we cannot possibly cover every eventuality. The book aims to give you some frameworks that will stimulate your thinking, provide you with some ideas and help you to translate these ideas in the light of your own understanding into what makes sense for you in the situation that you find yourself.

Finally if we do have an ambition with this book, it is that you will find it practical and down to earth. We hope we have written it in such a way that it will invite you to develop your understanding and separate the big issues from the mundane and trivial, so that you can understand what really matters for you and your company.

HOW HAS THIS BOOK BEEN WRITTEN?

We started from the point of view that many marketing books represent something of a paradox. Marketing is fundamentally concerned with understanding and responding to the needs of customers. Yet we felt that many books are written by academics and sometimes for academics rather than for practitioners. In other words, marketing authors have been competitor focused (other academics) rather than client focused (managers). To try to avoid this trap and to demonstrate our commitment to marketing principles, we decided that we would talk to our potential customers. That is why we carried out a series of interviews, focus groups and questionnaires with marketing managers in order to understand three things:

1. What are the real problems that managers encounter in their day-to-day jobs?

2. What kind of material would they expect to find in a book designed to help them in their everyday professional life?

3. What kind of layout and design would make a book inviting to read and pleasant to use?

What we did not want to do was describe an idealised view of the job of industrial marketing. We wanted to deal with the reality of your job, and the sort of problems that you have to face up to on an average Monday morning when you go into the office. That is why you will find only very few direct references to marketing theory in this book, despite the fact that as academics we deal with the theory and models of industrial marketing as part of our everyday jobs. Relying on our experience as managers and consultants we have hidden the features of the theory within the book but want to deliver to you the benefits of its application. The last and main assumption on which this book is based is our belief that a lot of industrial companies survive very comfortably without consciously thinking about marketing. At least, not the kind of marketing that you read in the venerable tomes on your bookshelf.

How can we explain this? Firstly, not all the business situations that we encounter need sophisticated marketing solutions and the involvement of people that do something that sounds like the job of marketing. Secondly, managers within companies may not be marketing experts but will bring other significant and worthwhile skills to the job which enables them nonetheless to achieve their objectives.

This book has been designed around these central observations. We will take you progressively from a first level of understanding to an area of greater competence, thus whatever your marketing knowledge we hope that you will be able to identify your position on this continuum and make positive progress in developing your skills. Also our research with managers has shown us that skills other than marketing are essential to do the job of marketing; therefore this book will also discuss what we have called personal skills. We believe that these are just as essential in doing the job of marketing. Finally, this book deals with marketing rather than with sales, which means, for instance, that very little will be said about salesforce management or about sales techniques.

WHY IS THIS BOOK DIFFERENT FROM OTHER MARKETING BOOKS AND WHY SHOULD YOU BUY IT?

Firstly, this book is centred on the reader, yourself, on your concerns and the hundreds of small frustrating problems that you have to deal with every day. The book is designed to help you to improve incrementally your understanding of marketing. As such, the book is not heavy and detailed in terms of concepts and theories because the job that you do is 90 per cent implementation and only 10 per cent thinking, analysing and planning.

Secondly, this book does not contain complex, structured, step-by-step, systematic methods and models. There is a very simple reason why not. In our research people told us that they hated these types of models, and when we asked why, we received the following answers.

- It takes a long time and a lot of concentration to understand how to use them.

- They do not intuitively fit with the way that you work so there is a gap between theory and practice.

- If you miss a step or take a short cut does this mean that you don't achieve your objective?

- You don't necessarily know where to start and where to stop. For example, if we ask the boss what is the company's mission statement and he replies 'don't worry about mission statements and all that marketing nonsense – just get on with it', how does that fit into a model, and which box do we start from now?

- Our respondents said they had an uncomfortable, sinking feeling that models did not work and that they may well be wasting their time.

- The method starts to overtake the objective as you struggle to use and apply the model.

- Because the model is difficult to use and you are unsure about your expertise in using it, in the end it reduces rather than increases your confidence. The model has managed to reduce you from expert to dummy!

- Many managers said that they rarely read a marketing book from cover to cover. They found it heavy going, difficult to read and dull. Most of the time they just gave up.

So, to summarise, this book does not contain idealised models and elegant explanations of theory because when you get into the office on Monday morning nothing looks as it is often described in the books. On Monday morning what do you actually find? A heap of incoherent bits and pieces of information, yellow stickies, fax messages, telephone calls to return and all sorts of other demanding and conflicting priorities. The jigsaw puzzle has been turned upside down and half the pieces are missing. Not only do you not know where to find the missing pieces, you do not even know which pieces are missing! In other words, the reality of business life does not fit comfortably with the models and frameworks conventionally taught in marketing texts. The Monday morning reality is not untypical and you can see a big gap between that and the models and framework. So big is the gap that it seems a daunting task to start to apply some of these step-by-step models.

Nevertheless, in the seventh part of this book we will give you an outline of the main tools usually presented in other books. Obviously you need to be aware of their existence and use. You can also read much more about them in the references provided. What Part VII will provide you with is enough information to describe to your boss or colleagues what a segmentation or SWOT matrix is, for example.

Thirdly, this book is neither a textbook nor a course support text but a book that you can use on its own without any additional information or explanation. It does not prescribe an ideal marketing position as a goal to reach. Conversely, we will try to explain why you cannot cope with a situation that other books so readily offer to resolve, the reality is that in some cases it does take three times longer than you originally thought, it is very difficult really to understand your competitors' strategies and maybe we cannot understand our clients' cost base. Many managers in small and medium enterprises and big companies experience the same feelings, you are not alone. If we understand that, then we can help you to understand your current situation and how you can incrementally improve your effectiveness.

The fourth reason why this book is different, is the layout of the book. It has a zig-zag layout which invites you to wander around and find some unexpected and interesting nuggets of information. In some respects this book acts as a warehouse and you can shuffle through the lanes picking items off the shelf as you go along. We certainly would not suggest that you have to buy everything that you see but hopefully it is laid out and explained in such a way that you can make sensible, pragmatic decisions that are relevant to the specific circumstances you find yourself in.

We also suggest through the design and layout of the book that marketing is a very large toolbox, but as in any toolbox there are probably a few tools that we use much more than others – the screwdriver, pliers and hammer. You do not have to use all the marketing tools at your disposal; one of the things that we find with our students is that their assignments come with a complete suite of marketing tools with a poorly developed sense of how to use tools which are appropriate to the situation. We hope to be able to help you to recognise the relevance of tools. This point will be expanded in Chapter 13.

HOW TO USE THIS BOOK – THE ROUTE MAPS

This book is not a book to be read from the first to the last line. It is a book to flick through, and browse around, you can wander through it from reference to reference, much as you would move from link to link on the Internet. You can also use the spiral, or the ladder, given here at the beginning of the book as a route map to find out where you want to go. You will see that the left-hand part of these route maps contains marketing skills and is mainly concerned with things external to the company. The right-hand side of the route map discusses your personal skills and refers mostly to things internal to the company (Figure 1.2).

To denote the fact that the book is primarily centred on you, the spiral starts in the middle with you – you and this book. The logic that you will follow if you choose to read each part sequentially is this:

Part I – You and the book

This explains how to use this book. This is not a conventional book to be read from the first to the last line. In some respects this chapter is your 'owner's manual'.

Part II – Finding your way through the company

Put your head round the office door and see what is happening in the corridor, that is to say, inside the company. Understanding your immediate environment is indeed the first thing you learn in survival lessons; this is the base on which you will build your expertise.

Part III – Finding your way through marketing

Open your office window and have a look outside at the external environment, just make sure that marketing is right for you before signing up for the job.

Part IV – Your working skills

OK, you are ready to start. So let's start by understanding some universal and best-practice ideas that everyone is supposed to know by heart but that are unfortunately rarely taught in management books. Why learn by trial and error at your own expense the basic principles that we have spent years testing and sorting from the mass of what has been written on the subject? In some respects, this chapter gives you a selection of the most efficient working tools available for marketers.

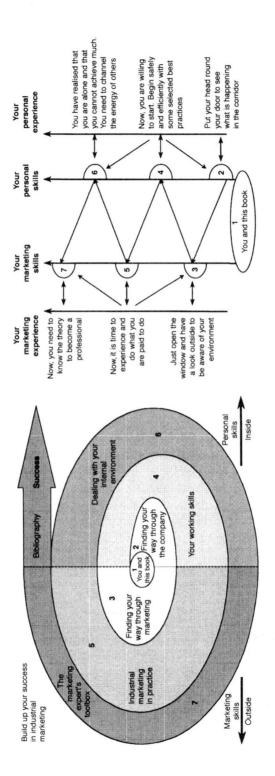

Figure 1.2 Route maps for this book

Part V – Industrial marketing in practice

Now it is time to experience what you are paid for. This is when you start getting to grips with the realities of clients, markets, competitors, etc.

Part VI – Dealing with your internal environment

After some initial experience you will find that you cannot do the job on your own and that you need the support of others – sales, R&D, your boss – to achieve your goals. This part will help you to overcome some of the internal difficulties that marketers often find and help you to build on the energies and enthusiasm of others.

Part VII – The expert's toolbox

Until now you have played marketing just as you might play the guitar, though without any knowledge of music theory. This is the time to get into detail and become a professional by really understanding as well as just knowing. As this suggests as you progress through the book, if that is how you choose to use it, then the depth and detail of the discussion increases. This is illustrated by both the ladder and spiral. As you move from the centre of the spiral in a radial fashion or climb the ladder the ideas are expanded and new ones introduced so that you can choose how far you want or need to go.

A REMINDER

If you have to remember one thing about how this book can be compared to others then it would be this. Based on our long practical and consultancy experience and the comprehensive survey we undertook with marketing managers before writing, this book is geared to help you tackle the real, day-to-day, concrete problems that you encounter or will encounter in your job. It has been written with the thought that you can say: 'That sounds just like my job! I seem to be struggling with all these problems, it's nice to know that someone understands me and that I'm not alone.'

Lastly, this book is underpinned by two main foundations: 'Personal skills' and 'Marketing skills'. A fundamental principle illustrated in Figure 1.3 summarises each of these pillars.

Personal skills	Marketing skills
Keep your eyes on the	Be obsessed by the consistency between what the company
• Big pictures	• Wants to do
• On what really matters for you	• Could do
• On what makes sense	• Is able to do

Figure 1.3 The two main foundations of this book

PART II

Finding your way through the company

INTRODUCTION: YOU AND YOUR COMPANY

Your company is your first and possibly one of the most important parts of the environment. Your company plays the role of launchpad for your career success. It is important to understand this environment and become 'streetwise' as a basis for future success. Likewise, all survival manuals teach you that the first thing to do when you are lost or isolated in hostile surroundings is to establish your base camp and explore the immediate environment. In this sense, Part II will be your manual for surviving in the business jungle. First, it will enable you to establish your base camp by giving you the boundaries of your job. Second, it will help you to explore your immediate environment and recognise your position in your company. In this way, this second part will take you on a short journey around the office building.

Your job outline

2

KEY POINTS

After discussing some common problems and issues that you need to be aware of, this chapter goes on to discuss the outline of your job

- *to sustain current activities; which means*
  - *managing the product range*
  - *managing the market segments*
  - *managing the portfolio of clients*

- *to prepare for the future; which means*
  - *differentiating the products*
  - *designing new products*
  - *managing new markets.*

- *The ways to achieve this are to*
  - *obtain and analyse management information*
  - *co-ordinate activities*
  - *support sales activities*
  - *consolidate and gain experience*
  - *develop and manage a network.*

THE REASON FOR THIS CHAPTER

The purpose of this chapter is to give an outline understanding of your job. It is designed to help you understand the functional boundaries of *your job* so that you can be clearer about what your job actually should be.

Why is it so important that you are clear about your job function? First, if you are unclear then it could take several months or even years before you develop your own solution and achieve a degree of efficiency.

Secondly, if you are unclear about where the boundaries are with respect to your job then there is a very real risk that others will decide your job instead of you, with implications for your future career in the company. This vicious circle starts soon after you have been appointed, in fact as soon as somebody pops into your office:

So, can you do something for me please? I need the names of the key
distributors of electrical components in Italy. As you are the new marketing
manager I'm sure you'll be able to help me with that!

As you have just started in your job and are maybe not very confident about precisely
what you should be doing, how nice that somebody takes an interest and asks you as the
'marketing expert' to deal with this obvious marketing question.

The problem is that you do not know the main distributors of electrical components in
Italy but, of course, there are all sorts of sources of information that any good marketer
would be able to access. In any case you do not want to make a bad impression as soon
as you start with the company. So you set about the problem and try to find the answer;
it will probably take a week or so as you work on and off with this problem. At last you
come up with an answer which you give your new-found colleague. He is delighted, not
only has he learnt who these Italian distributors are but he has also learnt something else.
That you are somebody who will help when he has problems. The next time he needs to
know something, for example, how many tonnes of acrylic fibre is imported into Italy
each year, he will no doubt come back and see you again.

By virtue of the theory of commitment, this says that if you have helped him once then
you will almost certainly help him again. No matter how much it costs, the next time a
question arises you will help in resolving it. Your colleague, having been delighted with
the way the marketing department helps him out, will no doubt tell his friends what a
nice person you are and before you know it you have become the human embodiment of
an answering machine.

However, that is not your job and in doing so you have missed your actual added
value for the company. There are all sorts of other sources of information that your
colleague could use, after all what did he do before you arrived? It is also quite likely that
such information will be cheaper to obtain elsewhere. But your colleague does not see
this, because as far as he was concerned, you gave him the information for free.

By responding in this way, not only have you lost some time that could have been
properly invested elsewhere but you have also preconditioned your colleagues about
how they can deal with you. If your time is free, then nobody will value it. Inevitably you
will receive more and more inquiries which will take up an increasing amount of time.
The danger of the situation is that it is difficult to rewind the tape. You have allowed the
situation to develop and it will be very difficult to change this unfortunate habit (Figure
2.1).

A variant of the situation, where you unwittingly set yourself up as 'the mug', is when
your job description does exist. Someone wrote this before your appointment to the job
but unfortunately it happens to be wrong, meaningless or useless. So this inappropriate
job description becomes a strait-jacket as you try to work within its constraints. After a
year or two you notice that nothing has actually changed, for your investment of your
time you have achieved nothing.

Unfortunately these situations are all too common in industry, as marketing is a much
more recent and unknown discipline in industrial companies compared to other sectors such
as FMCG (fast moving consumer goods). In industry the technicians are often the kings.
Marketing often has a low status as highlighted by a recent Cranfield study. In this study,

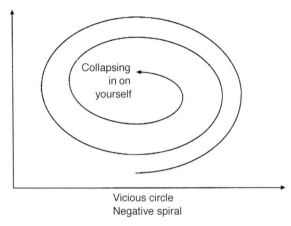

Figure 2.1 A risk of implosion

marketing was not ranked at the bottom of the list in terms of functional importance, but just above HR, hardly a vote of confidence. What this illustrates is that marketing is not well understood and therefore it could well be the case that your colleagues will not know exactly what to expect from you. The roles and functions of the sales department, production, accounts, etc. are very clear, but marketers? What do they do?

Nobody would ask a salesperson to design a new product, we all know that a salesperson's job is to sell. As nobody really understands what a marketer does then you can ask a marketer anything about whatever. So, little by little, day after day the marketing function shifts a little more and not surprisingly the final result of this experimental muddling through is 'whatever'. And, still worse, our research and observation of organisations shows that when things are not clear, not said, not written, people tend to keep for themselves the most exciting and rewarding tasks and leave the boring stuff to others.

 To avoid this pitfall, this chapter will give you an outline of the marketing role which will help you to define your own mission statement. Setting your personal mission statement will give you a framework, a reference point that will enable you to say what is appropriate or inappropriate for you to do.

It is not only important for you at least to be clear about your job description and feel comfortable, confident and therefore efficient in what to do. It is also vital for another reason. Bear in mind that as long as everything runs reasonably smoothly in an industrial company few people ever think of marketing. In other words, if they have decided to appoint you it is presumably because there is some problem or issue that needs to be resolved. Are you clear about what this problem or issue is? It is quite likely that it has not been articulated particularly well, and that there will be a wide range of views on the nature of the problem and the potential solutions. So the onus is upon you as you enter the job to understand the nature of the problem.

In summary, you need the strength of will to avoid slotting into the routine of the system. You must be clear about what your job is and not allow others to drive your activities. If you want to do a real marketing job then it is quite likely that it is up to you to define your job and make it clear to others within the company.

YOUR JOB BOUNDARIES

Before thinking further about your job description let us make an analogy to explain it. Your job outline can be seen as an empty jar. You will later fill it with all the things that constitute your job, but the size and shape are given. To make up your job there will be a mixture of things and it is important to differentiate between

- **what to do**
- **how to do it.**

We will now consider this in more detail.

What to do – your two main missions

From a general viewpoint your job consists of two essential missions:

- to sustain the current activities
- to prepare for the future.

Sustaining the current activities will essentially be achieved by

- managing the products and the product range – this means constantly ensuring that the product offering is more attractive than that of competitors
- managing the market segments – in order to target those that are most profitable for you by taking into account their attractiveness balanced against your abilities to serve them
- managing the client portfolio – choosing only those clients that suit you and that you want to deal with while balancing the client portfolio and managing the risk of client loss.

If managing the present seems challenging, a wide range of the marketers we interviewed agreed that actually you are dead if you look only at today. You must also look to the future which means

- differentiating products – the world is fast moving and dynamic. We should continually seek to make our products different from, and more attractive than, those of our competitors. Our current range of products represents today's income and tomorrow's investment. Failure to manage the current range of products will limit our future.
- designing new products – and making the most of your marketing and technological assets. This means creating value for customers, embodied in the product.

- defining and managing new markets – perhaps creating new demand by customer education and market development. This is especially important in industry where technology plays such an important role. A technological breakthrough can often encompass as much danger as it does potential. New technology means a change in habits on behalf of clients. Your role is to train and educate clients to make product adoption easy and painless for them.

How to do it – your means to succeed

To achieve your two essential missions, sustaining current activity and preparing for the future, there are a number of tasks that you can consider as a route to this.

- Information: this is the raw material of marketing. It helps you to understand the environment in which you work and is the basis for future decision-making. Your job is to collect, analyse, process, store and disseminate marketing information.

- Co-ordination: marketing inevitably has to work through and with other functions within the organisation. In order to bring about improvements this often means change. To achieve this you have to channel resources and plan activities all with the aim of client satisfaction in mind.

- Support: this means providing all those things that are required before during and after the sales activity, for example, sales support materials such as brochures and catalogues together with the underlying arguments that support the sales proposition. This can also be expanded to include, for example, training and after-sales backup.

- Consolidation: learn from previous experience in order to build on best practices and capture new ideas. The most effective way of doing this is to develop and manage a process and apply appropriate measures within the process. By doing this a large task can be broken down into a series of smaller ones and measures can be applied at each stage. This gives a much greater understanding of the reasons for success or failure. You must also write down, (or have written down) a log of successes and failures. We learn as much from our failure as from our success and – when written down and read – history can become your best teacher.

- Team building: this applies not just to your own marketing team but all those within the company involved in the marketing initiative. This is a subtle art as not everybody in the organisation appreciates that they may have a client-facing role to play.

- Build and manage a network of external partners on which you can rely to provide extra resources and specialist services at times of peak demand or in particular circumstances (e.g., PR services, market studies, product launches).

Figure 2.2 is a diagrammatic representation of the preceding text.

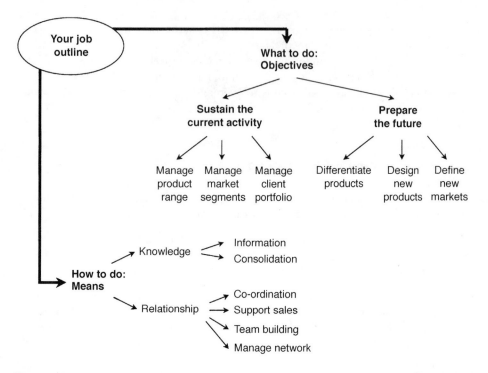

Figure 2.2 Your job framework

WHAT YOU ARE NOT

We have previously seen the elements that make up your job. Yet, it is not enough to design the job properly. You must also be aware of some of the things that you are not in order that you can manage these as well. So some of the things that you are not would include being

- A super sales person. Your job is to support sales, not to make them. You should obviously visit clients when required, and you will no doubt take a strong interest in client's views and opinions but that is different from selling. Do not be caught in the trap of 'reverse delegation' by your salesforce. This consists of saying 'As you are really better than me at this kind of negotiation with this kind of difficult client, I think you'd better go instead of me'. Ask them what is actually so challenging with this client, ask what solution they plan, make them find other solutions or suggest something, make them think through the alternatives and ... let them go!

- An inquiry service. Our original example illustrates this.

- A fortuneteller. Marketing inevitably deals in the realm of uncertainty. You will never know everything and the only thing that we know about forecasts is that they are almost invariably wrong. This does not mean that you should take guesses but formulate your response on the basis of carefully, systematically gathered and analysed information. Do not let others believe that you know everything. Always give your sources of information, assumptions and assessment of risk.

- Everyone's slave. Learn to say no and do not get drawn into short-term, time-wasting activities.

- The Boss. In a marketing position you often have access to the most senior people in the company and to privileged information. This means that you have significant power. Much of your job needs you to work with other people and abuse of your power will lead to the discretionary effort of others being withdrawn.

- A one-man marketing function. You must be very careful with the differences between
  - yourself
  - the marketing department
  - the marketing function.

The marketing function — as previously defined — is the function by which the company understands the environment and specifically customer needs and, as such, everyone in the company should be concerned with this. When R&D works on a new product with a client, for example, that is part of the marketing function. Therefore you share this function with other people in the company, you do not have to and should not carry all the marketing burden on your own.

Likewise the marketing department, if it exists, is a group of people responsible for marketing matters and you share this responsibility with them. So, be clear about your job in the department. If you are head of this department make sure, again, that the marketing department is not carrying all the responsibility for conducting marketing activity.

BEWARE OF STILL WATER

What we are implying here is that you might feel very comfortable in your job as everything around you seems ordered and calm. This could also signify another type of problem. One of the managers we interviewed coined the phrase 'no relationships — no problem'. As people in your company, particularly when you first joined, do not really understand marketing and your role it is quite easy for them to simply carry on as before. If all around you seems passive and quiet it may mean that you are failing to build relationships and are actually on the fringe of the organisation. You are not involved and do not contribute, ultimately a career-limiting prospect. As Tom Peters (1989) states: 'Making waves is the alternative'.

Your position within the company

3

KEY POINTS

Marketing usually has a low status in industrial companies. Nevertheless you can considerably improve your efficiency and your role within the organisation if you have a clear overview of what a marketer should achieve. To help you with this, Chapter 3 is based around two criteria:

- *Your marketing expertise (low–high)*
- *Your company's marketing maturity (high–low)*

The advice in this chapter will help you to understand your position within your company.

POOR ME!

Poor me! That is probably what you are thinking, or will be thinking, after a few months spent in your new marketing position. You may well start to wonder why you left your familiar and comfortable job in production or sales to take on this difficult and challenging task. Do not worry if you are or have been feeling unhappy with your job. Why do we say this? Because virtually everybody that we interviewed experienced these feelings and concerns at some stage in their new marketing role. Why?

LOW STATUS

Marketing usually has a low, or even very low, status in industrial companies. Unlike your counterparts in FMCG (fast moving consumer goods, e.g. baked beans and hair shampoo), who are the barons in their companies, your function in an industrial company is poorly perceived and sometimes poorly rewarded as well. How can we explain this difference?

Firstly, the difference in perspective between industrial and FMCG companies relates to the importance of marketing in such organisations. In FMCG companies such as Unilever, the power of the brand is predominant and a wide range of activities – TV campaigns, sports events, promotions, etc. are focused on supporting the image of the brand in the eyes of the consumer.

Conversely, in industry, the business is traditionally articulated around production and sales. There is something of a cultural gap with marketing. Sometimes even the word 'marketing' is banned in some companies where it is disguised under another name. Marketing is seen as lightweight and inconsequential, synonymous with advertising soap powder, manipulating clients and generally indulging in marginally unethical practices. Marketing in industrial organisations is a more recent phenomenon and is not so central to the focus of the company. In these circumstances we can understand that marketing is not so highly rated as a contributor to business success. The co-ordinating role of marketing is sometimes interpreted as marketing trying to take over someone else's job in sales, R&D, etc.

The situation may be worse still if you are relatively young although this is a self-correcting fault compared to the wily old dogs in sales and production. They will sit back and entertain themselves by seeing you struggle with all the obvious facts that they have been coping with for years. Needless to say they probably will not volunteer any support, and perhaps you feel a little nervous about asking for help.

Another significant factor affecting the perception of marketing is that marketing is seen as a cost to the business. On the profit and loss account marketing costs are classed as 'expenses' and you manage a cost centre, unlike colleagues who manage profit centres. You are a luxury for the organisation, widely perceived by many as something that cannot be afforded when times get tough. Paradoxically, times probably are tough, as that was the initiative for your appointment in the first place!

From this we can certainly understand that life is sometimes not easy for a recently appointed marketing person in an industrial organisation. Therefore you will have to be more than careful before doing anything of significance, and should take care that you understand how the organisation works before you attempt to intervene. Nevertheless, this rather gloomy picture will not be found in every company. Some are much better than that, and then again some are worse, as Figure 3.1 suggests.

Of course, reality is more complex and no two situations are the same. To help you understand this we can define three factors that will influence how you are perceived in the organisation.

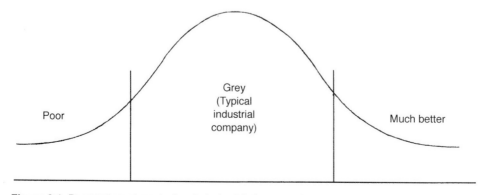

Poor

Grey
(Typical
industrial
company)

Much better

Figure 3.1 Perception of marketing in industrial companies

1. *The seniority of your position in the company.* Are you the marketing director at a corporate level, a divisional product manager or a marketing assistant?

2. *Your level of expertise in marketing.* Is this your first real job in marketing? Perhaps you bring previous experience from contrasting organisations.

3. *Your company's marketing maturity.* Is marketing a new job in the company, prone to all the problems that we have outlined, or is marketing established and driving the company's strategy?

You need to take into account these factors in order to understand how you are perceived within the company before you can really get to work. Taking this discussion a little further, how can we apply these factors to your own situation? What are the consequences for your job? To help you understand how this might develop we shall now discuss in a little more detail some typical situations which may relate to your own.

CHECKING YOUR OWN PERSONAL SITUATION

Where are you now? Let us draw up a chart to give you a map based on the previously discussed factors.

Firstly, your *position in the company*. If you are an experienced marketing director at corporate level you may need only Part VII of this book, but perhaps you may otherwise need to refer to all of it.

Your *expertise in marketing*. Do you bring significant previous experience of your new role, or is this your first job in marketing with only a vague definition of the objectives.

These factors give us Figure 3.2.

Now let us consider the third factor, your company's *marketing maturity*. If your job is the first marketing position in a company traditionally driven by sales or the technicians then marketing maturity is low. If the marketing department is strong, well structured and highly perceived then perceptions are conversely high. Adding these to Figure 3.2 we get Figure 3.3.

Your job level				
	Top		Top level	Marketing director
	Other than top	Your marketing expertise	Good	Previous marketing experience
			Poor	New to the job

Figure 3.2 Your level in the company and marketing expertise

| | | | | Your company's marketing experience | |
				Low	High
Your job level	Top			5	6
	Other than top	Your marketing expertise	Good	**2** Steer Give direction	Sustain Develop **3**
			Poor	Understand the mess	'You've been framed'
				1	**4**

Figure 3.3 Six different situations

Thinking about the underlying reasons for this book, we do not feel that we can add as much value to marketers who define themselves in boxes 5 and 6 of Figure 3.3 as opposed to those in boxes 1 and 2, where we think marketers really do need support. We shall briefly consider boxes 3 and 4 where there is a reasonably positive environment within the company. Although there are some strong differences, the four categories that we shall focus on have some things in common as well. Whatever the level of your expertise and the company's maturity there are some jobs and tasks that are the same in

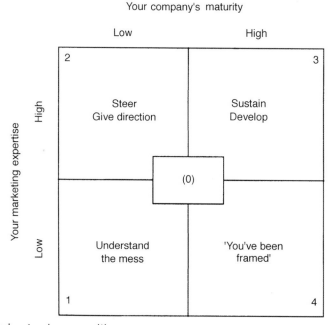

Figure 3.4 Understand your position

any organisation. To make this more explicit we will transform Figure 3.3 into Figure 3.4 where we have removed boxes 5 and 6 and added box 0 in the centre. This is the area of marketing tasks that is common to all the situations that we describe and which you will almost certainly encounter when you take up your job.

Let us now expand on each of these boxes to consider the specific issues in more detail.

BOX 0: YOUR FIRST DAYS IN THE JOB

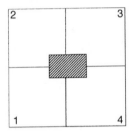

Whatever your company and your level in the company, when you first start in a marketing position there is some basic groundwork to be done as preparation for the future. What should be borne in mind at this stage can be summarised by two questions: *The fundamentals; where to start?* and *What do you have to achieve in this job?*

Fundamentals; where to start?

This helps you to understand the basis of the job, the foundations on which you will build your marketing expertise. Start by asking yourself if

- this is a new position in the company

- there is a written job definition

- you are replacing somebody who has moved on

- the person you are replacing was actually doing a marketing job.

Do not underestimate this last point; it is crucial for two reasons. Firstly, if marketing is not a core discipline in the company, then the term 'marketing' may have been applied to what is in fact an administrative role. For example, sales administration or tactical implementation of marketing activities such as direct mailing or a campaign. Also, if the marketing role did not previously exist, then it may be that you will have to sell to your boss and others the need to do something rather different from what has been done up until now.

At this point try to elicit a list of all the marketing-related activities:

- What are the products, product range and the product lines? How many of these are manufactured and stocked?

- What are our core technologies? Are they at the leading edge or becoming obsolete?
- Where are our manufacturing sites and what are the capabilities?
- What markets are we working in and where are they? How big are they? What products are sold into which markets?
- Of our customers, who are the more important ones?
- Who are the main competitors in each market?

By asking a series of questions such as these we can start to understand the scope of marketing within the organisation. It is often useful to draw up a chart or table of each of these points. In this way we can produce a visual representation of the market, our product range, etc. It is surprising how often that information expressed in this way gives insight and meaning. It is one of the ways in which we can stand back from the trees and really understand the nature of the wood. Typical examples of what we mean are illustrated in Figure 3.5.

Make the time to stand back metaphorically from the day-to-day business and prepare this sort of analysis. What you really want to know is 'how it works', both outside and inside the organisation. The way to do this is to keep asking questions.

- What are the essential 'rules' of doing business in our industry? What are the critical success factors? Who are the big players? What are the industry drivers? Who are the influencers?
- Whom are you dealing with internally? Sales, your boss, R&D, sales administration, etc?
- What are the main problems within the company? Ask everybody you meet this question, compare and contrast the views that you receive. Be prepared to exercise a

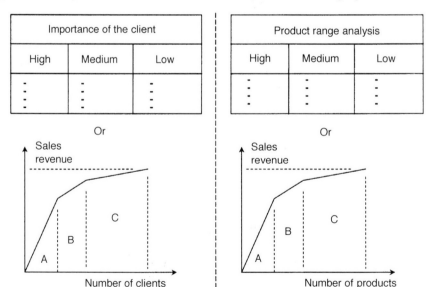

Figure 3.5 Weighting your clients and your products

little cynicism and scepticism here. There may be reasons why people do not want to disclose certain types of information.

- Who are the decision-makers in the company?

- Who gets on very well with whom? The organisation structure is one thing but the natural groups and cliques within the company often determine the informal way in which things actually work. This also helps you to understand who is ineffectual and ignored in the organisation.

- On what will I be judged at the end of the year: turnover, margin, market share, client retention, number of new clients gained, number of new products launched? In other words, what are they expecting from me? Once again no two companies are alike and it is very difficult to forecast from outside what they will expect from you. If you work for an international company, you may be surprised to realise that people from different countries will expect different things from you. For instance, we interviewed marketers in a multinational chemical company:
  - The UK expects good field support from marketing. They expect marketing people to accompany the salesperson and visit the client.
  - In France, salespersons primarily expect written support from marketing (leaflets, brochures).
  - In Germany, they need both field and written support.
  - In Italy they say 'Come whenever you want but mind your own business' but do not hesitate to ask for support when they need it.
  - In Scandinavia they demand little or even no support at all.

We would not wish to generalise about cultural differences. This is just to illustrate that sales might expect different things from you in different countries.

Write these lists down

As long as the ideas are just turning round and round in your mind they are valueless for your job, they are fuzzy and liable to change because they are not grounded.

What do you have to achieve in this job?

The starting point here is to ask if there is a job description and if so what is it? Also what marketing activities have previously been undertaken in the firm? Bear in mind that a written job description is not a bible, it may well be wrong. What has been done before may not have been appropriate and certainly it should not be taken for granted that this is what you should do in future.

To try to resolve this conundrum you need to understand the basis upon which you will be judged not only by your boss but also by your peers and colleagues. Of course you should not slavishly follow this, what you are judged on and what you ought to do could well be two different things. Think of it in this way, the tip of the iceberg is the

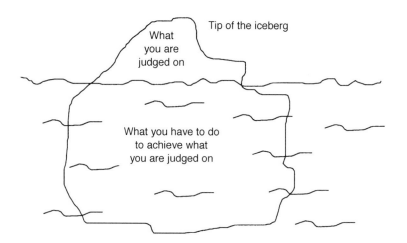

Figure 3.6 The visible part of your job

visible part of your job that drives the perceptions of others (Figure 3.6). The actual task of marketing may well remain hidden but you will need to respond to the requirements of others whilst getting on with the real task of marketing.

The point that you need to arrive at is that you understand three important factors:

1. What you can influence and change.

2. The degree of freedom and responsibility that you have to exercise your initiative.

3. The resources that you have available, both financial and otherwise.

To visualise your sphere of influence and what you can actually change in the organisation start by drawing an organisational diagram of the company (Figure 3.7). Indicate by boundary lines things for which you are responsible, e.g. product ranges 2 and 3. Another possible picture could look like Figure 3.8, where you work with a range of people in the organisation in order effectively to manage your product range. This

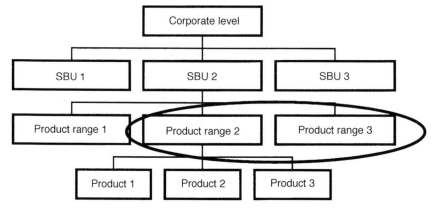

Figure 3.7 Your sphere of influence

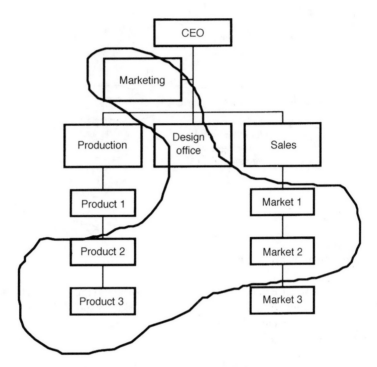

Figure 3.8 Your place in the organogram

gives you a good indication of your influence and also the people whom you need to work with in the future.

In principle we are arriving at an understanding of *your* zones of influence in the organisation. If we think about the things that we have to do for each of these we can test our influence with this question: 'Can I change or influence this?' If the answer to this question is 'yes' or 'no' then it is quite clear where we place that on our zone of influence. If the answer is 'yes and no' then we will put that in the 'I can' box. However, if the answer is 'neither yes nor no' then it would go in the 'I cannot' box (Figure 3.9). This helps us to understand what we can and cannot do on the basis of our responsibility, and

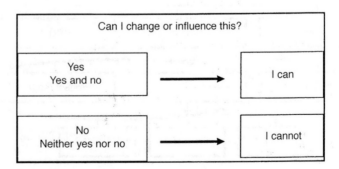

Figure 3.9 Identifying what you can influence

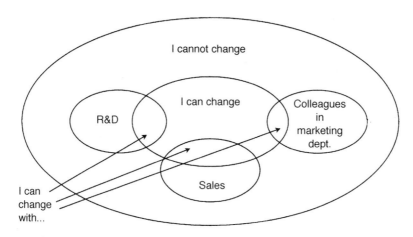

Figure 3.10 Sharing the burden with colleagues

to identify those people whom we need to work with. This also helps to clarify what you can do personally rather than the general role and function of the marketing department. Having done this analysis you should arrive at a very clear view of what needs to be done and whether this is a task that is 'focused in' or 'focused out'.

Once you have determined what you can change, try now to define what decisions you can take on your own and what decisions you must share and implement with others. Test also at a very early stage whom you can rely on in your company and who is a 'rotten egg'. In other words, who are your allies and whom you should avoid (Figure 3.10).

BOX 1: UNDERSTANDING AND SORTING OUT THE MESS

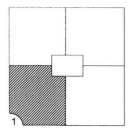

Not an easy box! You are new to the job, have no previous experience and the job is indeed a new one for the company. If by chance your company is a very traditional industrial company, perhaps an electrical component manufacturer or a company dealing in raw materials, it will tend to be focused around the production and sales interface. Is your organisation like this? Congratulations, you've hit the jackpot!

Let us make a representative list of what you find in the company.

- There is either no job description, or if there is it is fuzzy or inappropriate.

- Very little or no marketing has been done in the company, there is no marketing perspective and all sorts of anomalies can be identified. For example, products are sold with inappropriate technical support, the salesforce has few controls and sets its own objectives, product prices are based largely upon production costs. As one of our interviewees said: 'When I took my job, the marketing was literally upside-down. They were neither efficient nor rational. They were rather annihilating each other than helping each other.'

- Nothing is ever written down, it is just not possible to plan in this type of organisation and you must find your own route through the jungle.

- Everyone seems to be overwhelmed with a mass of detail and work with no co-ordination. For instance, manufacturing never gets commercial information or customer contact.

- R&D people regard their job as to guard the technical information for reasons of commercial confidentiality.

- The technicians and engineers seem to know precisely what clients want, but as marketing people we know they are obviously wrong.

- The salespeople base their power around their commercial information; try asking them for any details about customers!

- Relationship problems exist all over the organisation but nobody ever surfaces and addresses these issues. The ability to do the job is based upon personal relationships, informal liaisons, politics and grudges. This problem is often reinforced by the fact that you have to work with the people in place. Whether they are good or bad, hiring new competencies and skills will almost certainly be budget restricted.

- Nobody ever feels that they are listened to, yet everybody feels misunderstood.

- Do not expect any support from anybody. Perhaps, but only perhaps, the boss who appointed you will provide support.

In other words your organisation seems to function despite itself rather than because of itself, and you are left with very little idea about what you can actually do to sort things out. The first piece of advice in these circumstances is:

DON'T HURRY and DON'T PANIC

Start by watching carefully what is happening around you; until you really know what is going on in this organisation you should be walking on eggshells. The principle to follow here is to gather information by talking to people.

 Spend a lot of time in discussions with the people you will have to deal with. Listen to them, to their problems and the challenges they think they face. You are not yet in a position to decide anything so listen, listen, listen.

It is always worth while to spend some time with the salesforce and to understand the issues they face as well as being able to talk directly to clients about the products and service. It is quite likely that you will pick out some persistent problems perhaps around product quality but more likely in the area of service and the reliability of deliveries. Also take some time to spend time with outsiders – suppliers, consultants, distributors – and gather their views about the problems they have and how they see your company. At all times make sure that the door is open to the boss so that you can keep him/her informed about what you are doing and why you are doing it. At this stage you are simply gathering all the parts of the jigsaw puzzle.

It is quite likely that some of your colleagues will be suspicious about the role and function of marketing and you may well find it difficult to be accepted and trusted by them. You should be prepared to demonstrate some evidence of your skills and your ability to add value (Palmer and Meldrum 1998). Try to sell the idea that marketing is useful not only for the company but also for individuals. You will almost certainly be under the microscope and you can expect some jealousy and ill feeling. As you develop your role in the organisation take some time to note what you are doing, why you are doing it and how this has improved effectiveness. These early demonstrations of effectiveness will help to build your credibility.

At this stage you have nothing to gain by being arrogant and attempting to impose your views on how things should be done. You cannot afford to make 'take it or leave it' type comments, as the reaction of people will be to leave it, thank you very much. By listening to your colleagues and understanding the issues that are important to them you can start to identify those people who will be interested in some of the work that you will be undertaking. This is your opportunity to start to involve them in what you are doing by asking for advice and opinions. In this way you will gradually be able to build up the dialogue and establish some common ground.

At this early stage be prepared to cope with hundreds of petty frustrations before you think about developing a ten-year corporate strategy for the company. At this stage you are outside the system and you are subject to the scrutiny of your new colleagues. The challenge here is to avoid making mistakes, as very few people have any expectations of delivery from you.

BOX 2: STEERING AND NAVIGATING

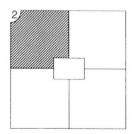

This describes the situation where you have previous marketing experience and have been appointed to a position in a company with little previous marketing maturity, but one that perhaps feels that there is a role for marketing to perform. As stated during an interview: 'We have relied on "word of mouth" growth. In order to achieve a high growth rate or at least maintain the growth, we need to market our organisation.'

It is often the case in such organisations that the CEO was tacitly undertaking the job of marketing. Typically this could be a company with good potential, perhaps a hi-tech company. The company could well have developed on the basis of an original idea successfully implemented that has allowed growth to take place. Now it is time to be more professional as the competition is catching up and the original good idea is no longer unique.

As discussed, start with a comprehensive review of what is being done in the company in order that you can understand the issues. The next step is to rank these in order of importance; following this diagnosis there is now a call for action. You are the expert, and there are high expectations of you. By ranking the issues in order of importance you can focus on the critical factors that match with the distinctive competencies of the company. Focusing could avoid you wasting your time on less profitable issues.

If your company has been product or technology driven it is a fair bet that the products have grown like bamboo in a forest – wildly and anarchically. We have seen many companies that consistently introduce new products, but without the resources to sustain such a wide product range. What would you do in such a case? Make a thorough analysis of the product portfolio and reorganise the range. The portfolio tools discussed in Part VII can be applied here. This is the first step in building competitive advantage. In other words your job will be to

- organise or reorganise
- channel the energy to where it will be more effective (Figure 3.11)
- drive the company forward on the basis of client demand
- take big decisions
- increase market share and profitability
- drive change within the company; this will require diplomacy and interpersonal skills.

These are large tasks and almost certainly you will need to build a team to share the load and improve efficiency. You will have to work closely with your boss to get commitment and approval of the big decisions as well as the necessary resources, particularly money, to achieve your goals. You must be prepared to challenge the status quo and overcome the inertia within the system in order to bring about change. This is an exciting challenge and a big opportunity for your own personal growth and development.

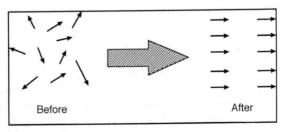

Figure 3.11 Channelling the energy

BOX 3: SUSTAIN AND DEVELOP

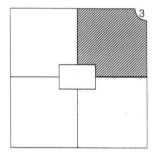

In this box you personally have a high level of marketing expertise and work in an organisation with a high perception of marketing. Most of the teething problems associated with the introduction of marketing into the organisation have been resolved and typically your job consists of sustaining and developing the activity for which you are responsible. You may wish to consider rationalising some of the activities in order to improve focus and cost effectiveness. This would be quite normal in an organisation of this type.

There may also be the need for some reorganisation, you might perhaps have been appointed to reinvigorate the department and to introduce new ideas in the light of change in the industry. The primary need here is to understand and respond to some of the 'big picture' issues and to demonstrate your high level of expertise, using the marketing tools described in Part VII of this book. You are accepted as part of the system, and are indeed someone who constitutes the system. Companies that will be typical of this box would be, for example, 3M, Hewlett Packard and IBM. The typical marketing role would be at marketing manager or senior product manager level.

BOX 4: YOU'VE BEEN FRAMED

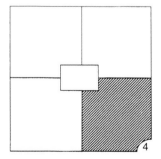

In this box you have little or no previous experience of working in a company with a high level of marketing maturity. A strong marketing framework exists in the company and there is significant ongoing support from your colleagues and boss. You would not be expected, at this stage, to take big decisions but you will certainly be expected to act professionally and in line with the normal practice of the company. It is quite likely that you will have been on a formal training or induction programme, either internally or externally, or will have received individual coaching.

At this early stage of your career it is quite likely that you will be working on existing projects and developing your experience by working with others. In the circumstances you will not have to worry too much about your job definition. This is likely to be reasonably clearly defined and most of the time you will be appropriately supervised and given clear guidance on what is expected. Here the system takes over and your best course of action is likely to be to work with it, develop your experience and learn from what is likely to be a rich and positive environment. Typical jobs in this box would be a product or brand manager, marketing assistant or junior assistant in a specialised area such as PR, market and sales analysis.

HOW TO DIAGNOSE YOUR OWN SITUATION

At this stage we have now understood the circumstances within the company using the diagnostic tool. The next step is to extend this diagnosis to your own personal circumstances by comparing what you should be doing with what you actually do (Figure 3.12). We can think of it in this way, with three zones

1. The 'overlap' zone – where you do what needs to be done. The objective is to increase the size of this zone.

2. The 'time wasting' zone – these are things that you are doing that are not contributing; you need to discontinue these activities as soon as possible.

3. The 'to do' zone – this is where you will make a difference, your future efforts should be directed to this zone.

To achieve this, once again list the things that you do and compare this with a list of the things that you should be doing (Figure 3.13).

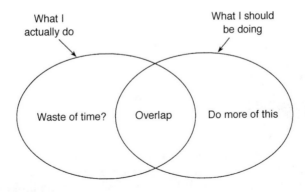

Figure 3.12 Are you doing the right things?

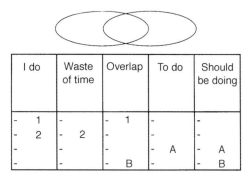

I do	Waste of time	Overlap	To do	Should be doing
- 1	-	- 1	-	-
- 2	- 2	-	-	-
-	-	-	- A	- A
-	-	- B	-	- B

Figure 3.13 Working smarter

A major pitfall at this stage is that you believe that everything that you read in a marketing book must be done. Theoretically this may be true, and it is often presented in this way. But in practice you cannot do everything at the same time and not all problems admit the same solution (for instance, if you sell military aircraft engines you will focus on lobbying the government whilst you will concentrate on rationalising your product range if you sell electrical components). You must rank the tasks from the most important or most relevant and focus on these key activities.

Success on these key tasks will then allow you to move forward.

Understanding your position within the company is useful and essential, but rather static. In other words, like so many marketing tools that are used, it is analytical in nature but does not necessarily suggest to us where we should go in future. To develop a more dynamic view of your job let us have a look at something that we call your trajectory.

YOUR TRAJECTORY

Very few people – it is safe to say no one – has a linear and progressive trajectory. The trajectory could quite likely look like Figure 3.14. There can obviously be some differences in the trajectory. Your trajectory could be quite predictable, for instance in a big structured company in which 'your job is framed' (Figure 3.15a). Conversely, in another company – in which very little procedure exists – it can be anything. You can take the responsibility that you want, whenever you want; you build your own job (Figure 3.15b). Anyway, we can see that there are roughly eight phases in the way that your job develops within the company.

1. You have recently started in the job, you perhaps have a technical or sales background but really have little idea how to tackle the problems that you find. Things look a lot different on the inside than they did from the outside. You actually find that you get little support and for all the difference that you are making you might as well work for the competition!

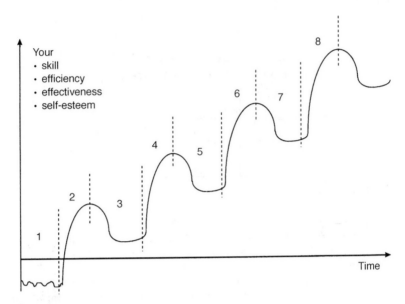

Figure 3.14 Your trajectory

2. It is pretty difficult to make any sort of progress in these circumstances so you attend a course to learn the basics about your job. Ninety per cent of the managers that we met in preparing this book attended a course as a basis for future development in the job. All of them admitted that reading a textbook on marketing was actually very little help to them.

3. You come back to your company invigorated with new ideas and enthusiastic to start to implement what you have learnt. Unfortunately your company does not seem to fit any of the case studies that you worked on during the course. In fact you sometimes find that the messy, inconsistent nature of the organisation does not lend itself to the models and diagnostic tools that you have brought back with you. You do not know where to start, where to stop and furthermore, you are constantly harassed by telephone calls, meetings, e-mail and all the things that prevent you from thinking and reflecting about how to do your job better. This is often a plateau stage as your enthusiasm subsequently drops.

4. In struggling to cope with the situation you find yourself in, you start to apply some of your new-found knowledge; despite all the problems you start to generate some results. Encouraged by this, you learn by trial and error and start to feel more confident about your marketing skills.

5. Winning a series of small battles is commendable, but it is not going to win the war. You are now dealing with a succession of small issues that you can successfully handle, but perhaps starting to feel a little discouraged as you are deluged in work but still not bringing about the change that you envisage is required. This can be a lonely time and perhaps you need some help, you cannot do everything at the same time all by yourself. Again your enthusiasm can wane at this point.

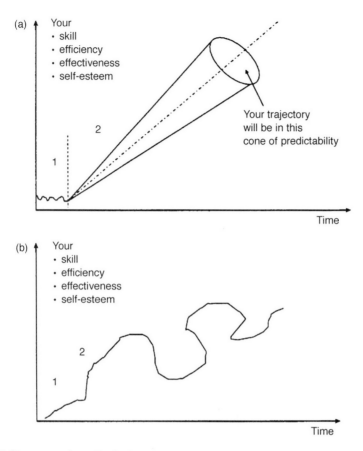

Figure 3.15 Two examples of trajectory

6. You start experimenting with some simple, different ways of approaching the issues perhaps by using external help. For example, conducting some market research, implementing a PR or direct-marketing campaign, and as a result you generate some success.

7. Working with outsiders is all very well, but the effectiveness is limited as you have to rely on others and are working on a continuous succession of short-term projects. It is now time to change gear again.

8. It is important that everybody within the marketing team develops their skills and teaches and shares their skills with others so that everybody can build on what they have learnt so far. The power of the team helps in the next breakthrough.

By this stage you should at least understand much more about how your job is positioned within your company, and indeed how marketing is perceived by the company. This analysis helps to set priorities for your job in order that you can achieve personal and professional objectives.

EXAMPLE 3.1

An experienced industrial marketer, working for a multinational petro-chemical business, described how it took him nearly four years to find his way through this process. The first 18 months or so were spent in knee-jerk reaction to the salesforce, often responding to minor issues around price, usually reductions. It took another 18 months to two years for him to redefine his role not in terms of managing price but of managing value delivered to clients and recognising that the salesforce was his tool for communicating that value, rather than vice versa.

Very few people enjoy a straight-line career progression, and understanding how we manage our business and personal lives and success and failure means that we are much more in control and personally empowered actively to address these issues.

EXAMPLE 3.2

A recently appointed Product Manager in a low-technology food-manufacturing business had a lot to do to establish his credibility. Previously a technical guru he had left the company to seek opportunity. Recognising his intelligence and high work rate the Marketing Director enticed him to rejoin the firm. He had two jobs to do initially, to demonstrate his own commitment to the company and develop marketing skills in order to have credibility in his new role.

The Marketing Director counselled him to understand how to manage his own personal trajectory within the organisation, to the extent that a graph complete with dates was placed over his desk. This served as a visible reminder of progress and motivation for success. He recognised that hard work was not enough and that he had to manage his position with the company. After a tough start he went on to great success, heading the largest business unit within the company. He has now moved on to work for the industry association and successfully manages industry sector affairs at a national and international level.

PART III

Finding your way through marketing

INTRODUCTION: WHAT IS MARKETING?

Some experts say that there is just one perspective of marketing. By this they mean that the same marketing principles can be applied to every situation related to trading something with somebody. Others say that marketing principles are more specific depending on the discipline. Well, yes, but then again, no. We would say that the marketing of products is different from the marketing of services and FMCG from industrial products. Certainly not-for-profit enterprises are seen to have unique challenges. Do big companies face the same marketing issues and require the same type of marketing solutions as new business start-ups?

Everybody is entitled to their point of view and we would hesitate to say that these views are either right or wrong. If pushed we would suggest that the truth is probably somewhere in between, by which we mean that some principles are universally applicable whilst others depend very much upon circumstances. We can summarise the situation as shown in Figure III.1. As this book deals essentially with industrial marketing, when one company sells to another company, in this third part we will discuss a more general framework for understanding industrial marketing:

- basic marketing principles – those which can be applied in virtually all circumstances

- industrial marketing principles more specific to the industrial environment

- marketing of technological innovation.

However, this will have an emphasis on three main aspects relevant to industrial marketing – technology, uncertainty and market development. In other words where the business is led by market needs and its ability to generate new technology.

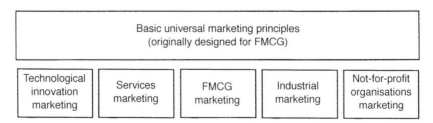

Basic universal marketing principles (originally designed for FMCG)				
Technological innovation marketing	Services marketing	FMCG marketing	Industrial marketing	Not-for-profit organisations marketing

Figure III.1 Several marketing disciplines

What is marketing?   **4**

KEY POINTS

The essence of marketing involves understanding the client's needs and requirements and how these, together with the continually changing business environment, can best be addressed by the company. Marketing people are not fortune tellers. They need to collect and process data to understand the clients, the markets and the competition together with the wider environment. This is in order that appropriate decisions can be taken in both the short and long term.

Marketing strategy is the linkage between doing the right things and doing things right. The aim is to achieve consistency and compromise between what the company

- *wants to do*
- *is able to do*
- *may do.*

The marketing process in principle consists of five main areas

1. *business review or audit*
2. *information collection and analysis*
3. *definition of objectives*
4. *implementation*
5. *monitoring and control.*

ROLE OF MARKETING

From a general perspective marketing primarily consists of understanding the environment to which the company is exposed. Marketing helps the company to adapt to the environment and to influence the environment in favour of the company (Figure 4.1).

Taking a more commercial point of view, the job of marketing can be defined as being customer orientated within a competitive environment. Marketing could also be described as understanding and satisfying the client's requirements whilst taking into account the presence and actions of competitors and understanding their position in the market-place. However, marketing is not selling. Marketing's role is to anticipate and co-

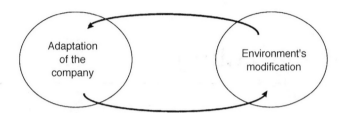

Figure 4.1 Adapting the company to its environment

ordinate the activities necessary to meet client needs and company objectives but not to sell the products. If marketing has performed its task well then selling is made much easier, but remains the task of those primarily responsible for client contact.

To grasp what being customer orientated means in practice we suggest that you hold at the front of your mind one of the fundamental axioms of marketing

'WHICH MEANS THAT'

As Professor Malcolm McDonald (1995, p. 103) says, 'being expert in technical details is not enough. The customer may not be able to work out the benefits that particular features bring. A simple formula to ensure that this customer-orientated approach is adopted is always to use the phrase "which means that" to link a feature to the benefit'.

- The maintenance time is reduced from three to four hours 'which means that' maintenance costs are reduced by 20 per cent.

- Our engines are made of aluminium alloy 'which means that' they are lighter, 'which means that' more units can be carried in a standard container 'which means that' transport costs can be reduced by X per cent.

'Which means that' brings customer orientation to the forefront. Every time these words are used it encourages a client-based point of view. Eventually the only point that really matters for clients is their point of view – rather than yours.

Consider the following example to understand the situation that a lack of customer orientation can lead to. Take the example of a client who makes plaster tiles (Roqueplo 1983). Would you think the client will understand if you suggest that 'we want to sell you a second-to-none product which generates high-frequency electromagnetic waves from a magnetron through a wave tunnel to excite water molecules'! Alternatively, what do you think the client will understand if you say 'which means that you can dry your plaster tiles more quickly, more thoroughly, with no cracks and much cheaper than using your conventional oven'. In other words, we are selling the benefits rather than the features of a commercial microwave.

Being client orientated can sometimes simply mean 'speaking the client's language' as shown by the following story. A very successful bank with a strong rural presence could not really understand the reason for their success. So, they carried out a marketing survey and were very surprised to learn that the reason for their success was the incompetence of their personnel! Why? In fact the cashiers in the rural branches were themselves

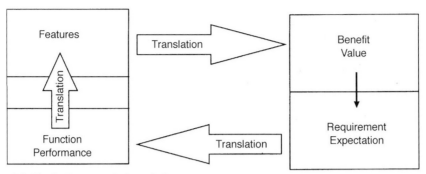

Figure 4.2 Marketing equals translating

country people, brought up in the same environment as the clients and speaking the same language. As stated by one customer 'We like them because they understand our problems and don't use the same complicated words as other bankers!'

To summarise, 'marketing' a product means 'translating' technical features into a benefit for the client (Figure 4.2). It also means that before we do this we have to understand the client's requirements and translate these into the function and performance factors associated with a product in order that we can provide the appropriate features and hence benefits.

Presented in this way, marketing is somewhere between the client and the company. In fact this is one of its main characteristics compared to many other functions in the company, as only marketing has the prime responsibility of standing outside the company and looking both at the external environment and customers and linking that understanding to the company. Marketing can be thought of as listening and responding to the needs of the client. There is a danger, in that by taking this principle too far we become too reactive to the demands of the client and they end up managing us. Our role as marketers is to identify the optimum match of our needs against those of the client using our available resources.

ORIGINS OF MARKETING

At one time communities were self-sufficient and provided, more or less, everything that they needed from their own resources. The prime requirements were for food and shelter and this was the era of subsistence farming. Markets developed as a way of trading surpluses, a glance at a map will show how roads radiate out from the early market towns. At this time survival was more or less a full-time job, it was not until agriculture became more efficient that there was an opportunity for labour to specialise. The agricultural revolution was the predecessor of the industrial revolution and it was at this time that workers moved from the country to the developing industrial cities. The generation of wealth meant that there was an emerging demand for consumer products.

The satisfaction of this early demand involved neither a client orientation or much competition; in fact there was no need for marketing. Henry Ford was the father of the production line making millions of his ubiquitous model T cars. His famous comment was 'you can have any colour you like as long as it is black'. Hardly a customer-orientated approach, but then when you could sell every car that was made, why worry? The reason to worry was given by Alfred Sloane who was Henry Ford's equivalent at General Motors. He offered cheap and reliable cars but with a choice of colours, and as a result eventually gained market leadership from Ford.

In thinking about marketing we can see that it is different from a simple trading exchange. Marketing starts when the exchange is focused on the client and when the common effort of all those working for the company is dedicated to client satisfaction. Competition can explain a marketing approach, but some monopolistic companies also demonstrate this. EDF in France, the monopoly provider of electricity, is a good example of such a company practising marketing. EDF has a monopoly to sell electricity, but does not have a monopoly on energy. Electricity has to compete with gas, oil or even wind power. Of course monopolies are traditionally unpopular, but EDF shows a real commitment to developing its image and to client satisfaction in order to maintain and increase the share of energy fulfilled by electricity.

ART RATHER THAN SCIENCE?

Marketing is often considered as an art, an elusive skill rather than a science, with its ability to demonstrate relationships between inputs and outputs and a strict set of rules governing behaviour. In industrially- and technology-orientated companies, which have developed on their ability to understand science and apply technology, it is perhaps not too surprising that marketing has not been fully appreciated. Let us consider this point further.

In any business situation there is a high degree of uncertainty. However hard you try, you will never be able to gather all the information necessary to take a decision with a guaranteed outcome (Figure 4.3). There are simply too many variables in the equation for us to predict with a high degree of certainty.

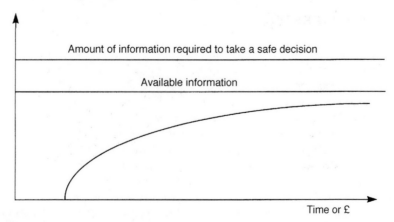

Amount of information required to take a safe decision

Available information

Time or £

Figure 4.3 Is it possible to collect all the information required? (Millier 1989)

Of course, to gather all the information that we might possibly require takes time. Even if we go through this information gathering and analysis process to try to improve the degree of certainty, it is unlikely that we will achieve a science-like level of probability around the decision. Why is this? Because we live in a dynamic environment, one that is constantly changing. Our clients and our competitors will respond to our actions or even our lack of action. This comes as no great revelation; as Francis Bacon said in 1625

'he that will not apply new remedies must expect new evils'.

In a dynamic and changing environment the 'do nothing' option is not an acceptable strategy. You may be the best in the world at making your particular product, but as the world changes around you mere technical capability and production efficiency is not enough. NCR (National Cash Register) were world leaders in the production of mechanical calculating machines as their name implies. The advent of the electronic calculator has led to their demise and take-over. Retail banks with branches in every high street now find that competition is coming from telephone-based banking services and even supermarkets, whose brand reputation and credibility has enabled them rapidly to build a share of this market. The manufacturers of photographic film are having to compete against digital technology. This allows the photograph of the winning goal at a football match to be sent via a mobile phone back to the head office of a newspaper. The photograph can be placed on the electronic page of the newspaper before the match has finished.

To compete in this ever-changing and fast-moving world means that information, technology and manufacturing capability are not enough. We also need the ability to understand our competitors' actions, interpret that into the implications for our company and apply our judgement on the best solution. Let us take another example. In this case, rather than looking at the current market-place, how do we understand and manage emerging markets? For example:

- How can we understand our client's need for a CD system based on a laser technology before we are able to demonstrate the product to them?

- How can we manage our entry into the market-place with genetically modified products? Who could have predicted the position of the government and other influencers before the research started and the products were coming to market?

- Will our main competitors roll out a new vacuum pressure gauge next year? Maybe yes, but if we launch ours first, maybe no!

In summary, business is fraught with uncertainty and no amount of market research will guarantee complete knowledge. In turn you are partly responsible by your actions for the very information that you seek; you are not just trying to understand the future but help to create it (Figure 4.4).

Regrettably, no matter how hard you try or how complex and sophisticated the market research that you employ, there is no single, best solution that will guarantee business success. Indeed, if you spend too much time and money collecting market research this could be harmful as whilst you are chasing information, you are not making decisions and driving forward.

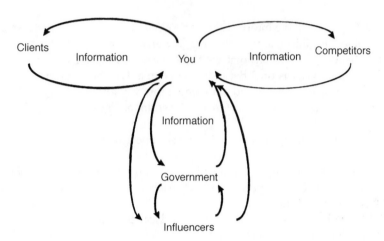

Figure 4.4 Many relationships

Inevitably market research and investigation will be supplemented by experience, expertise, intuition, judgement and the ability to take a calculated risk. Perhaps combined with a little good fortune. All of these subtle skills and complex interactions could help to account for the reasons why so many supposedly rational and scientifically driven people are inherently distrustful of marketing.

This fundamental difference between science and marketing can be put to the test. Any particular problem can have a range of possible solutions, ask the same question of five marketing professionals and you will almost certainly get five different answers, perhaps more if one of them has an MBA. The reason for this is that everybody is different. Inevitably their answers will be based on their marketing skills, background and experience and this will differ from one person to another. Furthermore, there are so many variables influencing a particular marketing question that you can never be sure of the precise parameters. An important factor that would influence your decisions and conclusions may remain obscure. Added to that we must also take into account the fact that marketing involves a series of trade-offs and compromises. For example between:

- short-term–long-term
- investing for tomorrow–profits today
- security–innovation
- added value–competitive price
- volume–flexibility.

Once again all these trade-offs require not just analysis but experience, intuition and judgement.

Lastly, marketing problems are rarely linear and pose a particular problem to those of a scientific orientation who have been trained to find the single, best solution (Figure 4.5). It is dangerous to believe in marketing that everything can be explained by a series of equations, although this was a popular pastime as the 'science of marketing' was being

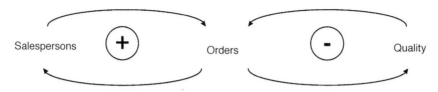

Figure 4.5 Marketing is not linear

attempted in the 1950s and 60s. A small example helps to illustrate the lack of linearity that exists in marketing problems.

To increase the number of orders you appoint a new salesperson; and it works. There is a linear relationship between the appointment of the salesperson and the increase in orders. The increase in orders requires an increase in production. The requirement to produce more influences quality, which starts to slip as the plant comes under more pressure. Quality drops and as a result orders tail off. The net result was that the greater the selling effort the lower the number of orders.

A BIG DIFFERENCE

A very important maxim to bear in mind is this:

Remember the distinction between:

Doing the right things
and
Doing things right

Following McDonald (1995, p. 23) we diagramatically summarise the distinction in Figure 4.6. Drawing this distinction more finely is summarised in Figure 4.7.

In marketing terms the objectives should only be about products and markets. What markets or what clients do you want to deal with and which products do you wish to sell? Although of course, we start from where we start from (Figure 4.8). Inevitably you will have a current range of products for which you will have to find a market. So what comes first, the product or the market? To be successful these products and markets will both have to meet in the market-place. Hence, marketing is sometimes referred to as a matching process whereby we continue to refine our understanding of the market and adapt our product offering accordingly.

The role of marketing strategy is the linkage between doing the right things and doing things right in order to achieve a competitive position in the market. Marketing strategy helps to resolve the tension that inevitably exists between what your company wants to do, is able to do and may do, a consistency between these sometimes divergent points is required (Figure 4.9).

Achieving a competitive position means optimising your market share by managing the few key factors that managers have to understand in order to succeed: the critical success factors. We shall consider this in more detail and in particular the principle of

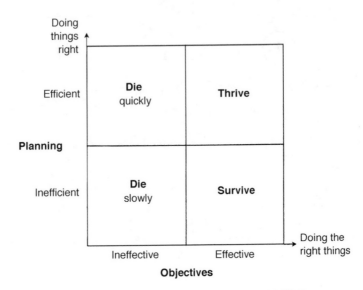

Figure 4.6 Right things and things right (adapted from McDonald 1995)

Doing the right things refers to	Doing things right refers to
Where are we going?	How do we get there?
What do we want to achieve?	How do we achieve this?
Long term	Short term
Objectives	Means
Alternative	Improving
Vision	Planning
Steering	Managing
Giving direction	Carrying on

Figure 4.7 Difference between doing the right things and doing things right

Figure 4.8 The product/market loop

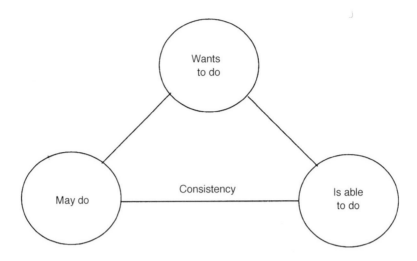

Figure 4.9 The consistency principle (Millier 1999)

consistency in Part V. For the time being let us conclude by saying that you need to achieve consistency between the marketing objectives and

- the company's business aims
- the sales objectives
- the resources at your disposal
- the market signs
- the intensity of competition.

MARKETING PROCESS

As with many marketing principles the process of marketing is easy to understand but its implementation is somewhat more difficult. In this chapter we shall outline the process, but will devote a further chapter to each of the important steps of the marketing process in Part VII.

To understand the marketing process, let us take a simple analogy. Assume that for your next holiday you are planning a trip to the USA, India or wherever. What will you do first? Check the atlas, or perhaps go to a bookshop and buy a book on each of the two or three possible destinations. Perhaps you might visit a travel agency to discuss your ideas and requirements. In other words your first task is to get some *information* to enable you to make a more informed decision on your destination. This information-collection phase is, of course, *market research*. It consists of collecting and analysing market-orientated data in order to be clear about your current position, your future options and how to set and achieve the objectives.

Once you have collected this information you might read the books and consider several possible options of how you will spend your time at your holiday destination. You want to spend your time near the sea or perhaps in the country or city. Will you take a backpack and hitch-hike, travel by train or hire a car? The USA is just one possible destination but there are so many possibilities once you arrive there. In other words, you have to think about your trip, elaborate a number of *scenarios* and then check these scenarios against a range of criteria. For example, there are cost implications depending on your choice and this might be an important consideration.

Once you have decided on one of these alternatives you can then get down to the detailed planning with a map in one hand and your diary in the other. The first day you will arrive at your destination, pick up your hire car and then spend a couple of days driving across country to reach your ultimate destination. You are now *planning* the detail of your trip, taking into account the time you will spend on each element of the trip and balancing this against your budget.

Having done all the background preparation the time comes when you can climb aboard the aeroplane and enjoy your holiday. Your are now *implementing* the project you have been preparing for so long. Whilst on holiday everything goes well until the car breaks down. You are towed to a garage but it takes a day for the rental agency to replace the car. A day is lost in your itinerary, which means that you must reconsider your plans. In other words there is a *control and feedback mechanism* which manages the implementation of the project. Well, marketing in process terms is just like one big holiday, although it may not at times feel like it. We can diagramatically describe it in Figure 4.10.

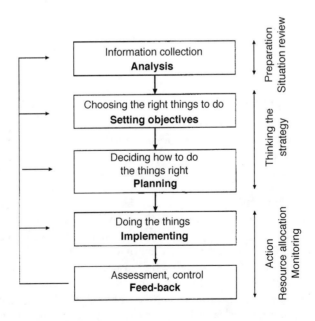

Figure 4.10 The marketing process

Step one: information collection

This is the market research phase of the process, conducted as a precursor to the next steps. The objective here is to summarise the current position, be clear on future options and understand the resources available that can be committed to future objectives. In principle, there are three types of information that are required.

1. Information about the type of business that you are in. The characteristics of the industry, business and broad understanding of the market.

2. Market overview information. This will describe the characteristics of the market-place. You should aim to understand the market segments and critical drivers of the market-place. Not only will this process help you to understand who the clients are and their needs but also why these things are important to them and how they can be delivered. The greatest and most common crime is to think you know what the client wants rather than to know.

3. Information about your current activities. Within the company you should have a reasonable amount of appropriate information about sales volume, margins and trends, relative performance of products, distribution channels and market. You should also have a summary or audit of your resources such as products, people, technology, plant capacity, etc.

The principal information is summarised under three broad headings. The industry audit, the market audit and the internal audit.

A common question that managers often ask is how much information is enough information? This can often be a significant problem for managers particularly if they are undertaking this for the first time. This is quite understandable as of course we do not know what we do not know. Our natural instinct is to gather as much information as possible in order to achieve a higher degree of certainty when we eventually start to take decisions. Our advice would be to aim to understand the critical factors affecting the market, for example, segmentation, market drivers and your current performance as measured by volume, value and trend against the market. Experience has a big part to play here as managers often see this as a very challenging task when they first undertake it.

Step two: setting objectives

The starting point for strategy development is one of the most critical and essential tasks in marketing; market segmentation.

 Marketing segmentation is the most important and critical task in marketing. It is likely to solve 80 per cent of marketing problems *as long as it is a proper marketing segmentation.*

We would like to draw your attention to this vital point. Poor segmentation leads to inappropriate strategy. Yet, very often, segmentation is not carried out with what really makes sense in the market but with information easy to find in the company. This means that if you take for granted that the industry is divided into groups such as 'Aeronautics, car, machine tools, chemical industry' (which is often the case in a general-purpose database) you might miss that your real market segments are 'R&D laboratories, production control managers, IT specialists'. A pre-existing segmentation in your company often acts as a barrier rather than an aid to segmenting the market properly.

Market segmentation involves understanding your customers in such detail that you can group them together on the basis of their similar needs and behaviour. These groups are known as segments. A good segmentation will almost suggest the appropriate strategy to meet the expectations of customers. Following on from this we can often identify that marketing problems arise from either a poor initial segmentation or a failure to respond effectively to the messages that each segment sends to the company. Segmentation is a particular form of market description and helps you to form a picture of that market-place. A good segmentation will help you to understand not just the 'what' of each segment but also the 'why' so that we can really understand client needs and means to satisfy their needs. Even this is not enough as you must have a clear view of your strengths and weaknesses in each segment in comparison to your competitors. Only when you have done this can you then start to target appropriate segments (Figure 4.11).

Having chosen the appropriate market segments you must now *position* your product offering in order that you meet customer needs better than competitors. This positioning is achieved by *differentiation*. The basis of differentiation is understanding which element of the product offering gives better value to our clients compared to that of our competitors.

For example, Jaguar and BMW are not equally positioned in the executive car market. Jaguar has an image more associated with classic British coachbuilding skills and understated, yet class-leading performance, whilst BMW is renowned for the quality of its engineering, handling and performance but not necessarily for the overtones of luxury. A common mistake when defining the market position is to consider this in product terms, positioned against competitors, rather than market terms positioned

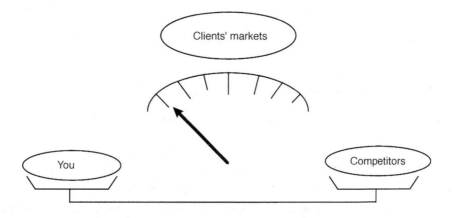

Figure 4.11 Positioning your offer compared to competitors

against customer needs. This means that we need to understand the market as otherwise we could make the mistake of positioning our products in the wrong market. Ford has never been particularly successful in the executive car market and therefore acquired Lincoln in the US and Jaguar in Europe to achieve presence in this market.

 There is a danger of being too customer orientated or too competitor orientated. If you focus too much on the client's expectation you may miss a dangerous competitor. Conversely, being too focused on your competition may lead you to lose the client's viewpoint. You might either spend all your money in innovating to keep ahead of the competition, which can become an aim in itself. Or alternatively condemn yourself to follow your competitors. Being competitor focused is, therefore, a good way to become product orientated rather than client orientated. It is just as if you were driving your car following the car ahead of you. You can do this but it is dangerous, and you let others drive you.

We usually recognise that there are four levers, the four Ps, that can be pulled to differentiate the product offering.

1. **Product** (or Service): features, performance, design, quality, packaging, service.

2. **Price**: high, low, discounts and rebate structure, value for money.

3. **Place**: the route by which your product reaches the market. Distribution channels could include direct to clients, retailers, Internet.

4. **Promotion**: all aspects of communicating with customers. Advertising, trade shows, telesales, direct mail. The salesforce could be included under this heading, the reason we employ salespeople is because of their unique ability to communicate with and respond to the specific needs of customers.

Positioning is achieved by the appropriate blend of these four elements, the four Ps, which constitute the *marketing mix*. The specific marketing mix targeted at a customer segment is sometimes known as a product offering. These four Ps are in fact supplier rather than client driven. From a client perspective we can think of these as the four Cs (Lauterborn in Schultz *et al.* 1993).

1. Product – **Customer's** – wants and needs.

2. Price – **Cost** – what does the client have to give up in order to obtain your product? Not just the purchase price but perhaps also the time involved in driving to the shop or in learning about your product. Think, for instance, how much it would cost your client to adopt your computer system instead of your competitor's product.

3. Place – **Convenience** – how can your client more easily access your product?

4. Promotion – **Communication** – what does the client want to hear?

In order to manage risk a sensible strategy should consider working with a number of segments, perhaps in different markets with different products. In this way the company can gain some insurance against rapid changes in the market-place while still benefiting from economies of scale and market presence.

Step three: action planning

Action planning involves the allocation and direction of resources. In simple terms this means

- what will be done
- who will do it
- what means are available
- with what resources
- when it will be done.

It is often appropriate to break down the action plan by segments. After all, the reason for segmenting the market is in order that the product offered can be more closely matched to the needs of groups of customers. At the risk of generating a confusing number of plans we would suggest that the action plan is considered in three main stages:

1. The product plan – the products to be targeted to the segment and whether any further product development is required. Will it be necessary to introduce and launch a new product?

2. The communication plan – describes how the product is to be promoted to the target segments. It describes the promotional techniques to be used and the messages that need to be communicated. This creates the environment for successful sales.

3. The selling plan – this directs and targets the sales resource which includes not just the salesforce but also demonstration and merchandising material, for example. The sales plan will identify and target customers and set objectives for the sales activity.

This can be broken down into a step-by-step approach as illustrated in Figure 4.12. As there is no best solution the process is often iterative, trading off activities and resources between segments as the cost implications become clearer and the budget eventually emerges, or as frequently happens, is imposed.

Market segment no. 1	Month 1	Month 2	Month 3	Month 4	Month 5	Month 6
Product						
Sales						
Promotion						

Figure 4.12 Breaking the plan down into several steps

At the end of this phase we would encourage you to produce a brief written report summarising the strategy. This is a great help in ensuring that you do really understand what you plan to do, to the extent that you can commit it to paper so that it may be communicated to others. This is the marketing plan and often contains some or all of the following:

- a market summary, an overview of the key market issues
- an overview of competitors, summarising the current state of play
- marketing objectives
- the detailed plans summarising distribution, production, communication and sales activity
- the timetable
- responsibilities
- the budget.

To conclude, planning gives many benefits by optimising use of resources and hence improving efficiency. A problem can arise if the plan becomes an end in itself and hence rigid and inflexible.

Despite the apparent simplicity that the marketing process presents there are some useful pointers than may help you, particularly if you are attempting this for the first time:

- The principles of marketing are easy to state and make eminent good sense. Implementation can be somewhat more challenging and at times discouraging. Approached in a workmanlike way, apparently daunting tasks can be broken down into bite-sized chunks. Particularly if you are doing this for first time, remember that 'better' is the enemy of 'good enough'. We would advise that you adopt a pragmatic balance between rigour and process.

- Sometimes decisions are made in advance of their implementation. This can often be three times longer than you think, hence it is known as the π factor. The problem with an extended delay is that there is always a temptation to revisit the decision. This is sometimes called the 'faucet effect' (Figure 4.13) (Senge 1990). If you have ever been in a hotel room where the shower does not seem to work too well there is a great temptation continually to adjust the temperature of the water which is

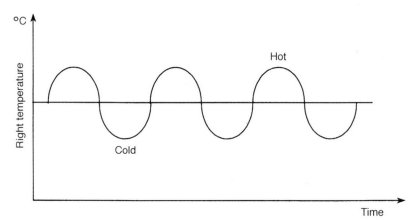

Figure 4.13 The 'faucet effect'

alternately too hot or too cold. In other words corrective action is applied before the initial decision has worked through the system.

- In the hothouse atmosphere of a busy company the temptation is always to deal with the almost overwhelming daily pressures but lose sight of the big issues and critical objectives. This leads to confusion between what is urgent and what is important. The opposite extreme of this is the condition sometimes known as 'analysis paralysis'. In order to make a critical decision you collect more and more information, this is then processed with the wide range of analytical tools available and eventually managing data becomes the end rather than the means. The extensive array of data analysed in every conceivable way serves to dazzle rather than illuminate. A sanity check is provided by asking the question 'what am I going to do differently or better as a result of obtaining this piece of information?'

- A real danger in marketing is to think that we understand what the clients want, rather than systematically gathering and analysing their requirements. In our experience this can be a particular problem in companies where research and technology are the strongest focus. If we remain firmly rooted within the company and either do not seek information from the market or selectively receive the information that fits our view of the world then inevitably our understanding will be fractured. We can then deceive ourselves into thinking that there is a huge market for our technically interesting but commercially doubtful new invention. If we make our own movie then it is easy to think that this perception is reality. Is anybody still using a Sinclair C5?

Step four: implementation

This is the point at which the planning stops and the action begins. By this stage it should be clear what is going to be done, how it is going to be done, who is going to do it and how it will be resourced. The plan not only serves to answer these points but also helps to establish checkpoints and objectives for the implementation phase.

Step five: feedback

This step consists of following up the field activity as it is taking place, checking that the implementation is going to plan or at least understanding and correcting for any variances. Inevitably there will be many useful learning points arising during this phase and appropriate feedback helps to improve experience.

IMPLEMENTATION GUIDELINES

Having had to do this ourselves we would suggest a number of practical tips which may help you to descend the learning curve a little less painfully than we did.

- Structure the information at an early stage. A number of books suggest checklists that can be used for audit purposes. Develop a framework for your data and ensure that it is properly referenced and filed either electronically or in hard copy.

- In the first round of this process you will inevitably collect too much information. As the process continues continually review and criticise the value of the data so that you can identify key market characteristics and drivers. This will enable you to reduce progressively the amount of data and will guide your data collection next time.

- Develop a 'black book' or 'bible' where you keep a summary of the data. This should be properly indexed and referenced and also contain material in presentation format. It is surprising the number of times that you may be asked to give a quick summary of performance, competitive activity, market-place trends, etc. Being able to refer to a consistent and regularly updated source of information will increase your credibility and improve your perception amongst colleagues.

- Use the marketing planning process as a way of structuring your work and making progress instead of drowning in analysis. You will almost certainly never have enough information and the temptation is to continue to gather information rather than to apply the '80/20' rule, push on and make progress.

- Define a timetable of activities with checklists, milestones, inputs and outputs. This is a planning tool that helps to structure your work and in doing so it will generate commitment.

Principles of industrial marketing

5

KEY POINTS

Industrial marketing is characterised by the following features:

- *Clients are few but large.*
- *Clients are organisations rather than individuals.*
- *Clients seek to reduce risk and are risk averse.*
- *The market consists of a chain of relationships.*
- *Relationships tend to be close and enduring.*

Therefore

- *Each client is valuable.*
- *Reputation is important.*
- *The behaviour of people in the organisation is important.*
- *Management of risk is important in relationships.*
- *All levels of the industrial chain should be understood.*
- *The relationship with a client should be considered as an investment.*

DEFINITION OF INDUSTRIAL MARKETING

In what way is industrial marketing different from consumer goods marketing? Industrial marketing is the kind of marketing you do when you want to sell your products or services to other companies or organisations, a hospital or car manufacturer for example. In other words, it is different from the so-called 'consumer marketing', which is relevant to selling washing powder or nappies to consumers themselves.

A continuum of clients

The markets can be located on an axis from the largest number of clients (consumer markets) to single clients (e.g. turnkey projects, the sale of a dam to Venezuela). In the middle of the axis is industrial marketing.

Number of customers	Large	Some	Single
Type of marketing	Consumer	Industrial	Turnkey projects

If we want to be more precise we can add a dimension to the diagram taking into account the order size (Figure 5.1). The smaller the size in general the more advisable it is to use extensive distribution. The larger the size, the more specific is the method of distribution, introducing issues such as Key Account Management. Right in the middle is the appropriate order size to be handled by the sales force. Box 9 represents typically the so-called turnkey project marketing (one single order, 'one shot'). Boxes 1 2 3 correspond to consumer goods marketing, Boxes 4 5 7 relate to industrial marketing.

	Large number of customers	Some customers	Single customer
Small order size £s	1 Food (daily/weekly purchase)	4 Nuts & bolts	7
Medium order size £ks	2 Car, white & brown goods (occasional purchase)	5 Machine tools Flat glass	8 Fighter aircraft
Very big orders Several £ms	3 House (infrequent purchase)	6 Turnkey plant	9 Dam

Figure 5.1 Positioning industrial marketing

PRINCIPLES OF INDUSTRIAL MARKETING

Some principles of marketing have been discussed in Chapter 4. The principles of industrial marketing are consistent with these but there are distinct differences between the marketing of industrial products and of fast-moving consumer goods (FMCG). An overview of these differences is given in Figure 5.2, which compares these two types of marketing.

Segmentation is the heart of the marketing approach. Therefore, even in industrial marketing insightful segmentation must be carried out as the starting point of marketing strategy and, above all, the segmentation must not be made on the basis of what is easy to find. It is not a mathematical assignment. You should never use your existing database structure or your sales organisation as an *a-priori* basis for segmentation without very careful consideration. Segmentation must provide you with an overview, a picture, a map of your market.

	Consumer	Industrial
Clients	Many Widely dispersed	Few Concentrated
Market	Consumers directly served by retailers and distributors	Derived demand. Industrial chain, long and complex
Buying behaviour **Relationships**	Individual and family decision Low individual buying power	Group decision Formal procedures High buyer power
Product	Standard Psychological factors important Positioned on emotional and perceptual factors	Technical complexity Specification important Bespoke and customised Positioned on functions and features
Price	Low unit price 'Take it or leave it', no negotiation	High unit price Negotiation and bid/tender Standard items from price list
Promotion	Mass-media advertising Role of the brand	Emphasis on personal selling Reputation important
Place	Established retail chain Stock availability Seasonality	Direct Made to order Standard items in stock

Figure 5.2 Comparison between industrial and consumer goods marketing

INDUSTRIAL CLIENTS

How many clients do you have? Perhaps one or two? Ten? A few hundred? Perhaps even thousands but almost certainly not millions. That is the first and main difference between FMCG and industrial marketing. Not only are clients fewer, but that also means that they are relatively more important, perhaps when measured as a proportion of turnover. We cannot afford to lose these valuable clients, as not only would it take time to recover the lost client and hence the turnover, but as clients are fewer they are more difficult to gain. Of course, your potential clients are currently dealing with your competitors. If they are pleased with the quality of the products and services they receive why should they want to give you their business? A blunt weapon that can be used is price, but price competition is rarely a smart move.

A French proverb says that for every client lost in FMCG markets there are ten to be found; for every ten lost in industrial markets, only one can be gained. This means that consumers tend to be treated as a 'universe' – a market of largely similar, homogeneous potential buyers. So if we do not sell a toothbrush or packet of breakfast cereal today the chances are that we can encourage more consumers to purchase tomorrow, particularly if we run a promotion or advertising camapign.

In industrial markets losing clients is a much more serious issue. Markets tend to be smaller and clients are fewer but larger, hence the level of knowledge and understanding by clients of their suppliers is high. Reputations are hard to win but can be easily lost, as bad news travels faster than good. One dissatisfied client could well lead to others. It is something of an axiom that negative word of mouth is much more effective than any positive messages that we want to send out, but we suggest that you do not put this to the test! It is said one satisfied client will tell three others but a dissatisfied client will influence perhaps ten others.

As we tend not to deal with large numbers of customers there is an opportunity for us to talk much more directly to our clients, rather than to gather opinions and information through statistically managed survey techniques. There is a greater obligation on us to talk and listen to our customers and really understand what they are saying. But of course it is not organisations that do business, it is people. Has anybody ever shaken IBM's hand? Certainly not, because IBM is an organisation. Within that organisation it is quite likely that you would have a number of different contacts, perhaps at a range of locations. It is also quite likely that they will be doing very different jobs, for example:

- purchasing manager
- quality manager
- production engineer
- management accountant
- logistics manager
- etc.

The people that we speak to in our clients' organisations can have different responsibilities and skills, and each of them will have special concerns which will sometimes require an expert from our company who can talk their language. For example, one of our ultrasound specialists will be able to meet the manager of our client's 'Non-Destructive Test Laboratory'. The purchasing decision is therefore much more complex than in FMCG markets and the relationship with the client goes far beyond the purchaser/supplier relationship typically understood within consumer markets.

INDUSTRIAL MARKETS

Who are our clients? Have you ever stopped to ask yourself this almost superfluous question? And why is it worth asking? Consider the following example.

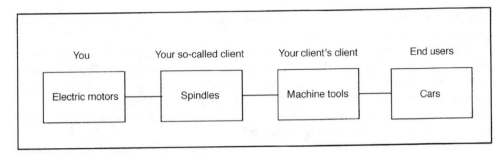

Figure 5.3 Example of industrial chain

Your company makes electric motors for a client who manufactures machine-tool spindles. Whose need are you satisfying with your motor? The spindle manufacturer's, or the machine-tool manufacturer's? If a machine is very specific for one particular application should you be talking to the end user who decides the specification in terms of the job that they want it to do? This could be a car manufacturer for example, the client of the machine-tool manufacturer (Figure 5.3). This illustrates another important characteristic of industrial markets. Industrial markets are in fact industrial chains, which means the real client who actually purchases your product has their own client, and so on, until we reach the end user or consumer. Our client is just a link in a longer chain and if we really want to be successful in our market-place we need to understand requirements not just of our direct clients but of all the other members of the chain. This chain has a number of implications for us.

- We must take into account the requirements of every constituent of the chain when formulating our product.

- We should understand the requirements at every level *that makes use of our product*. If we take the example of an automotive supply chain, an end user or consumer is hardly likely to be too concerned about how the cylinder head in the car engine has been machined!

- We should also communicate not just with our clients but with our client's client. In that way we can sell to our direct client and also generate demand further down the chain to both 'push' and 'pull' product sales. An excellent example of this is the 'Intel Inside' campaign whereby Intel branded their processors and then generated awareness of their products at end-user level, and effectively managed communications with all the links in the chain.

This is easy to say but difficult to put into practice. Sometimes your clients place orders but you do not know what they use your product for. This is dangerous in the sense that you can sell your product for years and be complacent that next year will be even better than this year. But the client can suddenly stop buying with no explanation. Maybe their own products have been improved and your product does not match their new requirements any longer. As there is no communication you are not aware of this, and the only thing you can do is weep over your lost sales. This 'screen effect' has cost the life of many car and aircraft sub-contractors in the 1980s.

Collecting information at different levels in the chain is one of the most difficult trade-offs in industrial marketing. It can be much more difficult than you think to get downstream information, as of course we do not have direct knowledge or contact with our client's client. There is also the possibility of upsetting our own clients who may well be suspicious of what we are doing, and can be fairly forthright in telling us to mind our own business. Finally, as we attempt to gather more information and build relationships at different levels, this could become more expensive and more difficult to manage as we try to sort the relevant from the irrelevant and determine what is useful and useless (Figure 5.4).

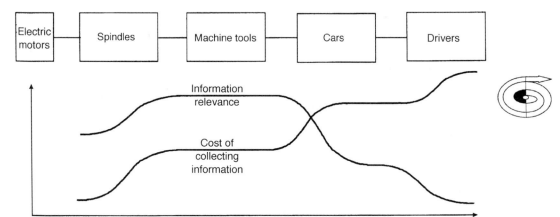

Figure 5.4 Collecting information along the chain

The consequence of this linkage through the chain is that our product contributes to the quality and reputation of our client's products. As our client base tends to be composed of few but large companies then there are significant implications if product quality is variable or unsatisfactory. A good example of this is a paint manufacturer who eventually had to pay for the cost of re-painting a number of sea-going vessels as the paint was blistering after just a few months' exposure to sea water. This linkage is particularly important if we are working with continuous manufacturing processes where the consequences of a line stoppage can be very large indeed.

The other point that this demonstrates is that all industrial markets ultimately depend upon a consumer to buy a product. In the example we have used, unless a consumer purchases a car then there will be no demand for our electric motors. Demand for our products is derived from that of the consumer as it passes back up the chain. This is an important point, because by understanding the nature of the industrial chain in which we are working, we can understand the factors that contribute to the demand for our product and hence this will help in forecasting and forward planning.

HOW CLIENTS BUY

Unlike consumers who may buy products just on a whim, industrial purchasers are often thought of as having a much more rational pattern of purchasing behaviour. The significance of industrial purchases is often greater due to the size of the purchase and influence of the industrial chain. Industrial purchasers are often careful, risk averse and even distrustful of potential purchasers that they do not know very well.

The purchaser may well establish testing and qualification procedures and check that the supplier can consistently and reliably deliver products of the appropriate specification. It is usually considered that purchasing behaviour is aimed at reducing risk. Following Michel *et al.* (1997) these risks can be thought of as:

- Technical – will the product meet specification? Will it meet all my requirements?
- Financial – what is the purchase price compared to comparable products? What is the cost-in-use? What is the payback period and are there any hidden costs?
- Service – is the supplier reliable? Can I be assured of supplies in the future? Will the product be delivered on time?
- Relationships – how well do we know the supplier? Do they have a reputation for reliability? Are they financially sound?

Obviously many of these risks are perceived rather than actual, but will be affected by:

The size of the purchase. Buying one PC represents a much lower risk than buying a fully integrated and networked system perhaps made up of several hundred PCs.

The significance of the purchase. A capital purchase fundamental to the client's business activity represents a big commitment by the client, and often an irreversible one. A stand-alone piece of test equipment, such as an oscilloscope, represents a much lower risk.

Relative risk. What is the risk compared to directly substitutable alternatives from competitors? Does a difference in price reflect the difference in risk?

A REASON TO SAY 'YES'

One of our consultancy clients asked us one day: 'We are a small chemical company surrounded by giant chemical companies – yet we survive. Why do clients buy our products?' This might seem a naive question but it is nevertheless an interesting one. Why don't suppliers ask this of themselves more often? We will try to understand why a cautious and risk-averse industrial client might say 'yes' to your product.

Firstly, your clients may well be dissatisfied with their current supplier and actively seeking an alternative. Also, not wishing to have all their eggs in one basket, clients may also want to reduce risk and dependency by actively managing a number of different suppliers. In the very competitive industrial climate of today it is not enough to win new clients and then stand still, clients seek continuing innovation from their suppliers. This is something of a paradox as clients aim to reduce risk and yet also want more innovation, which actually means more risk. Clients want to have their cake, or even your cake, and to be able to eat it too. So much for the rational buyer!

Thinking about this further, risk can be a reason or sometimes a pretext for rejecting a product, but the absence of risk is not necessarily a reason to buy. In other words the client needs a reason to buy a particular product from a different supplier. As it is people who make the buying decisions, they need motivation. We can identify (Millier 1999) a number of sources of such motivation.

- Production/technical. Research-based solutions can give a unique opportunity to solve a technical problem and improve productivity.

- Sales. Provide a better service to clients and perhaps assist them to sell more product or to sell into new markets. When working as a Marketing Director, a supplier provided one of us with considerable assistance in developing export market opportunities.

- Competitiveness. A product that offers a competitive advantage is a powerful motivation for purchase. Perhaps a new technology offers substantial cost reduction opportunities. Pilkington, a glass manufacturing company, became a global player due to their invention of float-glass technology, which reduced the costs of production very significantly. They generated substantial income by licensing the technology to other companies.

- Financial. There are a wide range of opportunities to demonstrate financial advantage, generating and selling value also enables a higher price to be achieved. Lower initial cost, higher throughput, less stock and work in progress, etc., can all be expressed as financial benefits.

- Social. Products which are easier to use or safer, quieter or do not require protective clothing and equipment will be preferred, particularly by users.

- Legislation. Changes in legislation can generate needs for better or different equipment. The makers of ink-jet printing equipment have seen sales boom as a result of the requirement to date stamp food products.

- Environment. Requirements to reduce waste and control emissions continue and firms are these days much more aware of their wider social responsibilities. In the automotive market there has been a switch to water-based rather than solvent-based paints in order to meet stricter environmental standards.

- Strategic shift. This is for clients actively seeking to make a step-wise rather than incremental competitive move. This requires a very good understanding of the client's business and the industry in which they operate. The use of group-ware products such as 'Lotus Notes' has dramatically changed the way that people work, salesforces are managed, etc.

- Personal. Do you really understand the basis on which the purchaser that you are dealing with is judged? Can you help them to be seen to be successful in their own organisation? A supplier of aero-engine components was consistently unsuccessful despite meeting quality standards and tough requirements for price. What they had failed to understand was that one of the factors on which purchasing managers were judged was their ability to negotiate discounts from list prices. Simply raising the list price to increase the discount was enough to gain the business!

- Fashion. Even in industry fashion has an influence. Supposedly rational and unemotional industrial managers will still be inclined to buy vogue products such as optical-fibre-based sensors, local area networks and e-commerce systems. Nowadays of course every self-respecting manager has a laptop, mobile phone and an electronic organiser with a solid business case to justify their purchase using the company's money.

ORGANISATIONAL STRUCTURE AND THE BUYING PROCESS

Why do some clients take quick decisions, but with others the purchasing decision seems to take forever? Clearly when it takes too long we can guess that this is unlikely to result in good news. Why is it that the longer it takes for the decision to be made, the more likely it is to be a negative one?

The explanation is fairly straightforward. The longer the decision takes the more time there is for reflection and discussion of not only the pros but also the cons. Human nature is such that the concerns often have a stronger negative influence that outweighs other considerations. It is *you* who have the best arguments in favour of *your* products and the greatest interest in selling them. However, if you are not involved in the discussions and not there to support those who are 'selling' the decision to the client, the longer this process takes and the more likely it is that the decision will go against you.

Secondly, no two clients work in the same way. In some large companies the decision-making process can be quite protracted as it is passed from one department to another, each of which has to have an input to the process (Figure 5.5). When working with a consultancy client on a relatively small assignment one of us eventually had to sign an 18-page contract, in duplicate, with a seven-page appendix but could not actually undertake the assignment on behalf of the client until the purchase order had been

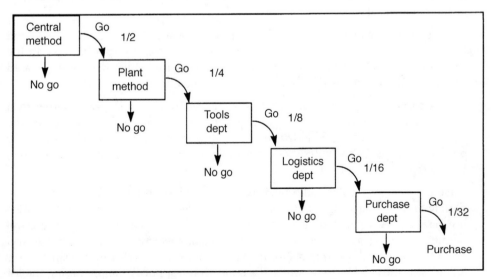

Figure 5.5 Smaller and smaller chance of success (Millier 1995)

received. Unfortunately, the bureaucracy continued as after completing the assignment the client then took nearly five months to make the payment.

There is a multiplier effect applying to the time that it takes at each level, the more decision levels, the longer it takes. Furthermore, if you consider that if you have a 50/50 chance at every level, at the end of a relatively short five-stage process there could be just a 1 in 32 chance of success. The more steps in the process, the more likely you are to be disappointed.

Consider the alternative of a company organised on the basis of project teams. Let us assume that the project team meets each month, and therefore all the key decision-makers are in the room taking decisions about the project at monthly intervals. If you have the opportunity to be there on the day when they may be discussing the investment in your ultra-high-speed milling machine, this gives you the opportunity to put your arguments and answer any questions arising. You can sell your machine without having to rely on a third party within the company to sell it for you. This also means that the decision-taking process may be much shorter than in the previous example.

DEVELOPING THE RELATIONSHIP WITH YOUR CLIENTS

Trust is fundamental to a client/seller relationship. How can that level of trust be improved? There are not too many solutions, but they are fairly intuitive and straightforward. A good product range, a sensible price and your reputation in the market are all factors which will give the client sufficient confidence to buy from you, but these factors alone may not be enough to ensure that you keep the client. The nature of the initial contact with the client is that they will test the supplier with a small and perhaps not too sensitive deal, gradually increasing commitment as trust increases. As this process unfolds it is important to meet the client's growing expectations and also work towards building a wider range of personal relationships at various levels between your own people and those of the client.

A relationship based on trust is almost obligatory as a basis for further, secure business. The client not only buys our product, but actually the company. In many cases in industrial markets the 'brand' is the company. This means that in addition to the product the client also buys:

- delivery reliability
- technical service
- maintenance and spares supports
- your ability to help the client improve efficiency and reduce costs
- opportunities to gain new clients.

If all of these factors contribute to trust and confidence then the client can only test the supplier *in vivo*. Trust and confidence can only be demonstrated to an extent; for clients to really build trust they have to do business with the supplier. Unfortunately, you cannot swim without getting wet, but it is only when you get wet that you find out the temperature of the water.

From this we can see that the relationship is really an investment by both the client and the supplier that matures after a period of time; sometimes this can be measured in years (Salle and Silvestre 1992, p. 46). Relationships in industrial markets are enduring by nature, and this gives the return on the initial investment required to establish trust and confidence. This mutual approach actually offers the best deal for both the client and yourself. In return, clients will often be prepared to pay a little more for your product than for the competitors, if indeed it is possible in a complex relationship to compare on a like-for-like basis. Our experience of working with many clients is indeed that in long-standing relationships higher prices can be achieved representing, if you like, an insurance premium paid for the reduction in risk associated with a known and trusted supplier.

It is costly in time, money and in terms of personal commitment to build this level of trust. In these circumstances it is only with some reluctance that the client will switch suppliers. The cost of doing so is sometimes called the 'transaction cost' or 'switching cost' and is a real 'barrier to exit' for the clients and a 'barrier to entry' for competitors (Williamson 1975).

It goes without saying that you should do your utmost to take the greatest care of your clients and by progressing the relationship to raise the barrier for competitors and retain your clients for as long as possible. Some of our recent research has shown that relationships between supplier and client have endured for 20 years or more. This is quite typical of many relationships.

 It has been shown that companies can boost their profits by anything up to 100 per cent by retaining customers for longer. This means that investing in relationships, managing for the long term and avoiding customer defections is a much more effective and intelligent way of managing customers than simply cutting the price (McDonald and Meldrum 1995).

The nature of relationships and the importance of trust is an important principle in industrial markets. On average industrial companies do not gain or lose more than 20 per cent of their clients each year (Salle and Silvestre 1992). This means that 80 per cent of clients are retained from one year to the next. Even a relatively small increase in retention can improve both profitability and the strategic position of the company. Retaining customers for longer is a significant disadvantage for competitors. It reduces their opportunity to gain more business and also means that it is more expensive for them to manage the business they have, as the cost of investing in relationships is increased. Hence we should think in terms not just of share of the market, but also in terms of quality of the client. By gaining and retaining better-quality clients we restrict our competitors to the below-average clients.

SELLING AND VALUE

The pricing of consumer goods depends significantly on a range of psychological factors; the price of industrial products can be estimated on a rather more rational basis. The aim should be to price on the basis of the value delivered to the client, in other words not how much this product costs us to make and sell, but how much money extra profit the client can generate as a result of using it. The value can be demonstrated in many different ways, for example:

- short payback period with respect to a capital purchase
- improved levels of process performance
- reduced costs for the clients perhaps by reducing storage, wastage, etc.

We see many more examples of organisations that price on the basis of cost plus rather than in terms of a value in use, which produces sub-optimal price realisation, in other words, selling too cheaply.

ME-TOO PRODUCTS

Products do not last forever! Even products that at one time were unique will eventually find that there are competitors that are near substitutes or perhaps even better in terms of performance. This is a particular problem in mature markets where products are similar and differentiation has decreased – there has been a progressive drift to commoditisation (Figure 5.6). As they gain experience and product knowledge clients become more familiar with products and confident of their ability to use them. The increasing similarity of products makes it easier for clients to make comparisons, and eventually this means that price can become more and more important as a major feature of the comparison.

As the discussion becomes more price focused margins come under pressure. The challenge is to find ways to prevent price being the main focus of discussion, for example, by innovation and product development and also by enhancing the service package – warranties, technical advice and support, excellent delivery, etc. and by continuing to invest in the relationship in order to stay close to a customer. It has been said that at the extreme the only difference between you and your competitor is the quality of the relationship that you enjoy with the client. Trust, confidence and the management of the relationship are central issues in industrial marketing.

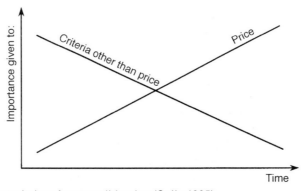

Figure 5.6 Characteristics of commoditisation (Salle 1985)

INTERNATIONAL ASPECTS OF INDUSTRIAL MARKETING

There are a number of excellent books on this subject and it is not one that we intend to cover in any depth. As a manager new to the subject of marketing, the basics of the subject will both engage you and serve you well in many market circumstances with which you may have to deal. Why do we say this? Because industrial marketing differs from FMCG marketing in a number of important aspects. Unlike FMCG marketing in which the cultural, linguistic and symbolic aspects of marketing are of prime importance, these characteristics are of much less importance in the context of industrial marketing. Industrial marketers usually sell products based on technical and functional characteristics.

It is often argued that the differences between countries are diminishing, and some academics would argue that there is really no such thing as a distinctive subject of international marketing. This is on the basis that the principles of market and customer analysis and understanding as a precursor of implementation are just as relevant in the domestic as the international context. There could be more differences between selling laboratory analytical equipment to, say, university research laboratories or government establishments than to selling the same products to multinationals in different countries. On this basis we would suggest that there is a lower level of sensitivity to international issues in industrial markets, although more obvious issues such as channels to market, logistics and service provision are clear priorities for a marketer.

MARKETING BUDGET

It is good to be able to give a clear and categoric answer to at least one question that arises in the complex and sometimes confusing subject of marketing. In answer to the question 'How should I set my marketing budget?', our clear and unequivocal answer is 'We don't know'. Perhaps not the answer you were seeking and we should explain why we remain obscure on this subject.

The marketing budget receives a high profile in many companies. It can represent a significant expenditure and individual items of cost can be very high, such as market research projects, trade shows and advertising campaigns. Inevitably this attracts attention. In addition it is often difficult to 'prove' a link between expenditure and return. This is because there are many factors that contribute to sales success, and in any event incremental sales as such may not be the objective of the expenditure. Salesforce training, raising awareness and market research, for example, will not necessarily demonstrate the cause and effect simplicity sought by the scientists and technologists or even accountants whose attitude can dominate industrial companies. In addition marketing expenditure is often regarded as discretionary, as is training, for example. So when times get tough these costs, or perhaps we should say investments, can be dramatically cut. A short-term expedient but both 'costs' may well represent, if properly implemented, a positive solution to the dreary and dispiriting mantra of cost cutting. Of course, continued attrition of costs is necessary in many companies but does not represent a positive strategy for growth. Cost cutting merely provides a little headroom during which time more beneficial strategies can be brought forward.

There are a number of formulae suggested as a basis on which to set a marketing budget; these include for example:

- A proportion of sales revenue. This begs the question of whether extra sales cause marketing or vice versa?

- An absolute sum fixed at the discretion of the Managing Director, representing the maximum amount he or she is prepared to consider.

- Last year $+/-$ as determined by differences in planned activities.

- Last year $+/-$ a fixed factor, perhaps inflation upwards or an efficiency factor downwards.

- Zero-based budgeting, in which the marketing budget is built each year on the basis of the marketing plan.

Some years ago, to try to provide more guidance on this subject and in response to a request from a pan-industry group, one of us undertook a series of interviews with the Marketing Directors of a number of large and sophisticated manufacturing and merchanting companies. The results demonstrated a complete lack of consistency between the companies interviewed. Indeed each Marketing Director felt unsure about their own approach and would have welcomed further guidance.

In managing your budget there is some general guidance that we would offer based on our experience as managers and working with many different companies.

- Remember that marketing expenditure is not just the budget of the marketing department. In regionalised or divisionalised companies where profit centres are split amongst product or geographical regions, it is very common for each profit centre to have a marketing budget, although it may exist under different names. Be sure that you fully understand all sources of marketing funds. Such 'hidden' funds can often be substantial and may even match or exceed central or corporate funds. It may well be that such diffused funds may not be as professionally managed as those for which professional marketers are responsible. They could even be regarded as the 'slush fund' for activities not formally approved within the company, such as entertainment or 'incentive payments' – discounts by another name – to trade partners. Equally, rebates from supplier may also be regarded in this light.

- The marketing expenditure is a cost rather than a revenue figure. As such, exceeding budgets is regarded very unfavourably and should be avoided if at all possible. At all times make sure that your budget is visible and understood by those who may make harsh judgements on any shortcomings.

- Keep the Finance Director or Financial Controller fully briefed and informed on your plans and activities. By its nature marketing expenditure occurs in peaks and troughs. Plan the phasing of your budget over the next financial period and ensure that this is shared with others. Accountants are comfortable with positive variances against budget and are unlikely to question this; however, large and unanticipated expenditures not planned and allowed for may upset their cashflow projections even if this is within the overall budget umbrella.

- Ensure that you have a rigorous system for authorisation of expenditure and that those responsible for committing funds are aware of their limits. Act decisively if you uncover any variances from procedure. There are really no prizes for bending the rules however expedient this may appear at the time.

- When dealing with invoices from suppliers, the marketing function may use a range of specialist services; make sure that goods and services invoiced for have been received. Where necessary, due to the size of the sum involved, two or more signatures may be required.

- Conduct the occasional spot check on the expenditure and invoice approval process. It is much more desirable that you should address any anomalies before these are uncovered by an audit procedure, for example.

Technology and marketing 6

KEY POINTS

Seventy per cent of new products fail, yet we cannot afford to rely just on current products. Technology is often inherent within many industrial products and this can cause us to mistake the technology for the product. Technological developments and innovation can lead to a multiplication of development projects.

    To avoid the dissipation of resources incurred by piecemeal and unplanned product development it is necessary to describe comprehensively and understand the market. This allows us to focus our efforts on the few but high potential segments that will lead to business success. Due to the role of technology in products and the opportunities that innovation can present, this may allow us not just to compete for market share against competitors but to create new markets as well.

IMPORTANCE OF TECHNOLOGY IN INDUSTRIAL MARKETING

The reason for dedicating an entire chapter to technology in a marketing book is that technology is both critical and omnipresent in industry (Millier 1999). Technology is a powerful weapon to

- guard against product obsolescence
- keep ahead of the competition
- rejuvenate your product range
- respond to your client's requirements.

This last point is particularly important in our modern economy in which marketing becomes more and more the marketing of ideas together with constant adaptation to more rapidly changing client requirements. Whatever the industry, even the most mature ones, you need technology and innovation as a defensive reaction but this is not enough to gain competitive advantage. Being a follower these days means in many cases being a loser.

Risks and rewards

Another reason for dealing with technology is that both risks and rewards are high. Technology and innovation are indeed difficult matters to manage since innovation fails to translate into products in 70 per cent of cases. If we just consider for instance the pace of innovation, it is a difficult trade-off. Too little innovation and you fall behind the competition, too many innovations and you are overwhelmed by the number of potentially good ideas and cannot afford to launch and maintain so many. As with innovation, being client responsive is a desirable characteristic but being too responsive to clients' needs means that in the end your clients manage your company instead of you, as they decide what innovation is required. In effect, you become an innovation sub-contractor.

Whilst risky on the one hand, innovation is rewarding on the other. For instance we know that

- Leading companies make 70 per cent of their turnover from products less than ten years old.

- Twenty-five per cent of their turnover is from products less than five years old.

- Top-performing companies, such as Hewlett Packard, have 15 per cent of their turnover coming from products less than one year old.

To summarise, innovation is costly but potentially very profitable. However, we do not want to sell the idea that innovation is a good thing *per se*. As a matter of fact a lot of innovations are due to ignorance of the company's true competitive position! After all, if you do not really understand your competitor's position in the market, then continuing to introduce new products as fast as you can is one way of trying to stay ahead. It would be much more insightful to ask ourselves if competitors really are ready to bring out new products and above all whether or not a client actually needs or expects a new product.

Our message is:

Innovate smarter rather than harder

Why should we be concerned by technology?

Technology is almost by definition the concern of technicians. Why would the marketer choose to be involved? In fact there are several reasons.

- You must be aware that whatever the industry, an innovative technology is almost never a sufficient argument on which to sell a product.

- R&D people will, unconsciously but sincerely, believe that they truly have a 'second-to-none' product. As we have seen this can be 'too good to be true'.

- R&D staff can become deeply involved in the project. Their concerns are very different from yours and it can be very difficult indeed to find common ground on which to share a conversation.

- The up-front costs of research in technologically-based markets can be enormous, and a significant amount of this investment can be wasted due to the lack of marketing focus. Your involvement can encourage re-allocation of research funds to more productive areas.

TWO KINDS OF INNOVATION

Not all innovations are alike. We can identify two types of innovation and will give an example of each to explain this.

EXAMPLE 6.1

Hitectronics' engineers have developed a new type of oscilloscope in response to their clients' requirements. Its sampling speed is 1 GHz instead of 500 MHz as with the previous model. They will launch the product at the Telecom exhibition in Geneva at the same time as a competitor.

EXAMPLE 6.2

Bio-organ is a new project based around cell encapsulation within a membrane. The encapsulated cells are then implanted in the body and substitute for a failing organ. The Bio-organ could cure diabetes as well as some 25 other diseases. The project is still under development and there are numerous uncertainties to be addressed:

- There are three or four options that can be offered for each disease, including the possibility of also encapsulating drugs.
- The bio-organ can be produced in different shapes in order that it can be implanted in different parts of the body.
- The bio-organ can be implanted adjacent to the diseased organ that it is replacing deep inside the body, or alternatively just under the skin.
- No surgeons have yet been trained in this new technique and there is little expertise in this advanced type of therapy.
- The NHS has yet to state if this type of implantation will be offered.
- Without further feasibility testing there is no clear understanding of the success rates.

Two types of projects		
Project type	New product	Technological innovation
Project idea originating from:	The observation of customer needs	The supplier (R&D, research laboratory, etc.)
Uncertainty level	Moderate	Very high
Project duration	Predictable	Three times more than planned
Actions and requirements	Accurately defined	Unknown
Potential	Moderate	High
Disruption to market	Low	Very high

Figure 6.1 Two types of projects

Our instinct would tell us that the style of innovation captured in the first example is most likely to succeed. In this example the clients themselves have asked for a product of this type. The company knows the market and already has established channels of distribution and a customer base.

In the second example there are a multitude of possibilities with 25 diseases that could potentially be cured, different types and shapes of bio-organs – a range of nearly 4000 permutations surrounded by large uncertainties. The product has enormous potential to bring about major change or, indeed, upheaval in the health world.

We could call the first example a new product, the idea and demand for which is coming from the market-place. The second example we could call technological innovation. The technological innovation originates from the scientist and has higher potential to surprise and disrupt the market. We can compare both types of innovation in Figure 6.1.

HOW TECHNOLOGICAL INNOVATION CAN BE MARKETED

Technological innovation is a very particular case. Is it possible to elicit some general principles? The answer is relatively straightforward, as nothing can be taken for granted with technological innovation. Nothing is given, nothing is fixed and everything must be checked. For example, in the case we discussed of the bio-organ, some of the things which would need to be checked include:

- the type of membrane

- the type of cell

- the most appropriate disease to be cured

- the implantation technique

- post-operative recovery and complications

- complications of rejection

- acceptance by the NHS.

All of this has to take place in a competitive environment as, for example, there are therapies available for diabetes today. The market must be comprehensively analysed and even constructed if the bio-organ is to have a chance of success.

In a similar way, if you have the skill to market technological innovation then almost certainly you will be able to sort out and resolve less complicated marketing issues. In other cases at least something will be known about the product, the market or the competition. In some cases it can be appropriate to be a follower as some of the major unresolved issues in the market are clarified by the time you enter. To market technological innovations successfully, do you really understand your client's requirements? The nature of the markets and segmentation? The way to approach the market and sell the product? Any further research and development that may be required? Requirement for investment in additional technical and commercial assets? If you can answer yes to all these points with respect to your technologically innovative product then read no further!

MARKETING ISSUES CONCERNED WITH TECHNOLOGICAL INNOVATION

The innovation axiom: the bigger the potential, the bigger the risk.

What most technological innovations have in common is promising potential. Take for instance a new product that can be described as ultra-thin glass wall. It is basically glass fibre, the sort of thing that is used for insulating your loft. But it is white, soft and silky just like cotton wool. The applications we can think of for this product include:

- babies nappies

- earplugs

- tissues

- air filters

- water filters

- fabrics.

This list could easily be two or three times longer; there are almost countless applications for this new technology. As the list grows so enthusiasm mounts at the tremendous market opportunities that there are for this amazing new product.

 Beware of the above list; it is dramatically deceptive as it does not differentiate between these applications for ultra-thin glass wool. It conceals the fact that there is a need for different products for different types of problems, and there is a completely different positioning required from one application to another.

The next step is to take this list and fully describe and explain how the market is organised. It could, for example, look like Figure 6.2. In this figure we can see the project mushrooming out with ever-branching clusters of applications in all directions. This

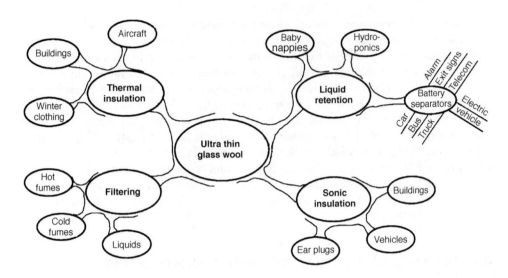

Figure 6.2 Project proliferation

mushroom overview is obviously not made at random but is built up from our understanding of the applications for this new product. What this really tells us is that each cluster of applications corresponds to the requirement for technical investment. For example, 'thermal insulation' will require us to focus on the fibre's thermal conductivity whilst 'liquid retention' means we will have to improve its hydrophilic properties. Applications for insulating aircraft, buildings and winter clothing will require specific additional properties to fit the application requirement. The aircraft application for example, will require a hydrophobic fibre to avoid water accumulation when flying in damp or cold layers of air.

Two attitudes

Project managers tend to be either enthusiastic or confused when they are faced with this proliferation of ideas. Over-ambitious companies get sidetracked, driven on by enthusiasm at the prospect of so many potential project applications. They try to develop the perfect all-purpose product that will satisfy everyone and end up with an all-in-one product, the sort of device that does not satisfy anybody.

In contrast, other companies with muddled methods and no helpful criteria will choose their application quite arbitrarily. Not only do they risk coming to a dead end, but they may miss more worthwhile openings in doing so. One especially pernicious type of 'opportunity' consists in letting yourself be inveigled by a particular customer into developing the product that customer needs. It is sad to say, but that customer may be the sole person who needs it, and additional demand is non-existent. You risk spending as much on one customer as you would on a whole market.

Reasons for failure

The following two factors account for 95 per cent of the failures of technological innovations. These are:

- developing technical devices instead of products
- the myth of the big markets.

The device

One of our clients had developed a world-beating pressure gauge of remarkable accuracy; it could measure pressure to 10^{-9} bar. It was suggested that the chemical industry would use pressure gauges of this type and our client asked us to carry out a market survey to demonstrate the size of the market. The client was convinced that they could do nothing but succeed as they undoubtedly had the best pressure gauge in the market!

It took at least 15 days to identify that users of pressure gauges needed an accuracy of only 10^{-2} bar in the best cases! So not only was there a gap between the actual and required accuracy, none of the market's requirements were suited by the pressure gauge (Figure 6.3). In other words, none of the pressure gauge's features suited the market's requirements. Therefore we could define a device as an object with outstanding performance for which potential clients have no use. We can illustrate these differences between a product and a device in Figure 6.4.

This example illustrates that the product's outstanding performance is more a handicap than an advantage and brings home to us the fact that technology is not enough to sell a product. Marketing should aim to meet clients' expectations, and not substantially to exceed them. It is counter-productive to over deliver on performance leaving the client with the thought that they are paying for useless features.

Great devices are invented in laboratories.
Great products are invented in the marketing department.

W. Davidow

	Pressure gauge features	Market's requirements
Accuracy	10^{-9} bar	10^{-2} bar
Temperature range	$-80°$ to $+80°C$	$0°$ to $450°C$
Mechanical resistance	Acceleration 10g	Hammer shocks
		Resistant to impact damage
Chemical resistance	Petroleum and oils	Strong acids and bases
Miscellaneous	–	Compatibility with industrial automation systems

Figure 6.3 Missing the market's requirements

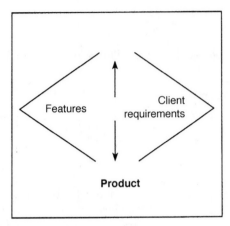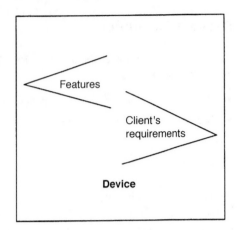

Figure 6.4 Product vs device

The myth of the big markets

Once you have developed your amazing device it is easy to believe that the market is the 'pressure measurement market' since you have the best product. Unfortunately the big, safe, uniform, open, expectant market everyone seeks can justifiably be called a myth until you actually test your product and establish the market. In fact, whenever you think you are solving the problem you are usually just raising a dozen other unexpected ones. All of this undermines your chances of launching the product soon. Let us take the example of fibre-reinforced concrete.

The adventure began in the laboratory, where it was tested and found easy to use. All you had to do to reinforce your concrete was to mix fibre with it. The resulting concrete was very strong and evenly reinforced. Once the manufacturers were convinced it would work they made a trial offer of their miracle product to a building firm. 'You just need to mix it with concrete, and that reinforces it!' There were none of the usual problems with steel reinforcement (corrosion, difficulty, implementation time, etc.). But it is a tradition with builders to mistrust new techniques because they have seen others fail. However, with a little luck and perseverance, the fibre makers eventually managed to root out a co-operative building firm that let them leave their bag of fibre and promised to try it later.

Left to their own devices, the builders did not take any precautions, thrust their hands into the bag and promptly cut their fingers. From then on, they just loved it! Having donned gloves, they threw a few handfuls of fibre into the cement-mixer. But the cement-mixer was not adapted for fibre, so the handfuls stayed in lumps. They turned into miniature hedgehogs which congregated around the blades of the cement-mixer, and the blades got bent as they turned. The product had no shortcomings at all!

So now they had to scatter the fibres one by one in the cement-mixer. This took ages, but the nightmare was not over yet. The fact is, they were using the same concrete as usual, with exactly the same composition as usual, but the fibre made it too dry. More water was necessary. Unfortunately, they added too much water in proportion to the cement so air bubbles and cracks formed in the concrete when it dried. This meant it was actually less well reinforced than it would have been without the fibre. The builders had had enough. When they removed the shuttering and saw fibres sticking up in sharp spikes all over their new wall, it was the last straw. They just could not bear the sight of it, threw out the bag and cursed the day someone left it with them.

The innovators believed they had solved the steel problem but in fact they had unexpectedly raised a dozen others. And each of these problems was an additional and permanent deterrent for the builders. After all, they had never asked anybody for anything and were quite happy with the steel rods they had been using for the last 30 years.

This example demonstrates clearly that if you consider the market as either

- the concrete reinforcement market or
- the steel rod market

you are caught in the trap of the myth of the big market. Why? Because in the first case you are describing the market-place by reference to the functions of the product, reinforcement, hence you do not describe the market itself. In the second case you are describing the market by reference to the main competitor, steel bars, and again are failing to describe the actual market.

The consequence of using your product's main function, or that of your competitors, to describe the market is that your perception of the market is bounded by the one-word description that it is given. Therefore you think of your market as a homogeneous whole. From this point you compete with steel bars for the custom of builders who have been satisfactorily using them for many years. You are very surprised that you are unable to replace steel bars in the market!

Secondly, by considering your market as a homogeneous whole you miss the real target for your product. In the case we are discussing, all these markets could be specific targets for the reinforcement fibre:

- cliff reinforcement
- sewer pipe restoration
- lightweight armoured doors
- radiation-proof containers
- tunnel stabilisation
- 'instant' overnight road repairs.

So, what is the point? The point is that it is easier to consider the problem from the outside than by adopting a more introverted approach. If by saying 'my fibre reinforces concrete' therefore my market is 'the concrete reinforcement market' you see the problem from the wrong perspective and adopt the 'it'll do' approach.

Conversely, to be able to draw up the above list of potential applications you must carry out in-depth market research and go out and talk to potential clients. That takes time, energy and money.

Information is not free

You will never find the specific answer to your specific question on the Internet.

The way to approach this is to adopt a perspective that there are some clients out there whom we do not yet know, who have problems that we do not yet understand, to which our fibre provides a solution that our clients are not yet aware of. In this way we can avoid preconceived ideas and inappropriate market understanding.

EXPANSION, SEGMENTATION, FOCUS PRINCIPLE

To avoid some of the pitfalls of technological innovation this principle can be used to help us to bring a technologically innovative product to the market (Figure 6.5). Let us now consider in more detail each of these three steps.

Expansion. Here we allow the potential applications for the technology to proliferate as we systematically test as many likely or even unlikely opportunities as possible to increase the potential field and range of choices. By all means undertake some market research and discuss the potential application with interested clients, but do not invest anything in development at this stage. To do so would be a waste of money. This proliferation phase may well be turbulent and chaotic but research shows that it is a necessary part of the success of the project. From an empirical, non-intuitive viewpoint projects that do not experience this turbulence are noticeably more prone to failure than others. This can be easily explained by the fact that this proliferation is driven by customers who suggest new ways of using the innovation. In this way we can avoid trying to guess what the clients want, because we allow them to tell us.

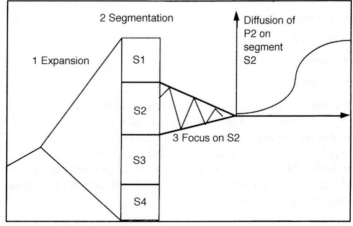

Figure 6.5 Expansion segmentation focus

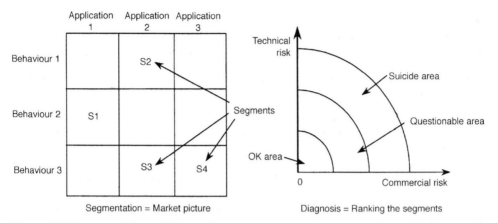

Figure 6.6 Segmentation and diagnosis

Segmentation. By getting as complete a picture as possible of the potential markets for the innovation we can now start to think about segmenting the market. After undertaking the segmentation process, segments can then be ranked according to their accessibility. We can diagramatically display the segments and diagnosis in Figure 6.6. A more detailed explanation of segmentation and diagnosis is given in Chapters 24 and 27 respectively.

Focus This is the phase in which we start to focus on a very few segments, possibly no more than three. The segments become the focus of our effort and commitment. By concentrating our energy we resolve problems as they arise and get our product to market as quickly as possible. By focusing our resources in this way we increase our commitment and determination to overcome any challenges that occur. It is extremely important in this phase never to give up until you are absolutely sure that the segment is unavailable. Otherwise if we jump from segment to segment starting from scratch each time, we will always confront difficult problems and eventually not achieve anything at all. In the focus phase it is highly desirable, if not essential, to have a partner to collaborate on the project. This partner would normally be a customer who can work with you on co-development. The benefit of this is that there is the opportunity to obtain the guidance and input of your customer and better fit the innovation to the needs of the market as well as sharing expenses and reducing the time for the product to be commercialised.

 It should almost go without saying that you should choose the partner rather than allow your partner to choose you.

TWO LAUNCH STRATEGIES

Launching an innovation traditionally consists of spotting a market and trying to take a share of this market against the competition. However, for your technological innovation you can use two complementary strategies to develop markets. The first launch strategy consists in penetrating niches with the unique technical solution to a specific problem. Competition is limited here, so you try to take the biggest market shares possible by highlighting your offer's potential. A niche strategy should be chosen when

- your technology has no equivalent (i.e. it involves having an entirely new vision of things and a new way of working);

- research or development teams are promoting the innovation within the client company, so in fact what you are trying to sell is performance and technology. Technicians are better at selling technology to fellow technicians than products to buyers.

The second strategy is the substitution strategy. It is also called volume strategy because your goal here is to reach a certain sales volume quickly by snatching share from competitors as fast as possible. When you choose this strategy, you need to know exactly how you stand versus the competition so you know what tactics to use against it. Volume strategy should be chosen when

- there is a market available for mass-produced or continuous-process products

- your company has a strong volume culture (i.e. it is used to making very large quantities at low cost) and does not intend to diverge much from its core activities.

These two strategies can be comparatively displayed in Figure 6.7.

Customer behaviour is fundamental in determining what action to take within the framework of these two strategies. In one case clients are dissatisfied with the present offer and in the other they are not. Potential customers in niches are said to be technically orientated. They are plagued on a daily basis by an acute, recurring technical problem and seek a solution at any cost. They are usually job competent, like talking about technology

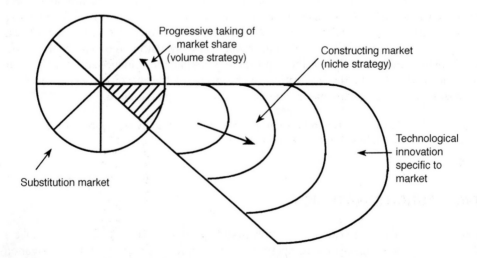

Figure 6.7 Creating the market; the runny cheese principle

Clients with technical logic	Clients with industrial buying logic
Half-full cup	Half-empty cup
Right brain	Left brain
Sees advantage first	Sees drawbacks first
Reference to positive aspects	Automatic initial rejection
Intuitive adoption	Bargaining
Technological approach to problem	Economical approach
Technical motivation (research of unique solution)	Socio-economic motivation (money, regulation)
Adoption decision	Buying decision
Global and systematic vision	Analytical vision (slicing salami)
Nothing to lose and everything to gain	Many things to lose and not much to gain

Figure 6.8 Two types of clients

and will be keen to collaborate with suppliers. This is the type of customer who likes meeting technicians (Figure 6.8).

The clients you target with volume strategy are said to be purchase orientated. They are usually pleased with what they use now and do not see any reason whatsoever for dropping their current product and adopting a new one, because they seek to avoid risk at all cost. Suppliers are generally handled by their purchasing departments and all new suppliers and new products are filtered by a series of procedures and predefined evaluation grids.

BUILDING YOUR ACTIVITY

We have seen that, as a marketing principle, to succeed you must focus on very few segments. However, you cannot make all your business in only a few segments. You must deal with more and more segments to be able to sustain your growth.

These are our guidelines for building up business around an innovation:

- Attack the market via the less important segments. These are your intermediary marketing goals. Midway objectives are more accessible than others so they give you an opportunity to achieve in your first successes. They help you gain the know-how needed to attack more important segments without taking the risks you would have taken before. It all amounts to starting where success is easiest to find.

- Exploit synergy and build upon your initial acquisitions before attacking segments with higher potential.

- Secure your position by grabbing the biggest possible market share you can before going on to new segments.

Let us come back briefly to each of these three points.

Small segments

First, why is it so important to start with small and unimportant segments and how fruitful is it? The intermediary segments are far from ideal, but they represent very little technical and commercial risk on a short-term basis. When you choose these first segments you are taking that 'easy way out' which makes us go where success is easiest to find. In fact you have a relatively high chance of succeeding here. There are several advantages to intermediary segments. For one thing, initial success boosts the morale and allays fears of failure. Expressed in a military analogy, if you want to win the war you have to win the fights first. Furthermore, these access segments are a real gateway to more important segments. They provide the opportunity for full-scale experiments, help you to make progress with your clientele, to get to know the market and find out how it works. Basically, they are a way to improve your experience without endangering your company if you fail, since any possible failure would be comparatively insignificant. In fact they amount to a sort of training process. Mistakes are still forgiven here, because any publicity made about you will be limited to small, quite insular segments.

Should we remind you that the Japanese car manufacturers first invaded Europe via Finland (Peters 1988). They were able to experiment at their ease on that small, 'invisible market', learning to adapt to the needs of European consumers. They launched their vast offensive on Europe against the big players (VW, Fiat, Renault) much later after a long period of trial and error in the Finnish test market.

People who start in a small way only go wrong in a small way and small projects aimed at small niches are soon stopped and soon modified. Pilot experiments do not cost much, yet they can be a quick way to success for your project.

Synergies

Let us take now another example to illustrate how to progressively build up a business from small to larger and larger segments: a product called 'Cruciform' that was developed by SEPR (Société Européenne de Poudres et Réfractaires). The product in question is heat resistant, has high heat capacity, is very resistant to heat cycles in an aggressive gaseous medium and has a very large heat exchange surface. SEPR developed cruciforms to equip heat regenerators for glass furnaces. These regenerators are chambers filled by a pile of refractory material that is alternately heated by the fumes and cooled down by incoming air. The pile deteriorates because of mechanical heat stress and chemical aggression, so production has to be stopped periodically for its maintenance or renewal.

SEPR offered its cruciform refractory material to the big glass manufacturers first. But the big glass makers judged the markup ($\times$ 250 per cent) excessive for the uncertain results of a new product, and they refused. Then the company identified some technically orientated clients among small foundries producing high-specification glass. These foundries had to stop production every three to six months to change their piles of refractory material. One of them was ready to pay any price to solve this major, recurring problem, and agreed to collaborate and help the company. They worked together on a test site. After conclusive testing, SEPR had easy access to other customers on this intermediary segment of high-specification glass furnaces.

When all the initial problems had been solved, the innovators were able to reach mainstream glass furnaces that had to change their material every year because of problems relating to the design and small size of the chambers. This penetration was possible because the company was able to prove that the chambers it had equipped on the first segment lasted three times longer in normal industrial running conditions. Factual evidence like this was much more convincing than any other arguments the innovators could have developed.

Then the oil crisis came. The big glass manufacturers were now convinced by these experiments that 'Cruciform' was more resistant in time and had greater heat-exchange capacity, so they finally agreed to test it. In fact it enabled them to restore profit margins that had been reduced since the rise in oil prices. Once again, it was the full-scale experimentation on prior segments that swayed their opinion in the new product's favour. But these difficult clients also needed proof that something which cost them three times as much really brought substantial savings.

Today, SEPR equips glass manufacturers worldwide with its cruciforms. The product has been largely optimised since then and is now sixth generation. The company hit the big markets, but it got there via the small intermediary ones. The business gradually developed with the see-saw effect of offer and demand, but it also forged its own way through knowledge acquisition, meaning that two different choices at the start can lead to the development of two different techniques, that these different techniques will give you access to different openings, and so on.

Securing your position

Basically what you need to do to secure your position is to concentrate your efforts on one segment until you overcome all the problems there, before going any further. The company who ran the reinforcement fibre project waited until they had solved all the implementation problems with drains and underground pipe networks before they went on to other segments.

Securing your position also implies improving your sales. The further you penetrate a segment, the more people know you and the easier it is to convince them. Your sales figures progress too, which reduces commercial costs and increases your margin. It is worth trying to do as much as you can on a given segment, trying to gain the biggest possible share of the market, if only for that.

Strategically speaking, it is of crucial importance to plumb each segment in depth before you go on to the next one. There are serious studies like those of PIMS (Profit Impact of Market Strategy)* by the Research Planning Institute which show that people with more than a 30 per cent share in the market have excellent chances of running their business profitably for a long time. This does not apply to companies with less than 15

---

* PIMS is a database of business-related information that demonstrates relationships between various items of data within the database; it is used for research purposes.

per cent of the market. These firms have no guarantee whatsoever of being able to maintain their business for any length of time. They survive only as long as they remain at the edge and appear harmless to competitors.

This is why innovators must try to take over at least 30 per cent of a small segment they are familiar with and in which they have a certain number of advantages. It helps them to master the game and control their segment well. On the other hand, it would be disastrous to plan on taking 2 per cent of a big market just because 2 per cent of a big market is enough to live on. You would be at the entire mercy of competitors and could be swept away at the snap of a finger. Furthermore, you have no control at all of the market if you just rely on luck to bring in those 2 per cent. Your share is anybody's guess: it could be 1.5 per cent or 6 per cent of the market. Firstly, customer reaction will be a complete mystery. Then you will find your sales volumes are only a quarter of what you predicted – or three times more, which means you will not have enough capacity to keep pace. That is to say, either your deals will not go through – or else they will but customers will be dissatisfied. And whichever way it is, you have no prior warning.

For example, if you intend to launch into car manufacturing, it is better to say you want to get 100 per cent of the small electric city car market than to say you want to get 0.0001 per cent of the car market. Maybe that comes to the same thing in terms of sales volume, but it does not mean the same in terms of commercial investment, attitude to the market and your underlying understanding of your marketing strategy.

According to the PIMS, strong market penetration and co-development combine to make profitable strategy. What happens is that when you co-develop you make a product that corresponds to customer expectations. This helps to raise customer opinion of its quality. And market shares and product quality are the two factors that best explain high returns on investment, as shown in Figure 6.9.

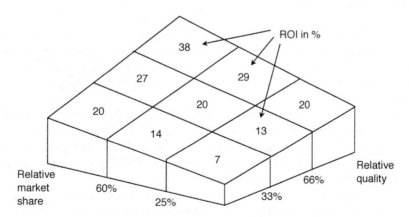

Figure 6.9 Relationship between investment returns, market share and quality

PART IV

Your working skills

INTRODUCTION

As stated at the beginning of this book, there is more than one company that survives with a low commitment to or appreciation of marketing. They do so because their personnel work with efficiency, effectiveness, professionalism, logic and common sense, perhaps utilising other skills that are just as important to the business. This means that marketing can presumably be largely reinforced by a range of skills that we could call 'support skills'.

The interviews that we carried out with marketers revealed that they derive great benefit by improving their skills in

- time management
- presentation skills
- personal skills.

They agree that these skills are important – even sometimes compulsory – and yet they admit that they are not often formally taught and that the managers concerned lack confidence or natural skills in these areas.

Despite the fact that these skills are not particularly marketing orientated we have decided to give you a brief overview of these techniques. We have selected those that we have personally used with success for years and have been used successfully by our respondents. So effective are these tools that if used properly they will change the way that you work.

Effectiveness and efficiency   **7**

KEY POINTS

- *Don't work harder – work smarter.*
- *There are only 24 hours in a day.*
- *You cannot be in two places at the same time.*
- *Nobody ever died wishing they had spent more time at the office, and graveyards are full of 'indispensable' people. Keep things in proportion.*
- *Be practical, realistic and professional.*
- *Take a day off sometimes, it does not mean that you will not continue to contribute to your objectives.*
- *Let the paper rot.*
- *Write and record your main issues and decisions.*
- *Take decisions.*
- *Keep it simple.*

ACTIVITY VERSUS EFFICIENCY

Are you a businessman or a busy man? That is a question we can ask of many people who mistake activity for efficiency. We must admit that it is more comfortable to spend one's time driving to the client's factory or speaking to them on the telephone than getting to grips with our business strategy. But is it efficient and effective? That is the point that we would like to deal with in this chapter.

The illuminating idea here is

'Don't work harder – work smarter'

when you have to work under pressure

To achieve this we would like to remind you of some common-sense points which almost have no need to be said, but which are none the less worth writing down. Some things are the way that they are, and whilst we might write them down there is not a lot that we can do to change them.

- There are only 24 hours in a day; you have only one brain and two arms so do not attempt to do more than you can sensibly hope to achieve. Reasonable success is much better than glorious failure. When one of us was working with the director of a large international Christian-based charity he said one of his major problems was encouraging staff to take on tasks that they could sensibly achieve, rather than to attempt to change the world and fail. Failure represents a waste of resources and considerable personal expenditure of emotional energy. The problem that the director of the charity had was that in the Christian tradition failure was somehow seen as acceptable because those who have failed could then seek forgiveness. Addressing this culture and mindset and applying professional management skills was a prime objective for this manager.

- You cannot be in two places at the same time and you cannot be all things to everybody. Focus on really essential points and practice 'management by inaction' as often as possible! Many busy people do this, often not replying before the second or third request arrives. By simply ignoring requests a significant proportion of the problems will sort themselves out.

- However much you might seek calm and inner peace the pressures of work will inevitably raise your stress levels. Within reason this is perfectly acceptable. Experience shows that we all need some pressure, of a deadline for example. Also stress helps us to work well, hence the old proverb 'if you want something done, ask a busy person'.

GOOD WORKING HABITS

Enough homespun common sense; let us think about some good working habits that you should try to adopt.

- Be practical, be realistic. As often as possible use the 80/20 rule. Use it to prioritise your time, and invest your time in those activities that are likely to yield the best results. For example, making time to meet an important client who contributes significantly to your business. Selecting those products that are really important contributors to profitability and focusing time, effort and resources on them.

- Take a day off from time to time. Once a month for instance take a day off in order to work really effectively! When do managers come up with some of their best ideas? Often they are generated on holiday, in the bath or when commuting. This means that some of the best ideas come when you are away from the pressures and daily turmoil of office life. So do not be afraid to take a day off, stay at home and perhaps start your weekend on a Thursday. Take time every now and then to really think about what matters in your job. We recommend a long weekend, this gives you time to unwind on Friday and clear your mind and perhaps your desk of all the small but time-consuming trivia. This time and space will allow you to think more creatively over the rest of the weekend and you will be surprised how many good ideas can be generated. These ideas are the things that you 'must do when you have some time'. So if we aim to be efficient and effective then there are some guidelines we can offer.

- Set yourself a few but important objectives at any one time. Do not be too ambitious and fail, generating a successful outcome or a series of outcomes is much better than failing to achieve the unachievable. Maybe three or four key objectives at any one time would be sensible.
- Take the time to relax and unwind, and clear your mind of all the day-to-day pressures that crowd in. Firefighting and responding to the demands of others will not necessarily help you to progress.
- Dare to switch off the mobile telephone; there really is no need to carry the office with you.
- Let the paper rot! Take a 'rot box' and put it under your desk. Every time a piece of paper lands on your desk aim it in one of three directions. The waste paper basket for those things that you will never need again, the filing cabinet for things that are important and will need to be referred to again. Finally, things that you are not sure about but which might have a short lifetime, do not hesitate to put them in the rot box (Figure 7.1). A similar principle works very well with the pernicious, time-stealing e-mails. There is enormous satisfaction in transferring somebody's effort to 'cover themselves' into a folder called 'deathrow'.

When the rot box is full up, take the bottom two-thirds out of the box and transfer them to the dustbin. Twenty years of experience using the rot box demonstrates that every time you need a paper it is invariably in the rot box when you need it. By the same token, you will almost never need a paper once it has been transferred from the rot box to the dustbin.

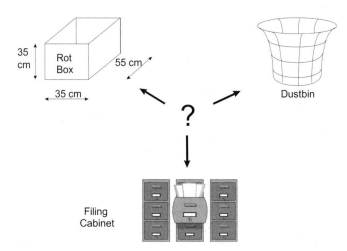

Figure 7.1 Sorting the paper

Be professional

What does being professional mean? At least four things:

1. Forget the 'it will do'. Never leave an important job half done. Never accept 'more or less'. Do not take anything for granted and check everything. It really is suicide to make assumptions about what you think your customers' needs are for example, or what your competitors' product offering delivers to the target market segments. Either get the right information or develop a range of alternative scenarios that match the most likely situations you will find. In your reports and presentation you cannot be indeterminate and equivocal. You must demonstrate, not just state. You must bring proof from credible sources; marketing studies, multi-client studies, industry surveys, scientific articles, economic reports, statistics, probabilities. You simply do not have time to do things badly; wasting time doing something badly prevents you from doing it well.

2. Be an expert in your job. Expertise is 'the body of specialised information and practical skills that make you good enough to do a particular job' (Goleman 1988). In other words, knowledge is one thing but expertise is another. You can read as many books as you like about sailing, but this knowledge will certainly not match the expertise required when it comes to taking to the water. Being expert means knowing all the inside information about your industry; who the key shakers and movers are, the history and mindset of the industry, the nature of the local and international market-place. You should aim to understand your industry and all its subtle nuances better than anybody else does. This innate knowledge will give you the ability to understand, interpret and forecast issues just that little better than anybody else. Otherwise you always run the risk of meeting one of those sly, wily old dogs who will state with conviction and certainty some assumption so dearly held for so long that it has become an axiom against which it is very difficult to argue. We are all familiar with the instant response of 'that will never work in this industry' and you really do need to master your subject so that you can convincingly argue against these long-held beliefs.

3. Be organised and make time to manage a range of activities properly. Comprehensive studies have shown that the best small and medium enterprises are driven by chief executives who actively develop a wide range of contacts, such as through discussion circles and business clubs. Here they pick up good ideas from others, and discuss their own ideas that can then be challenged and tested in order to develop a stronger argument.

4. Keep your word. If you say or promise something; deliver. This will enhance your reputation and presence in the organisation. A recent Cranfield study demonstrated that this was an important personal characteristic for a marketer to possess.

Do not let others manage your job

Sales, production, clients all know better than you; as a marketer you will never be short of advice albeit of distinctly variable quality. See also Chapter 11 on time management which will show you how to be determined in your use of time.

Write, write, write

Writing is essential in your marketing role. It leaves a trail of evidence of what you have done and demonstrates the linkage between your actions, done properly, and the results you have achieved. In other words, it leaves milestones along your way. Marketing is an intangible subject and by keeping comprehensive notes you can produce the data to support your actions. Writing acts as a jigsaw puzzle; it reveals what you have and have not done, what you do and do not know. Writing clears your mind of all sorts of things that are turning endlessly in your head. By writing your thoughts down and arguing them through you can make progress. Furthermore, writing down a memo, a report or something similar still remains one of the best means of communication that exists.

Take decisions

It is better to take the occasional wrong decision than to prevaricate and take no decision at all. Even if your decision may prove with hindsight not to have been the best one, then at least it is a learning opportunity. We can read books, watch videos and discuss the finer points of stroke technique, but if you are to learn to swim you actually have to get wet. Having done your analysis be prepared to commit.

KIS (keep it simple)

Einstein once said, 'make things as simple as possible and no simpler'. Keep things as simple as possible. We live in a world where an infinite number of factors endlessly combine and interact to produce complexity beyond our understanding. One of your jobs as a marketer is to reduce this complexity to something the human brain can consciously understand by selecting the key information required for decision-making. Use pictures, diagrams and visual tools rather than lists to assist in understanding this complexity (Figure 7.2).

Think 'loops'

Remember that most of marketing is concerned with complex social processes. These are looped rather than linear interactions; do not expect simple cause and effect relationships – if we spend £x on an advertising campaign we can generate £y return – but think about these recurring influences. By advertising our new product we increase the number of enquiries at the trade show and our sales staff can make more appointments to see better-quality potential buyers. Their sales visits are in turn more productive and increased sales result. Is this desirable outcome due to the advertising campaign, judicious positioning of the trade stand near the entrance, a recent sales training course or the fact that good potential buyers visited this trade show rather than the European event due to a strike by airport staff – or some other effect, or a combination of all of these?

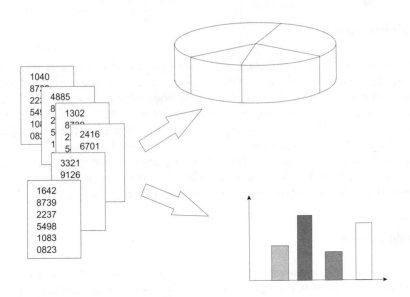

Figure 7.2 Drawing pictures rather than lists

Another example of a looped process is found in managing change. Get rid of the idea that the future will come true as you have dreamt it. Start with your idea, implement it then stand back and reconsider your assumption, rationalise the experience then start again (Figure 7.3).

Speak from a position of knowledge

Or the grass is greener syndrome. It is a common human failing to undervalue the things that others do. The jobs that other people do seem so simple, much simpler than the tasks you have to deal with. Gratuitous advice is therefore readily available. Those working for international companies may well be frustrated by the advice received from Head Office several thousand miles away. That clarity of understanding lent by distance not being shared by the hapless manager who actually has to do the job.

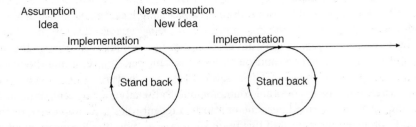

Figure 7.3 A looped process in managing change

The Business Team Manager for a world-class company entertained us with the story of the Vice-President back in the States who sent a helpful e-mail saying that the Division was under performing, and that their analysis had pinpointed the cause as low sales. Would the Business Team Managers please submit their proposals to increase sales? This particular manager was responsible for a specialist business area with limited manufacturing capacity. Having worked hard for two years to generate commitment from customers that capacity was now filled, and they were pursuing a margin rather than volume strategy by pushing through price increases. The net effect of the e-mail from the States was to reduce confidence in the Vice-President and make it more difficult for her to speak credibly in the future. Rather than demonstrating her grasp and overview of the business she had simply demonstrated her lack of knowledge and understanding, resulting in a loss of respect.

At a more parochial level this is often seen as a point of differentiation between marketers and those with a technical or scientific background. Marketing is often seen as conceptually simple, requiring only product superiority. Driving a car is conceptually simple, but requires skills to co-ordinate all the various activities – turning the wheel, changing gear, operating the pedals. It requires experience for these to become automatic, unconscious actions. This combination of skill and experience may often not be appreciated. This can be summarised in Figure 7.4.

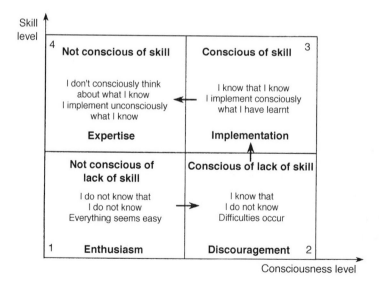

Figure 7.4 Skill development – the learning cycle

Interpersonal skills 8

KEY POINTS

There are three aspects of behaviour that we discuss in this chapter:

- *bounded rationality*
- *self before others*
- *the theory of commitment.*

Some personal skills and attributes important for marketers are also discussed:

- *acknowledge people*
- *refrain from criticism*
- *listen*
- *ask questions*
- *save face*
- *involve people*
- *reward people*
- *let it go.*

The principles of building power within the organisation are built around:

- *competencies*
- *understanding the environment*
- *communication*
- *the authority of others*
- *money*
- *influencers.*

WHY IS IT SO IMPORTANT TO HAVE GOOD INTERPERSONAL SKILLS?

Take a minute to think about your job. Whom are you working with and how are you working with them? Basically you are dealing with your clients and with other departments

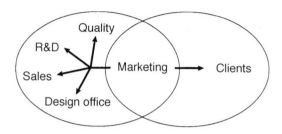

Figure 8.1 With whom are you in contact?

in your company. And what points in common are there from the relationship point of view? The one thing they all have in common is that you have no direct authority over them. You cannot force your clients to buy your products. Neither can you demand that your colleagues do anything for you that they do not want to do. You should always remember that your colleagues work with you but not for you. So to be effective, marketing competence alone is not enough. As a manager you also need the ability to enthuse and motivate people to work with you and help you achieve your objectives. The best tools for this purpose in convincing and motivating colleagues are your own interpersonal skills. Of course some people are naturally more gifted than others in this respect. Nevertheless, however gifted you may or may not be, this elusive skill can always be improved.

To look at this we shall first consider *three fundamental principles*. These help to explain how and why people behave in the way they do. Then we shall also look at some *guidelines* that can be used *to get people on your side*. Finally we shall see how this can be used to help you *increase your power* within the company.

THREE FUNDAMENTAL PRINCIPLES

Considering how and why people behave in organisations in the way they do, we shall look at three principles that will help us to get to the heart of this.

Bounded rationality (after March and Simon 1958)

In industry it is politically correct to be rational, so people attempt to explain their actions in this way when they take a decision. For example, if we consider the case of a purchase, you behave rationally when you

- draw up a comprehensive list of similar products for comparison
- decide the criteria on which to assess these products
- weigh and rank the criteria
- score the products
- compare the scores
- choose the high-scoring product.

But yet when you take a personal purchasing position do you really go through this process? Think about the last time you bought a piece of hi-fi equipment, a camera or made that unemotional decision about the company car. Do you go through a rational process by listing products, scoring lists of criteria, testing and comparing? Almost certainly not. The reasons for this being

- you do not have enough time
- you may not have the methodological tools to do the job (do you really use typologic or cluster analysis very often?)
- you are driven by factors that it may not be possible to score rationally (how can you rationally score for instance 'I want a nicer car than my brother-in-law')

So what do you do? What does this concept of 'bounded rationality' say? It says that

- you may review just some of the items available. For example, the nearest car dealer may have a reasonably good selection from which to choose.
- you make your choice of a product that you are more or less comfortable with and that fits a few, and perhaps unconscious, criteria that you have in mind. In other words, you might pick an item that, rather than being the best, is the least bad and will be good enough for the job in hand.
- the human brain apparently can take into account only a few criteria (7 ± 2) at the same time. This means that if you have a 'scientifically' drawn up mental list of multiple criteria then you almost certainly will not be able to use them effectively in exercising your choice.

From here your rationality consists of collecting information that justifies your choice – after you have made it – and of course you selectively forget information which does not afford support to your decision. For example, you may have chosen a particular type of car because it is cheap to insure, it is a reasonable size and is not sufficiently ostentatious to catch the eye of passing car thieves. In the process what you might have forgotten is that it is actually quite expensive to run as it uses rather a lot of petrol and this particular model has a below-average track record for reliability.

If we do not live in an entirely rational world, one where our rationality is 'bounded', then we really need to understand what it actually is that is driving our clients and colleagues. As a consequence how can we appeal to this particular need?

Self before others (after Berry 1986)

This principle says that people will optimise the things that they believe they will be judged on. If you believe, and of course you might be wrong, that you were judged more on market share than on margins then this will influence your behaviour. Imagine that the managing director of your company was judged by the shareholders not on return on capital employed but on an index of employee and customer satisfaction. You could perhaps imagine that the company might be managed in a different way. If we can understand how people are judged, or what they think they are judged on, then we are going a long way towards understanding their behaviour and motivations.

This also means that in the context of the company and what is good for the company, people will usually select what will favour them most in the first instance from a choice of options. Take the example of a company that manufactures expensive noise analysers for use with milling and turning machinery. One of the segmentation criteria was the quality director's age! Why? The answer was that the recently appointed director was buying noise analysis equipment for the functional things that it could do, but he was also demonstrating to the rest of the company how effective he could be at tackling the noise problem. This was an advantageous deal for the supplier as the quality director did his utmost to justify the higher price of the machines and their relatively better performance. Conversely, in the same situation, an older quality director who has nothing to prove any longer to anybody will not be likely to spend all this money. He has not worried about his prestige in the company for a very long time. We can therefore conclude that some people will buy the machine rather for their ego or personal prestige than for actual technical purpose.

Theory of commitment (after Moriarty 1975)

Imagine that you are at Victoria station in the middle of London and a beggar approaches you and asks for some money. Your response is to refuse. Suppose the beggar approaches you and asks not for money but could you tell him the time? There is no cost to you in telling him the time, and you do so. He then says that he has to make an urgent telephone call but does not have any change, would you by any chance have any loose change and could you help him? In this case a surprisingly large number of people would be prepared to give something.

The reason for this is that by making a small and inexpensive commitment in the first instance the theory says that you are then more committed by what you do rather than by what you think. In other words even if you think that you do not want to give the beggar some change, the fact that you have previously helped this particular person means that you will be more likely on this occasion to make a further gesture. In this way you will continue to help somebody whom you have helped previously. Having helped previously then you justify your previous actions by helping them in the future, even if it is more costly for you.

Why not generate your own evidence to test commitment theory? Ask for a small gesture from colleagues and then as soon as possible, so that your colleagues mentally link the two events, ask again for something more significant. Then ask for something still more significant. In this way you can eventually get what you want – unless you are too transparent and they also know of the theory of commitment! Of course this may sound a little manipulative, but is this actually the case? Or is this a way of understanding behaviour in order that you can work more effectively with your colleagues to achieve better results for you and your company?

One of our clients, a new business start-up, had developed computer-aided measurement software that was selling rather poorly. Industrial clients tend to be distrustful of 'here today, gone tomorrow' software houses. Using the principle of commitment theory we selected a large potential client in the car industry and targeted their 'tests and measures' department. They were contacted and told that software was in the development phase and the principles of how it worked were explained. We asked their engineer's advice on how we could further develop the software so that it would more precisely meet their current measurement problems. They were delighted to be asked for their expert opinion and were very responsive to this approach. There was no ready-made, off-the-shelf solution; the initial approach was to listen and understand the needs of the client.

A few weeks later we contacted the engineers again and said that we were extremely grateful for their expert advice and had now developed a prototype of the software for testing. Would they be interested in testing the software and telling us if we had correctly understood and responded to their comments? 'Why not, that sounds interesting' was the response. The test went reasonably well and the engineers made some further suggestions to make it more user friendly, and these suggestions were incorporated into the product.

After a month or so the company was contacted again and we told them that the software had now been fully developed and tested and had reached the stage that it was now a commercial product. Could we talk about their requirements for such a piece of software? A year later the company was using the software on three different sites.

     We could summarise the theory of commitment in one sentence:

He who has given will give!

INTERPERSONAL SKILLS GUIDELINES (PARTLY INSPIRED BY CARNEGIE 1994)

There are some very reliable principles of interpersonal skills that it is worth reminding ourselves about.

- *Acknowledge people.* People need to be recognised. The game is always the same, both inside or outside the company. You must acknowledge people for something special that they do or that they know. 'I have come to see you because you are the expert who knows better than the others.'

- *Do not criticise* – your clients, your competitors or your colleagues. Every criticism is a time-bomb that one day may explode when you least expect it. Likewise refrain from making personal comments or divulging confidences to a colleague. How do you think they will feel the next time they have something they want to discuss with you – are they sure they can trust your discretion?

- *Listen* – if words are silver, then silence is gold. The more you listen, the more you learn. At the same time the more you listen the less you speak, the less you speak the less you reveal. Information is the raw material of marketing and you will avoid giving away potentially valuable resources to others. Also, letting others speak is always appreciated, there is nothing we like more than the sound of our own voices, particularly if we are talking about our favourite subject – ourselves. To talk about listening skills seems almost bizarre. How can something so passive as listening be a skill? The skill is not so much in listening, but in providing feedback to the person we are talking to in order to indicate that you have listened and understood. A simple nodding of the head, very common in television interviews, provides feedback during a conversation. As do gestures and facial expressions. You also give feedback by paraphrasing what has already been said. Positive feedback phrases using words such as 'so what you are saying is' or 'I see what you mean' all help to maintain an open conversation.

- *Ask questions.* Questions demonstrate your interest in what people are saying. Ask a question in such a way that you will get a positive response; this will maintain the tone of the conversation. A 'yes' type response invites further discussion whilst a 'no' can turn a positive conversation into a more competitive discussion. Also, the asking of questions is much better received than an instruction. 'So I wonder if you will be kind enough to do this for me?' 'Do you think it will be possible to get this done by the end of the week?' In this way you not only make your point, but also gain the commitment of the respondent. You could go a stage further and invite good ideas by asking questions such as 'How would you think we could get this done within the available budget?' thereby respecting the professionalism and skills of your colleague.

- *Saving face.* In a discussion or perhaps an argument help the other person to back down with dignity. Make sure that they can save face and at all costs avoid statements of the 'over my dead body' type, which are extremely difficult to undo once made.

- *Involve people.* Nobody likes to be treated as a means to somebody else's ends. So involve people in what you are doing, make sure they are fully informed and invite them to share in the decision-making process. Involve them in building the project with you so that the project is not 'your' project but 'our' project. A wide-ranging study of 356 strategic decisions showed that more than half of them were never adopted or only partially implemented and subsequently abandoned (McNutt 1998). The common reason for failure was that the executive took an authoritarian view and tried to impose decisions rather than building and supporting consensus. Conversely, when people were involved, the strategic plans were adopted in 90 per cent of cases. This is because the people involved became missionaries for the project.

- *Reward people.* There are lots of inexpensive ways of rewarding people for their support and commitment. For example, let their boss know how helpful and supportive they have been and how their good ideas have made the project a success. As a marketing person you will recognise that this is an issue of internal marketing and we have a whole range of tools from the ubiquitous internal newsletter to recognition and reward schemes to help us in this. Do not forget that we sometimes need to stroke the clients as well. Clients are not some large anonymous corporation but human beings that respond to recognition just like everybody else.

Always reward people for what they have done and never for what they are. A judgement on actions is preferable to a judgement on the person.

- *Know the people.* Try to know people as people when you are doing business with them. Communication can be difficult because people do not give the same meaning to words. People understand according to their frame of reference. Try to understand their backgrounds and approach. This will make it much easier for you to deal with them on a day-to-day basis. Engineers and accountants for example, from a highly quantified background, may well adopt a different view from others, such as creative designers, who see things from a different perspective. An understanding of people in this way will help us to communicate using words and ideas that are appropriate to their view of the world.

- *Let it go.* Feel when to bend before breaking! As previously said, your hierarchical power is often low and you must endeavour to convince others with enthusiastic arguments and perseverance. But sometimes too much perseverance can upset your internal partners and it is time for you to give way to winning at all costs. It might be counterproductive.

GAINING POWER

Despite the position of marketing within the organisation having little or no direct line of authority a marketer can still gain power. This can come from a number of sources.

- *Distinctive competencies.* Your distinctive skills enable you to do things that nobody else in the organisation can do.

- *Understand the external environment.* Keeping in close touch with all elements of the external environment – clients, legislators, the trade press – can be an important source of power as it helps to reduce uncertainty. As a marketer you have the chance to be part of both the organisation and the external world and that gives you the opportunity to be somebody who always knows what is going on, a source of indispensable advice to others and somebody whose view is respected and required.

- *Communicate.* As we have discussed, strategic decisions may not be implemented because of lack of communication. Use your position to disseminate information about your projects and also to communicate the commitments that others have made. The public acknowledgement of commitments, perhaps in the minutes of a meeting, will increase visibility and accountability.

- *The authority of others.* Whilst marketers may have little or no direct authority over other people due to the strategic nature of marketing, you will often have access to senior people in the organisation. By keeping them informed and gaining their buy-in this gives you the opportunity to lever their authority to achieve your objectives.

- *Money.* The marketing budget by its very nature can be quite large. As marketing is sometimes, perhaps usually, seen as a cost then it is very important to manage the budget to meet expectations. Take the time to plan your budget well in advance and with care so that you can demonstrate how it will be allocated. By doing this you will gain the confidence and commitment of key players and this in turn will enable you to be more progressive in your ideas in the future, as you build confidence and a reputation for delivering.

- *Influencers.* There are always people within the organisation who have undue influence, either negative or positive. The salesman who is known to speak his mind in uncompromising terms about the support received from 'them' in head office, or the R&D Manager who is never wrong and has an encyclopaedic knowledge of the company's products and technology. Their status comes not from their position in the hierarchy but due to the respect that they have gained. Their opinion can be critical about whether your initiative will be successful or not. Identify and work with the influencers and use them as your 'innovators' and 'early adopters' (these terms are based on the 'diffusion of innovation', a concept that describes the way in which new products are adopted (Rogers 1982)). They can be part of your product development and marketing planning processes.

Presentation skills 9

KEY POINTS

- *An essential skill for marketing is that of communication. The principle to bear in mind when preparing a marketing communication is to use the 'which means that' principle in order to present your information from the client's viewpoint.*

- *Use your understanding of the market-place – segmentation – to tailor your communication approach.*

- *Written material that you may prepare could include client's records, product literature and sales presentation material. More substantial written materials such as reports should be planned carefully using a linear or mind-map approach.*

- *Oral presentations may provide a unique opportunity to discuss your views and ideas. To improve the quality of your presentation prepare carefully and rehearse; after delivering your presentation seek feedback. Manage the quality of your presentation using confidence cards.*

- *Marketing people are communication people. Therefore you are very likely to communicate either written or spoken information. As the presentation can be as important as the content you will find in this chapter some ideas on how to prepare successful written and oral presentations.*

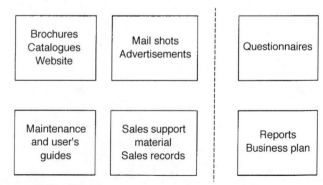

Figure 9.1 The marketing literature

WRITING MARKETING DOCUMENTS

There are all sorts of documents that you may well have to prepare in your marketing job. Brochures, mail shots, advertisements, user guides, commercial reports, sales literature, questionnaires etc. We can split these documents into various categories (Figure 9.1). A fundamental principle when writing any form of marketing document is that it should be written with the clients in mind.

Write from the client's viewpoint, not from your viewpoint

Use 'which means that'

SAY	DO NOT SAY
My product is made for drying up plaster tiles quickly, cheaply and with no cracks.	My product is able to excite water molecules with electromagnetic microwaves.
My paper holds its shape once folded, which means that you can slide it easily in the motor rotor's slot for the purposes of electric insulation.	My paper is made of thermostable, thermoformable fibre with a high 2nd degree transition point.
My product is able to detect flaws inside composite material without dipping them in water which means that the material is not spoilt by getting wet.	My product uses two pulse lasers and a Fabry-Perot interferometer.

When presenting your material always try to present your product in the context of the client. For example, try to illustrate the product on the client's premises or in a genuine working environment. This will convey what the product does much more effectively. It is always a good idea to test the message with the prospective readers. This is to make sure that it is

- understood by the reader in terms that they would use

- clear and conveys what is intended

- provided with sufficient information

- of an acceptable format.

It may be appropriate to use specialists to assist in producing communication material, for example, PR and advertising agencies. You should not be unduly concerned at having to use external specialists; it is not an admission of weakness on your part but a sensible exercise of managerial judgement. Marketing is a very catholic function and requires a wide range of expertise. A suitable and appropriate agency will be able to produce higher quality and more consistent work than you could yourself. However, it is always desirable to work with an agency that understands your business and what you are trying to achieve. It is your responsibility to make sure that you explain the context to the agency. This is often done in the form of a briefing document.

The agency brief

Unless you are clear in your requirements of the agency then how will you know if your needs have been met? The preparation of a briefing document acts as a discipline to your own thinking and the basis on which you can judge the quality of the agency's response. Typically a briefing document should run to no more than two or three sides of A4. It should contain

- a brief introduction and general description of the company, market and product
- specific details of what you want the agency to do
- the timescale
- budget
- key contacts and contact details.

A well-prepared brief is a valuable tool for both the client and the agency.

It hardly needs saying that when producing sales literature the underlying theme should be based on segmentation, our unique understanding of the market-place. Just as segmentation, explained in Chapter 24, allows us to design our product offering, this also allows us to tailor our communications approach (Figure 9.2).

Sales support document

One of the most efficient ways of helping the salesforce is to provide them with effective sales support material, often contained within the ubiquitous sales presenter or perhaps its technological counterpart, the laptop presentation. Either way information can be slipped in or taken out as the product range is updated and the literature changes. You should provide the salespeople with at least two sets of inserts. The first set contains client records and the second set should contain sales support material.

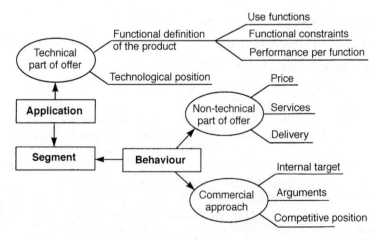

Figure 9.2 Exploiting segmentation (Millier 1999)

Account manager mr/ms:			Client record				

Group ☐	Activity		Client status	
Company ☐	Reference no. Town		Current ☐	
Plant ☐	Street Post code Direct line		Potential ☐	

Person's name	Tel e-mail	Function	Role played			Outside interests	
			Prescriptor	Decider	User	1	2

Figure 9.3 Example of client record (Malaval 1996)

Client records

An example of a classic client record is shown in Figure 9.3. This record can be completed by the more comprehensive document illustrated in Figure 9.4 (Michel *et al.* 1997). A further sheet (Figure 9.5) concerning account plans can then complete the set (Michel *et al.* 1997).

Product literature

The second set of literature included in the sales presenter should be useful to a salesperson in presenting the products to clients (Figure 9.6). Generally speaking, what we would expect to find in a sales presenter are examples and illustrations of products, a description of features, functions and performance and an explanation of how this delivers benefits to the clients. This enables the salesperson to use that magic phrase 'which means that' enabling us to link features to benefits by explaining not just what the product is but what it does. The sales presenter will also include competitor and market information and a list of FAQs (frequently asked questions).

When preparing sales literature for this purpose you should

- Consider how each insert can be used in the sales process.

- Define carefully the justification for inclusion of the insert, otherwise the sales presenter fills up with potentially useful but actually useless information.

Client history

Who is in charge at this client
(Function, name)

Major events in the past with this client
   Major sales
   Major problems

Client's strategy
   Global strategy
   Strategy per unit

Client's competitive position

Per unit
   Purchase history (volume, turnover)
   Purchasing trend
   Our competitors in this unit (name)
   Our position in this unit (strong, weak)
   Our strategy with this unit

Sales reports
   Date
   Who met whom
   Perception of our company by the client
   Report summary
   Relevant topics

Figure 9.4 Client history record

Action plan. Year :

Last action carried out
   Location, unit, application, TO, volume
   Objective, process, results, date

Current action
   Location, unit, application, TO, volume
   Objective, process, results so far
   Flag, comments, risk, delay

Prospect action
   Location, unit, application, TO, volume
   Objective, process, results, date

Figure 9.5 Action plan

**Product name
Satrack 2000**

Description
Antenna for Telecomunication
by Satellite
Sets automatically in the
direction of the selected satellite

Suitable for car, trucks, boats

Compatible with all
telecommunication standards

List price : £ 3500
ARGUMENTS :
The only telecom antenna
usable in mobile environment
+ very small size

COMPETITION

**Competitive product : HD 1000
Manufacturer : HD Ltd**

Description :
Antenna for Telecomunication
by Satellite

Suitable for ,trucks, boats but
not for cars due to its size

Only compatible with american
telecommunication standards

Need to stop the vehicle to be used

List price : £ 2000

Figure 9.6 Sales support material

- Prepare alternatives appropriate to the needs of each segment.

- Use diagrams, illustrations and colour to produce an attractive presentation.

- Keep the style of presentation consistent in terms of typeface, layout and use of logos and colour. This all adds to professionalism and corporate image.

- Ensure that the literature demonstrates value-in-use. If economic advantages from the use of your products can be demonstrated, this helps to overcome price objections on behalf of clients. This is a classic function of the salesperson, but appropriately prepared arguments and sales propositions are needed from you.

- Check the layout and design of sales inserts with sales colleagues; their involvement and commitment will mean that it is much more likely to be used.

- Ensure that each item of literature is coded and catalogued so that it may be easily referenced and updated or replaced.

- Ensure that the illustrations, graphs, photographs and accompanying text are consistent from sales presenter to advertisements, laptop presentations, etc. The information for all these means of presentation should derive from the same source.

- Discourage sales staff from preparing their own material, perhaps using their home computer and presentation software. This type of information may not be consistent with the overall marketing approach, make promises or statements that are inaccurate or cannot be met, or may in some other way make commitments on behalf of the company to the customer.

Writing reports

Having to write reports is regarded by some as a punishment, but is nevertheless a necessary evil. In order to achieve the objective of conveying information and actually being read a report should meet the following criteria:

- The report should have a clear objective that is explicitly stated. 'The purpose of this report is'. Why are you writing this report? What do you want to let the readers know? Who are the readers? How much do they already know? These questions help you to arrive at a clear and explicit objective.

- In preparing your reports collect all material, facts and key points. Organise the points in related groups and sub-groups. Whilst not everybody prefers to work in this way you can go as far as defining the headings and sub-headings of the report before you start writing (Figure 9.7).

If you are not the type of rational, logical person who thinks in this hierarchical way another very efficient method of organising your thoughts is to use mind maps (Figure 9.8, Buzan 1974). The centre of the map is the subject of the report. The major branches are the headings and the minor branches the sub-headings. The advantage of this method is that the data is organised in the way your brain works. Some people find this a much more intuitive and productive technique.

Structure your argument using the 4Ps. No, not those 4Ps, but these:

state your	**P**osition
define the	**P**roblem
outline the	**P**ossibilities
make a	**P**roposal.

Make your reports readable and stick to the KISS principle – Keep It Short and Simple. Readability can be improved by using wider line spacing and larger margins to create 'white space'. Use plain English and break the report into bite-sized chunks using

```
MARKETING PLAN

(1) GOAL SETTING
    (a) Mission statement
    (b) Financial summary

(2) SITUATION REVIEW
    (a) Market overview
    (b) SWOT
    (c) Portfolio summary

(3) STRATEGY FORMULATION
    (a) Marketing objectives
    (b) Marketing strategy

(4) RESOURCE ALLOCATION
```

Figure 9.7 A linear marketing plan

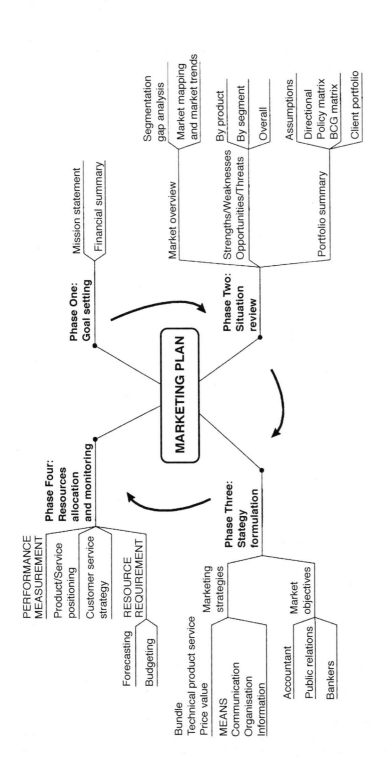

Figure 9.8 Marketing plan mind map

headings and sub-headings. Place all the heavy, boring information in an appendix and simply refer to it in the text. The use of pictures, graphs and charts makes the point very clearly and could save you the proverbial thousand words.

Package your report in an appropriate way making sure that you have

- Title, date, author's name.

- Table of contents; this is appropriate for the larger reports.

- A one-page executive summary for the busy or lazy reader.

- Make sure the objectives are clear.

- Define the terms of reference – what the report is and also what it is not.

- Have a clear conclusion or set of conclusions and try to avoid as far as possible 'further work recommended' or some such phrase. This is often an excuse for avoiding a recommendation or decision.

- Quote your sources; this adds authority to your report.

ORAL COMMUNICATION

There are some simple guidelines to follow if you have to make an oral presentation. In summary you should consider a presentation in three stages:

1. preparation
2. delivery
3. feedback and questions.

Preparation

Before any presentation ask yourself:

- *Why* am I making this presentation?

- *What* do I want to say? It is very helpful to write out the key points that you want to deliver.

- *Who* will be listening? What do they know about the subject? What might prevent them from understanding my presentation?

- *How long* will my presentation last? Do not be too ambitious. Do not try to say too much in too little time, this is counter-productive. Three to four points in ten minutes is more than enough.

The secret of any presentation is preparation. Many people are intimidated at the thought of having to make a presentation. The mere act of standing up in front of an audience causes the mind to go blank and the speaker to dry up. So if you have to make

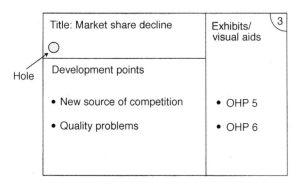

Figure 9.9 A confidence card

a presentation prepare carefully in advance. Novice presenters will probably want to write their presentation down word for word, the more experienced will none the less still feel the need for speaking notes. Even if you do not use them in the course of the presentation, they are there should you dry up or be thrown off course by a question or comments. They are a safety net should you need one and as such add confidence. That is why these aids to presentation are sometimes called confidence cards (Figure 9.9).

 Punch a hole in the top left-hand corner of each card and link them with a 'treasury tag'. If you drop your cards they will remain in order.

An alternative to a confidence card is a flipchart on which you write the points as you make them. If you have previously noted the points in pencil on the flipchart this cannot be seen by the audience but enables you to produce an impressive list of words, figures and statistics. You will amaze your audience with your fluency and success is guaranteed!

Another alternative is to use the mind-mapping technique discussed earlier. As a further development of this, different coloured sheets of paper can be used to colour code the presentation. For example red may mean 'negative points' and green could mean 'favourable points'. You can also use symbols and signs as shorthand on the map for transparency slides or visual aids to remind you of the material that you have available. Writing the mind map with a felt-tip pen makes it readily visible from some distance. The sheet can be left on the table as a memory jogger when needed.

The most widely used of presentation tools is the overhead projector, or its latter-day substitute the computerised presentation. Whilst these are largely substitute technologies the overhead projector still has some advantages compared to the computerised presentation.

- The transparencies can be drawn on to enhance a point or respond to questions.

- The order of the transparencies can be varied 'on the hoof' to respond to particular needs.

- The room does not need to be semi-darkened, enabling the speaker to maintain eye contact with the audience.

- The overhead projector is more reliable than computer-based presentations. We know this as many presenters using the computer bring transparencies as a back up, but rarely do users of transparencies bring a disk 'just in case'.

With the advent of computer technology it is possible to produce extremely high-quality transparencies for use either with overhead projectors or for computer presentations. We have suffered more than a few presentations where the presenter's ability to include graphics, logos, clip art, photographs, diagrams, etc. confuses and obscures the message. In preparing overhead transparencies the KISS principle should apply.

- Avoid using red or green colours for text as they are difficult to read and those who are colour blind find this is even more confusing.

- Use a consistent but simple layout.

- Use larger letters and fewer words to aid clarity. Do not use more than six to eight lines on each slide. Do not use more than six to eight words per line.

- Use pictures and charts wherever possible. Try to avoid transparencies which have only text on them.

- Readability can be improved by 'reversing out' text from the background. In other words, use light coloured text on a dark background, yellow on blue or white on green is often effective.

REHEARSE, REHEARSE, REHEARSE

All professionals will rehearse their presentations, although sometimes our students may not think so! Remember when rehearsing that the actual presentation will almost certainly take longer as you will present more slowly when under pressure. Try running through your presentation before going to bed the night before the big day. Your brain will keep working overnight and embed the presentation in your mind.

If you are making a presentation that involves the use of computer projection it is always advisable to check the equipment well in advance of the presentation. We have seen far more presentations that have been ineffective due to either poor functioning of the equipment or inadequate understanding of how to operate it than otherwise. One of us had the opportunity to see a faultless, three-hour presentation involving a wide range of media – overhead projector, computer projection, slides, Internet presentation, etc. given by an American professor, an expert in the field. In order to achieve this seamless presentation he came to London a week before the presentation in order to check the equipment, rehearse and brief the technicians on what was required, such was his attention to detail. For high-profile presentations it is well worth the extra expense to have a technician present to deal quickly and efficiently with any malfunction.

Delivery

This is the point at which the butterflies start to flutter, the mouth goes dry and unless you are well prepared mistakes can start to happen. This is the point at which you wish that you had prepared more. A feeling of nervousness before a presentation is not necessarily a bad thing, it helps you to focus and raises your level of performance. Even the most experienced of speakers feel uncomfortable before a presentation. To help to overcome this:

- 'Shake-out' any tenseness. Literally stand on the spot and shake your arms and rotate your head to relieve those aching muscles.

- Breathe deeply several times to relax.

- When you stand in front of the audience never, ever apologise. Should something go wrong just carry on, the audience does not know the script, so they do not know what is 'right' and 'wrong'. There is really no need to expose yourself by admitting any mistakes.

- Depending on the type of presentation, respect people's territory (Figure 9.10). In the U-shaped layout illustrated by Figure 9.10, you can violate the personal space of the audience if you stray into the centre of the U. You may want to do this in order to emphasise and make a point, but it is generally a trick that only a more experienced presenter would use.

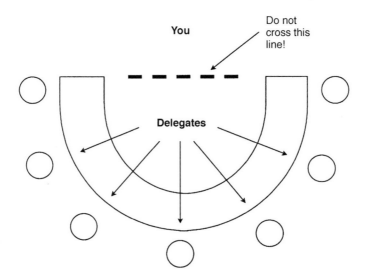

Figure 9.10 The delegates' territory

- Explain your transparencies but do not read them. You should add value to each transparency and be clear about the points that you wish to make with each one.

- No audience appreciates a dull speaker. This does not mean that you have to be full of jokes and repartee, very few of us are capable of that. But you can avoid dullness by not using jargon, using visual aids, not speaking for too long in one go. Try breaking off every now and then and inviting questions and checking understanding. Encourage your audience to ask questions by asking them open-ended questions. Instead of saying 'is that clear to you', which invites the obvious answer of 'yes', try asking questions such as 'can you think of similar circumstances that we have found with other clients', for example.

Use some simple but well proven presentation tactics:

- Start with an unexpected and attention-grabbing hook. One of us attended a presentation on one occasion when the presenter unveiled a foaming pint of real ale as a way of making his first point.

- Making clear what the objective of the session is. Prepare a suitable transparency or write it down on a flipchart.

- Deliver your message through three to six essential key points.

- Give practical examples – facts, statistics, definitions; to illustrate key points it is often useful to start with an example and then make a generalisation afterwards.

- Repeat what you have told them by way of summary.

- Finish with a concluding message. Presumably you would like them to do something as a result of the presentation; this is your opportunity to make your point.

- Do not be afraid of repeating points; everybody's attention wanders from time to time.

Feedback and questions

At the end of your presentation encourage your audience to ask questions to expand on points that interest them. This is the opportunity for them to choose what they want to speak about rather than to discuss what is of interest to you. Depending on the type of audience you may also want to get some feedback about how well the presentation went. Did the points come across clearly? Were the visual aids easy to read? What were the main points that they take away from the presentation? Did they make any suggestions for improvements?

The ability to make presentations is rapidly becoming an essential business skill. If you are intimidated at the prospect of standing up in front of an audience or have experienced what it is like to make a less than satisfactory presentation, then consider a presentation skills course as part of your personal development. This is a life skill that, once conquered, will be invaluable for the rest of your career. However, the lack of presentation skills may mean that your career is not as fulfilled as it might be!

Problem definition and decision-making

10

KEY POINTS

The first step in solving a problem is to define the nature of the problem. To achieve this

- *ask questions*
- *use the why-why method.*

To solve the problem

- *use the how-how method*
- *test alternative solutions.*

PROBLEM SETTING

It is one thing to resolve a problem, something which we all feel a sense of achievement in doing. It is entirely another to understand the problem that needs to be resolved. It is something of a paradox that most marketing books provide a wide range of sophisticated tools to assist in problem solving, but yet do not tell you how to understand the problem in the first instance.

Just why is it so important to understand the problem? Firstly, there are some simple principles that help us to understand this.

- A problem cannot be resolved if it has not previously been defined.
- A problem-solving tool cannot provide you with a solution to problems which are not initially clear.
- An analytical tool is of no value if the reason for using it is not clear.
- Inappropriate solutions may be more harmful than an unresolved problem.
- A problem that is correctly defined is already half solved.

Given these principles let us have a look at how to define the problem in practice. Before we do that let us first think about what a problem actually is. We can define a problem as a gap or divergence between what is happening and what should be happening.

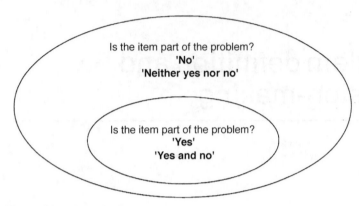

Figure 10.1 The problem boundaries

ASK QUESTIONS

There is wide agreement that the definition of a problem first starts with asking questions to stimulate thinking and help to understand the nature of the gap. Rudyard Kipling spoke about his six best friends – what, when, where, why, who, how.

- What is the problem? What is not the problem?
- What is happening? What should be happening?
- When is it a problem? When is it not a problem?
- Where do we find the problem? Where do we not find the problem?
- Who is associated with the problem? Who is not associated with the problem?

A simple series of questions, but answers to these questions will help to draw a circle around the problem to clarify what is within the circle and part of the problem and what is outside it. Every piece of information that we obtain should help us to contribute to the definition of the problem, that is to say it should be relevant. To carry that out, ask yourself the simple following question: Is this item part of the problem? If the answer is 'Yes' or 'Yes and No', then the item is included in the circle. If the answer is 'neither Yes nor No' or just plain 'No' then the information is not relevant to the problem and is placed outside the circle (Figure 10.1).

   Perhaps you have been in a meeting where the nature of the problem is being discussed. You can often see how irrelevant information or even red herrings are dragged into the argument, confusing the picture and not contributing to defining the problem and hence the solution.

WHY-WHY METHOD

Often, simply defining the problem is not enough to help us to understand how it should be solved. To do this we have to go a stage further and look for the causes of the problem. A good way of doing this is the so-called 'why-why' method illustrated by Figure 10.2 (Majaro 1992, pp. 137–8).

Figure 10.2 Why-why method

FISHBONE TECHNIQUE

A variation of the why-why method is the 'fishbone' technique. This is another way of breaking a large problem down into what may be multiple causes and is illustrated by Figure 10.3. (Developed by Professor Kaoru Ishikawa of the University of Tokyo.)

Reducing a problem into its constituent parts very often helps us to understand the most likely cause of the problem. Perhaps this may become more obvious at an early stage of the analysis, or there may be a clue in the way that the same types of issues repeat themselves. We can also apply a simple test to each piece of information, and ask ourselves if the cause that we have identified is within or outside the circle. By way of a shortcut we can suggest a short list of common marketing problems.

- The client's requirements are not clear, or at least not clearly understood throughout the company.

- Training is inadequate or inappropriate for the requirements of the job.

- There has been a lack of analysis to help to define the problem.

- There is confusion between the possible solutions perceived by the company and the often misunderstood requirements of the market.

- We are reactive and not proactive, being driven more by our clients rather than listening, learning and acting positively to meet client needs.

- We are efficient rather than effective. We may be great firefighters, but how much better it would be if the fire were prevented in the first instance.

- We manage by function rather than by customer-driven process.

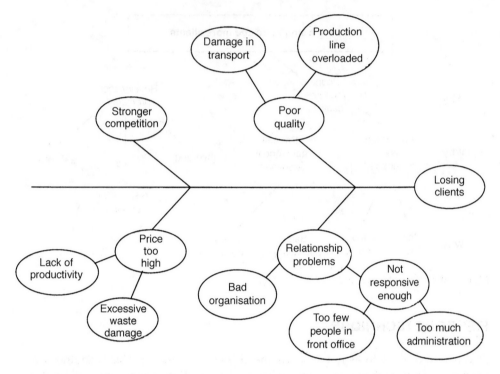

Figure 10.3 Fishbone technique

PROBLEM SOLVING

When you feel that you at last understand the problem, that is the point at which a solution can be sought. Having identified the nature of the problem using the 'why-why' method we can then build on the causes identified by using the 'how-how' method as shown in Figure 10.4 (Majaro 1992, pp. 151–3). In this way we can start to build a range of potential solutions. Looking at these alternatives we can then use our judgement to decide which is the most appropriate. Factors that we should consider when thinking about this are

- the effectiveness of the solution to resolve the problem that has been identified, within the limits of our capabilities
- the alternative costs involved
- the possible follow-on consequences of our actions
- fall-back and alternative solutions should they be required
- ensuring that there are follow-up and feedback processes in place to ensure sound implementation.

We depict this process in Figure 10.5.

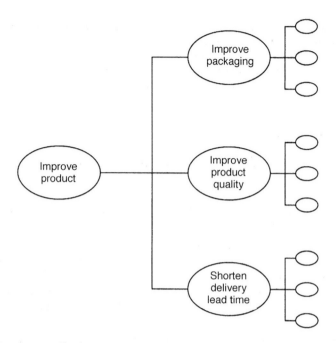

Figure 10.4 How-how method

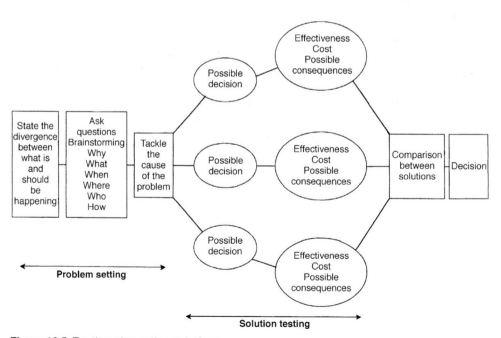

Figure 10.5 Testing alternative solutions

It is quite common in this process to feel both overwhelmed with information and yet not have the critical information necessary to arrive at a decision. In reality it is easy to become buried in data but lack information. The difference between data and information is that information is relevant, appropriately processed and presented and useful for decision-making purposes.

The information trap

There is never enough time to turn all the data into information, and we therefore end in a situation where we are surrounded by data but are unable to reach a sound decision — we have arrived at analysis paralysis. The danger here is to short-circuit the analysis stage and apply experience and intuition. In other words, using our knowledge of the past and gut-feel, applying it for the future.

The problem here is that perhaps our previous decisions were not so good either; in different and perhaps more complex circumstances this is hardly likely to be the key to success. However, the situation can deteriorate even further, as having taken a poor decision we then select information from the available data to support our position. In other words you took the decision 'a priori' and collected information to justify your decision 'a posteriori'.

To avoid this trap we suggest that you should adopt a 'comparison between solutions'. Far from creating work, it can enrich the information by giving a basis of comparison. By developing a range of different solutions they support each other and give you alternative options should expectations not be met. This reduces the risk of failure and increases confidence in the decision that you eventually make.

 Last but not least
Some problems seem so difficult that you cannot find a solution in spite of your efforts. In this case *give this problem a rest*. Let it rest for a night, or for a week, and see how elements of the solution emerge.

This can be explained by the fact that your relentlessness to solve a problem can become more a barrier than a path to the solution.

Give the problem a rest and let your brain work for you.

Time management

11

KEY POINTS

To organise your time effectively:

- *Decide what is really important for you and your company; your values.*
- *Define your annual objectives consistent with your values and write them down.*
- *Do the same for your monthly objectives.*
- *Each week decide the tasks necessary to achieve the monthly objectives.*
- *Take a little time to plan your week.*
- *Each day manage your tasks, distinguish between the important and the urgent issues.*

A BUSY AGENDA

- a meeting in Brussels with a major client
- the marketing plan to complete before the end of the month
- a presentation to prepare for an important shareholder
- a meeting with journalists to follow up on a recent product launch
- a meeting with a colleague to discuss the market circumstances in Asia Pacific
- a hundred and one other frustrating issues that absorb our time.

Does this sound a little like your working life? More like a Chinese plate juggler desperately running backwards and forwards trying to prevent a plate falling to the ground. If so, do not worry unduly as all marketing managers seem to face problems of this sort. One of the most common factors we found is that managers ask themselves how can I do a hundred and one things at the same time? Be in two places at the same time? Be several different people but with only one brain?

To help with this universal problem you will find in this chapter a selection of ideas to help you manage your time more effectively. These are presented in a clear and simple way that will at least allow you to go easily and logically from the 'big picture' through to the jobs you have to tackle tomorrow. Yes, we really do practice what we preach. Both the authors run variants of these ideas using both paper and electronic organisers combined with computerised diary systems.

BEFORE ANYTHING ELSE

Get an organiser, either paper based or electronic. If you choose one of the many types of electronic organisers – diary, database, word processing, spreadsheet, etc. – be sure to instigate a back-up procedure as soon as you start to enter data.

STEP ONE – THE BACKCLOTH

Draw up a list of

- your own values (honest, hard-working, modest, etc.)
- your company's values
- your company's mission.

If you find that a little too challenging then think about it in a different way.

- What you believe in – these are the factors which will underline the way you think and behave.
- What you know is legitimate in your company.
- What you know is forbidden in your company.

In other words what is 'politically correct' or 'politically incorrect'. You need to think about the boundaries that define the organisation and what should not be infringed (Figure 11.1).

STEP TWO – PAINTING THE BIG PICTURE

What are the three or four things that would dramatically change your company if you could do them regardless of the time and energy required. Now think about the three or four things that you will be especially proud to achieve for yourself. Imagine that the managing director or chairman is saying a few words of farewell as you leave to take up an appointment elsewhere in the organisation. What are the things that you would really like him to note as your achievements? These points constitute what is important for you to achieve. From now on, regard these as your personal big picture, the things that really matter to you (Figure 11.2). Write them down in your organiser and from now on everything that will help you to achieve this big picture will be important to you as well.

Good	Bad
Legitimate	Illegitimate
Authorised	Forbidden
Politically correct	Politically incorrect

Figure 11.1 What is good or bad in your company?

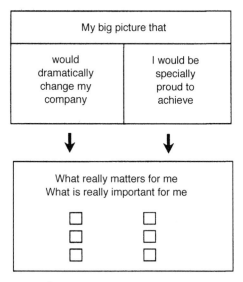

Figure 11.2 What really matters for you

Figure 11.3 A 'to do' list

Other objectives will not have this level of importance to you and are therefore ordinary day-to-day issues. That is not say that you should not address them, but there is a difference between what is important to the company and what might be important to you personally. So you can now sort your written 'to do list' into two categories, the 'important' and the 'ordinary' (Figure 11.3).

STEP THREE – ANNUAL PLANNING

Take some time at the beginning of each year to draw a list of the key objectives that you need to achieve, consistent with your value and with your big picture. This is your own personal checklist, not one that you necessarily want to discuss with the boss or other people. These points will be the objectives for the year, what really matters to you and the things that you will really commit yourself to do. These might seem so large and

Objectives	Sub-objectives
1 Developing sales in Middle East	1.1
	1.2
	1.3
2 New key accounts	2.1
	2.2
	2.3
3 Developing partnership with largest clients	3.1
	3.2
	3.3
4 Developing new product range	4.1
	4.2
	4.3

Figure 11.4 Split the difficulty

unachievable that it is better to break the objectives down into sub-objectives (Figure 11.4).

This can then be used as the basis for more detailed planning. You can start to think about the time, energy and other resources that are required for each subject. Make sure that thinking about the time and effort required does not involve more than 20 per cent of your available time throughout the year. If it does then you need to revisit the list of objectives and re-prioritise them. Almost by definition, not everything is important so you can continue to prioritise until the list is boiled down to the key issues. Then take your year plan and start to book out the time that you will need to achieve these objectives, making sure that you really do keep this time available and do not allow it to leak away on other activities. In fact, this is the most critical and difficult step of the process, being determined enough to keep these dates for the achievement of your objectives despite all the other pressures.

A manager working in the European office of an American multinational company was being drowned by calls on his time, as he bounced backwards and forwards across Europe, rushing from one meeting to another. Neil, his real name, recognised that he really was not achieving anything in this way. When he was invited to meetings he started to ask some direct questions, for example, 'so will you send me a copy of the agenda a week in advance of the meeting?' Of course, very few managers have even thought of preparing an agenda, let alone a week in advance of the meeting. The other question he asked was 'what specific contribution do you expect me to make to the meeting?' This often received a reply along the lines of 'well we think it's important that you are there'. If he could not obtain satisfactory answers to simple questions like this then he refused to go. In this way he was able to take control of his time and start to manage events rather than be driven by them.

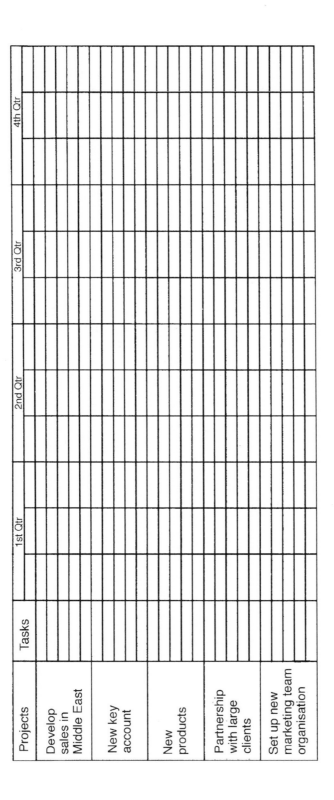

Projects	Tasks	1st Qtr			2nd Qtr			3rd Qtr			4th Qtr		
Develop sales in Middle East													
New key account													
New products													
Partnership with large clients													
Set up new marketing team organisation													

Figure 11.5 Planning projects on a one-year basis

Now that you have decided your objectives and time allocation you can now start to map this on a chart as shown in Figure 11.5. This overview reflects the time that you have blocked out in your diary in order to achieve your objectives.

STEP FOUR – MONTHLY PLANNING

At the end of every month come back to your diary and review next month's programme. To do so, review the important tasks that you have written down in your planning chart and decide the objectives for the month. This also prompts you to prepare for the next series of meetings, presentations, etc. Be careful to write down your objectives for the month in your diary.

STEP FIVE – WEEKLY PLANNING

At regular weekly intervals review your organiser and prepare your week, taking into account all the tasks that are necessary to achieve your objectives. At this stage the short term is beginning to encroach as you also need to take into account the tasks generated by current events. These are the hundred and one items that crowd in to steal your time – the meeting with the journalist, an unexpected visit from an important client, the accountant wants to discuss the end of quarter figures, etc.

On your weekly agenda start to sort the 'to do' list into the urgent and non-urgent. With this list you are now able to sort your tasks into four categories and think about how you will use your time. In reality the matrix could look like Figure 11.6. This will then act as a checklist for your weekly activities.

STEP 6 – DAILY PLANNING

Every evening take 15 minutes or so to organise your next day using your diary and the weekly planning sheet. In this time construct a list of the tasks that have to be completed

	Important	Ordinary
Urgent	15%	65%
Not urgent	5%	15%

Figure 11.6 Apportioning your time

the next day, and review today's lists. Experience the satisfaction of crossing through those tasks that have been completed.

PRIORITISING THE TASKS

As you probably realise in this process the two critical parts are firstly defining the objectives and secondly prioritising the tasks. In deciding priorities use the following questions:

- What tasks will contribute the most towards the achievement of my objectives?

- What are the consequences of not completing a particular task?

- What tasks must be done?

 Avoid the 'last in-first out' (LIFO) principle, which involves doing first the last thing that you had been asked to do and treating it as the most important. If you do this, then you are allowing others to dictate your priorities. Their priorities in fact become your priorities.

Planning in advance allows you to act instead of reacting. It allows you to preserve some time, we suggest around 20 per cent, for the essential long-term objectives which are otherwise sacrificed in a never-ending list of daily 'to do' lists.
The process could be summarised as shown in Figure 11.7.

SOME FINAL THOUGHTS ON IMPROVING YOUR DAILY EFFECTIVENESS

Finally, when it comes to actually using a system like this, here are some of the implementation principles it will be beneficial to remember.

- Complete the task you have started, do not come back to it.

- Do one thing at a time.

- Be prepared to delegate to others.

- Split large tasks into several small ones.

- Decide the objectives of a telephone call before making it.

- At certain times of the day have your telephone diverted to your secretary or a colleague in order that you can defend your time.

- Stand up when making telephone calls. This has the effect of encouraging greater attention and making the call shorter.

- Avoid meetings for the sake of meetings. If you work out, on the basis of your salary, your cost per hour it brings home how expensive meetings actually are.

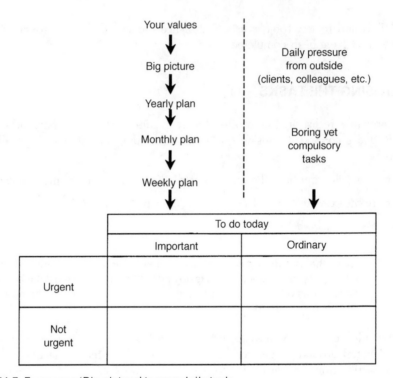

Figure 11.7 From your 'Big picture' to your daily task

- Always have something available to read or do in spare moments, perhaps when commuting or waiting in the airport lounge.
- Make use of e-mail as it is not intrusive; you can reach otherwise unreachable people and you can reply in your own time when you have developed the response. Do not take this too far as otherwise you will be e-mailing people in the next office, far better to talk to them. Manage your e-mails using directories and folders.
- Avoid long business lunches and dinners.
- Guard your time and avoid 'corridor conversations'.
- Dare to say no.
- Be prepared to invest both time and money in efficiency aids. For instance, a training programme to really understand how to use a certain software programme. Another example is this book which was 'written' using voice-recognition software.

Personal planning in this way is not a tiresome time stealer; it is the way in which you can make time. So many managers are content to be driven by events and fail to differentiate between being busy and being effective. A large part of marketing is concerned with the future, in other words, with planning. As a marketer, how can you manage the affairs of a company if you cannot manage yourself? And stop moaning that you do not have enough time. You have exactly as much time in your life as Bill Gates, Shakespeare or Winston Churchill.

PART V

Industrial marketing in practice

INTRODUCTION

We have seen in Part II how you can think about your job when we considered the job outline. If we think of the outline of the marketing function it is to

- make the company aware of the external environment in which it operates in order to
  - sustain current activity and
  - prepare for the future.

Then we saw in Part III

- some basic marketing principles
- characteristics of industrial marketing
- how the principles of the marketing of technological innovation can enable you to cope with conditions of uncertainty.

It is time now to put these principles into practice and see how to implement them.

 In summary, implementing marketing in practice consists of a two-stage approach:

- **thinking through and developing strategy**
- **implementing the strategy.**

The first chapter in this part will be dedicated to developing and thinking through the strategy and the next to implementing strategy through the planning process.

The principle of 'implementing marketing in practice' is that you should think of the whole and the details at the same time. Coping with this apparent difficulty is the purpose of Part V.

Industrial marketing in practice

Introduction

Setting a marketing strategy **12**

KEY POINTS

- *To build a strategy we need to make a clear distinction between doing the right things and doing things right.*
- *This means we need to identify our distinctive competencies and the key success factors.*
- *Marketing objectives are concerned with markets and products and should be defined in such a way that they close the gap between what the company*
  - wants to do
  - is able to do
  - could do.

PRINCIPLES

A strategy is 'a plan for achieving objectives through the development of scarce resources in the face of intelligent competition' (Webster 1974). What does this mean for you? How do we actually tackle this problem in practice? Where do you start, where do you stop? In this chapter we shall try to give you a simple and visual framework to bear in mind when thinking about your marketing strategy. As usual we shall try to stick to some basic but solid and robust guidelines in order to keep this as applied as possible.

The golden rule of strategy
To build a good, efficient strategy think about the GOLDEN RULE and make a clear distinction between

Doing the right things
and
Doing things right

At this point let us have a look at how to connect these issues. The so-called golden rule can be diagrammatically displayed as shown in Figure 12.1. Marketing strategy consists of achieving consistency between doing the right things and doing things right. On the one hand we can consider that the 'right things' are the marketing objectives that we set out to achieve. This means that we define clearly what we want to achieve in what markets and with what products. On the other hand we can consider that 'doing things

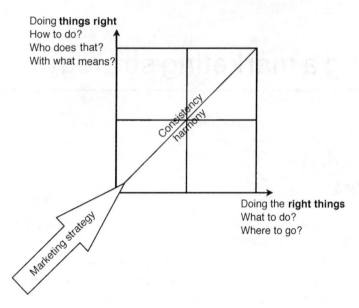

Doing **things right**
How to do?
Who does that?
With what means?

Doing the **right things**
What to do?
Where to go?

Consistency harmony

Marketing strategy

Figure 12.1 The golden rule of strategy

right' concerns how to do the things necessary to achieve our objectives. This means that we have to allocate resources, and of course we never have enough of those and so this means that we have to take decisions and make judgements. We also have to plan our activities so that we co-ordinate the way in which our resources are used.

However, defining strategy is more than that. We should also indicate the principles by which we intend to operate, to give guidance and direction to our actions. For example, is it our intention to be

- offensive – and enter new markets

- defensive – improve our current position, gain market share

- co-operative – to work with others to achieve our objectives

- technology leader – to invest in research and development

- price competitive – to position ourselves at the lower end of the market

- client responsive – to meet customers' needs and expectations better than anybody else.

The diagram of the golden rule can now be drawn as shown in Figure 12.2.

Consistency means defining marketing objectives that are achievable within a given time and with respect to the resources that are available. Therefore the first and critical point of marketing strategy is to define appropriate objectives that will enable the company to be competitive, but objectives which are nevertheless achievable. Easier said than done! Above all, why should you rather work with one particular market than with another and what will determine your success?

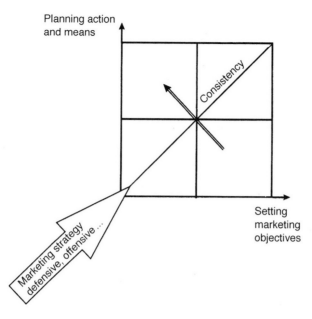

Figure 12.2 The golden rule of strategy in practice

KEY SUCCESS FACTORS (KSF) AND DISTINCTIVE COMPETENCE

There are several reasons for working with one market. The first is that the market is determined by the past. In other words you have already been working with this market and you cannot rewind the tape. The second is that you are driven by some critical factors called key problems, key success factors and distinctive competence.

One common mistake in marketing is to believe that everything you find in a book should be used and implemented in order to succeed. In reality, every situation is specific and can be driven by a few essential factors that make you successful and differentiated. Therefore, the game for you will be to find out what these driving factors are around which you will organise all the rest of your business. We could diagrammatically explain this in Figure 12.3. Key success factors (KSF) and distinctive competence are, in some respects, the spine of your business and hence the spine of your strategy. Let us give some definitions of these driving factors.

The KSF are obligatory factors defined by the market and client requirements. They are compulsory actions that you must take to succeed in a given a market. 'It is essential for the company to establish what these key success factors are and how well it compares with its closest competitors.' (See Figure 12.4 and McDonald 1995.) The KSF can be, for example, price, quality, reliability, service, innovation. The comparison of yourself with your competitor can be quantified in the chart of Figure 12.5.

Distinctive competencies are what really makes the big difference between you and your competitors. They allow you to be strongly differentiated from your competitors. They give you your unique characteristics and are those vital elements on which you

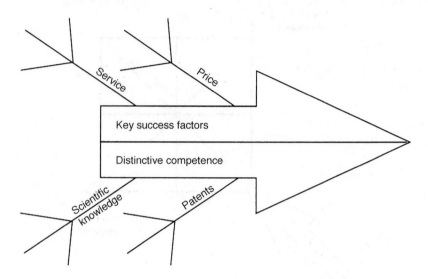

Figure 12.3 Organising the activity around KSF and distinctive competence

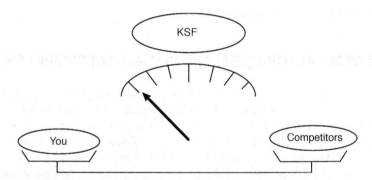

Figure 12.4 Be better than the competitors on the KSF

should allocate your resources. As stated by Webster (1974) they may be found in any area of the company, in R&D, in engineering, in production, marketing, distribution. They are defined as a 'set of capabilities that translates into products market strategy distinguishing the competitors in a way that is important to the clients'.

Distinctive competence can be

- basic scientific knowledge in the R&D group giving the ability to invent effective solutions to customer problems

- access to critically important raw material or components

- patents and related technical expertise

- production skills related to machinery or processes that allow better quality or cost saving

Key success factors	Relative weight %	You		Competitor 1		Competitor 2		Competitor 3	
		Score	Score × Weight	Score	Score × Weight	Score	Score × Weight	Score	Score × Weight
1 Price	50								
2 Product	30								
3 Reliability	20								
4 Service	5								
5 Innovation	5								
6									
Total	100								

Figure 12.5 Assessing your position on the KSF (Webster 1974)

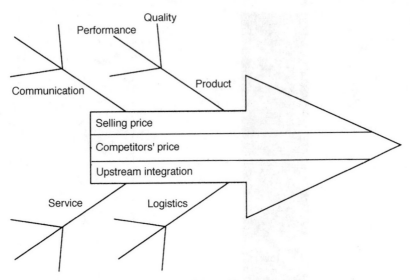

Figure 12.6 Example of organisation around the critical factors

- fixed plants, location and technology that produces cost savings or unique product characteristics

- distribution relationships that provides access to specific markets and customers that are not so readily available to the competition.

The key problems are those things that make your job difficult, those things that raise a big constraint around how you organise all your business (Figure 12.6). For example, in the flat glass industry the glass furnace is the big point. It must run 24 hours per day and 365 days per year during several years and never fail otherwise it is a nightmare for the company. Losses are very large and the plant must be virtually rebuilt. To be more explicit and to illustrate the variety of the situation, let us give some typical industry examples from our interviews.

- A company selling doors and windows for buildings and houses has 200,000 possible combinations in their catalogue. Their key problem is the price list, a real obsession that requires three people full time and takes a large part of the marketing director's time. Their key success factor is their distribution network.

- For a chemical company selling commodity polymers the key problem is the competitor's prices. How can they know at what prices the competitors are really ready to sell their products? A key success factor is invariably the price. How can I produce cheaper? The distinctive competence is to be found in the fact that the company is integrated upstream which means that it makes the monomer used as a component for the polymer. They make their profit on the monomer and can sell the polymer cheaper.

- In the military aircraft industry the KSF is preparing the ground and networking at both a political and industrial level. A first distinctive competence is to hire a former senior officer and another is the quality of R&D.

- A company working on big contracts for the public sector will find that the key problem is forecasting sales. As the contracts are very few and very big your year can be very good or very bad due to just one contract lost or won. No statistics can help you in forecasting your activity. One KSF is to bid as quickly as possible because the notice is always very short after the tender comes out. Most of the time it is too late to bid when you discover the call for tender. Therefore, one distinctive competence can be a network of trustworthy partners with whom you are prepared to bid jointly. Another distinctive competence is given by software and a database enabling you to work out a proposal very quickly.

- A company making equipment for the electronics industry will have difficulty in fore-casting sales. As with the climate and the weather, the company can predict the long term (warm in summer) but can hardly forecast the short term (rain or sun next weekend). The KSF is to have world-wide presence because your clients have plants all over the world and require the same products, the same parts and the same service in every country. The distinctive competence is to work extremely closely with the main clients to adapt constantly to the latest evolution of the clients' technology. The second distinctive competence is the information system that enables you to have a world-wide overview of the industry. You must, for instance, take a subscription to the SIA (Semiconductor Industry Association), which produces technological forecasting and road maps.

- A good example of a company building its success on a distinctive competence is 3M who articulate their strategy around innovation. Everything is organised around this distinctive key factor.

- A software company that we have interviewed was building its strategy around a distinctive competence called Business Development (everything was organised around generating and managing the change in the market).

Now, bearing all this in mind, how do we define marketing objectives?

DEFINING MARKETING OBJECTIVES IN PRACTICE

If marketing objectives are concerned with markets and products, then the first question to decide is which markets do we wish to be involved in. But how do we decide on this? Do we start by looking at the market or market segment and deciding on the basis of size or alternatively do we look at our products, such as an ultra high-speed machine tool, and ask ourselves what we can do with it? Perhaps you could take guidance from the boss, perhaps he or she has made a long-term commitment by saying that the company wants to be a big player in telecommunications in ten years' time. So how does that help us to decide which market to target and what products should be developed to achieve this long-term objective? Another tricky problem, but it is still difficult to know from where we should start.

We would not suggest that there is one single, simple starting point that we should use when defining objectives. If we consider the discussion so far we can conclude that there are three main points.

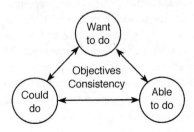

Marketing objectives golden rule

Figure 12.7 The marketing objectives golden rule (Millier 1999)

1. The MARKET − what opportunities may exist in the market and what is its size?
2. The PRODUCT − and by extension the other types of assets the company has available and which enable it to compete.
3. The VISION − a long-term perspective of where the company is going.

In fact, defining the marketing objectives means taking decisions based around these three areas so that there is consistency between what the company

- WANTS to do
- IS ABLE to do
- COULD do

That is a golden rule that we could apply to marketing objectives (Figure 12.7) and a set of criteria that we should apply whenever necessary. In reality defining marketing objectives means that we have to match and sometimes compromise in order to achieve consistency between these three points. A three-legged stool is always stable and our marketing objectives, like the stool, need these three main points to be resolved if they are to be durable.

Let us now take this one stage further and consider each of the three poles of the decision. What the company wants to do refers to

- what can be done in the company
- what cannot be done in the company.

What we are really saying here is that we have to decide what is acceptable within the company; we could use the phrase 'politically correct'. In other words, what can be done is within the political boundary of acceptability. If your company is more developed in terms of its marketing understanding you could refer to this as

- the corporate strategy
- the mission statement
- the vision
- the culture.

All of these describe what is appropriate and by definition appropriate within the organisation.

What the company is able to do refers to

- product
- technologies
- patents
- people and people skills
- organisational assets
- networks and alliances
- access to critical resources.

Here we are looking at things which both enable you to do what you want to do, but will also limit you. These are the assets and proficiencies of the organisation that we have to employ as effectively as we can if we are going to compete effectively. We can understand these assets of the organisation by conducting an internal audit.

What the company could do refers to

- market opportunities
- market constraints
- client needs and wants
- competitor exit and entry.

These are factors in the external environment that we need to understand if we are going to match our resources to them in order to be better and more competitive than other companies. Again, we understand this external environment by conducting audits, perhaps focusing on critical issues by using the market research and segmentation techniques.

The arrows in Figure 12.8 have significance. For example, the arrow between 'could do' and 'able to do' implies that we need to find an appropriate match between the market opportunity and capabilities of the organisation. Matching means firstly that we have to understand the gap between the market requirement and the offering. This is where we use marketing diagnostic tools such as the various matrix tools and SWOT analysis (see Chapter 27) which helps us to understand the gap and then to make a judgement about our future course of action.

The arrow between 'want to do' and 'able to do' refers to investment decisions (Figure 12.8). Investments in technical assets such as patents or plant, commercial assets such as developing alliances and networks, or perhaps engaging new staff with different skills. An understanding of this gap will ultimately help us to decide our allocation of financial and other marketing resources.

The arrow between 'could do' and 'want to do' resolves itself in our decisions about which markets we wish to participate in (Figure 12.8). In other words, our marketing objectives. Here we are attempting to get the optimum balance between the opportunity offered by the market and the capabilities we possess. Decisions about the markets, or market segments, that we want to engage in are threefold:

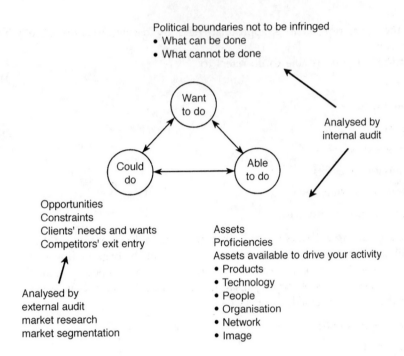

Political boundaries not to be infringed
• What can be done
• What cannot be done

Analysed by
internal audit

Opportunities
Constraints
Clients' needs and wants
Competitors' exit entry

Assets
Proficiencies
Assets available to drive your activity
• Products
• Technology
• People
• Organisation
• Network
• Image

Analysed by
external audit
market research
market segmentation

Figure 12.8 Implementation of the marketing objectives golden rule

- which segments or markets we want to participate in

- which markets we want to remain in

- which markets we want to withdraw from.

We could for instance display our market opportunities on a chart that helps us to summarise the options that we have with respect to marketing objectives (Figure 12.10).

A final word about the framework in Figure 12.7 that discusses marketing objectives. A line connects each element of the diagram with an arrow at both ends. This means that each element of the marketing objective framework influences the other elements. Whilst it might look straightforward on a diagram like this, in practice it is a messy, iterative process. There is no place from which the process starts or finishes. By saying that it is iterative we mean that we bounce from one pole of the diagram to another as we seek to

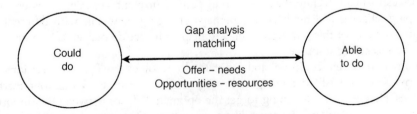

Figure 12.9 Relationship between 'could do' and 'able to do'

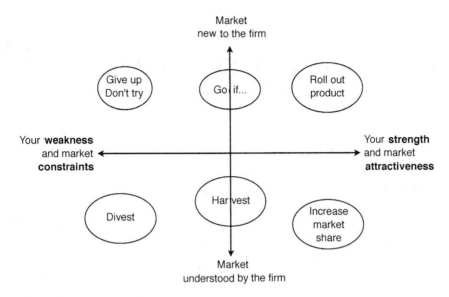

Figure 12.10 Mapping your situation

optimise the consistency between what we want to do (Figure 12.9), what we could do and what we are able to do. Defining marketing objectives is not a linear process. It involves trade-off, compromise and judgement. The good news is that you will know that you are right, the bad news is that it is invariably with the benefit of hindsight. Hence marketing depends on your experience and judgement as a manager of resources as decisions are rarely clear cut and straightforward.

Planning marketing action   **13**

KEY POINTS

- *Marketing planning is concerned with doing things right. It helps us to plan our actions and co-ordinate them from the corporate to the market-segment level.*

- *In this process we consider the attractiveness of each segment, which in turn helps us to allocate resources as we choose between segments in order to select those that are most attractive.*

PLANNING PRINCIPLE

In the previous chapter we saw how to decide the marketing objectives, that is to say, how to decide which markets we wish to compete in and what we want to achieve

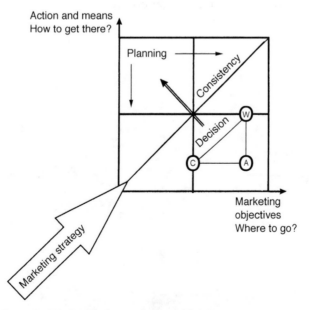

Figure 13.1 Planning consistent with the marketing objectives

having taken that decision. In this chapter we will see how to plan a course of action within our chosen markets and how to allocate resources in order to achieve the objective (Figure 13.1).

Planning should be done at two different levels:

- the activity or corporate level
- the market-segment level, for each segment that you have decided to serve.

SPYMAG

Planning at the activity level is particularly important when entering or exiting the market or segments. Care should also be taken to co-ordinate activities across segments in order to optimise any synergies. At the market-segment level you will need to decide which product offering you will provide clients with and how any subsequent back-up service can also be supported. As an example of how to build a marketing strategy let us take the example of SPYMAG (Millier 1999a).

SPYMAG is a company selling basic electrical and electronic components to industry. They recently added a new option to their range, magnetic tracing. This consists of leaving a magnetic trace on any base such as wood, plastic, paper, etc. so that it is possible to 'write' on objects and then subsequently to read and recognise the objects.

Segmentation

SPYMAG identified twelve market segments:

S1. taxi flow management in restricted areas such as stations and airports

S2. passenger information in public transport

S3. patient 'badging' in hospital

S4. sports event timing, e.g. sailing, cycling

S5. action counting, e.g. dustbin emptying

S6. large warehouse storage and management

S7. infrastructure management, e.g. tracing plastic pallets

S8. time management on a production line, e.g. determining product flow through machines

S9. access control

S10. fleet maintenance and management, e.g. cars and trucks

S11. car anti-theft device

S12. differentiating items in bulk.

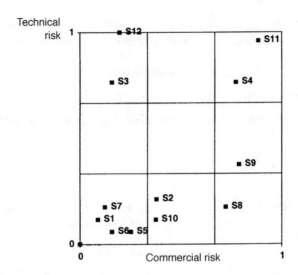

Figure 13.2 SPYMAG's situation diagnosis

Diagnosis and marketing strategy

Taking into account the market attractiveness and SPYMAG's main strengths and weaknesses displayed in Figure 13.2, it has been decided that:

- SPYMAG will concentrate its commercial investments on S1 and S5, segments with high potential which offer a good match with SPYMAG's core competencies. Due to synergies, such as the sales of different products to the same clients, passenger information, S2, and the access control segment, S9, can also be served with little additional investment.

- SPYMAG have decided to adopt an aggressive approach to segments S6 and S7. These two segments have a high potential as well as good synergy with the core activity of electronic components, as a number of the clients are the same.

- SPYMAG will also look for opportunistic sales in other segments but have decided actively to avoid segments S8 and S10, since they have little knowledge or understanding of these markets and the potential application of the product.

- SPYMAG also decided to continue to invest in technological innovation in order to look for a technical development which would enable them to offer a better fit with the requirements of S4, sports event timing, and S12, bulk item identification.

- SPYMAG have decided not to enter S3, patient badging in hospital, and S11, car anti-theft devices, as they do not have the appropriate competencies to serve mass markets such as these.

	Year 1	Year 2	Year 3
Number of contracts	8	11	11
Number of sales visits	38	38	33
Turnover (£K)	270	390	390

Figure 13.3 SPYMAG's commercial objectives

SPYMAG have now been able to take a view on their commercial objectives by activity (Figure 13.3).

The background to these numbers can be diagrammatically described in their global plan as shown in Figure 13.4.

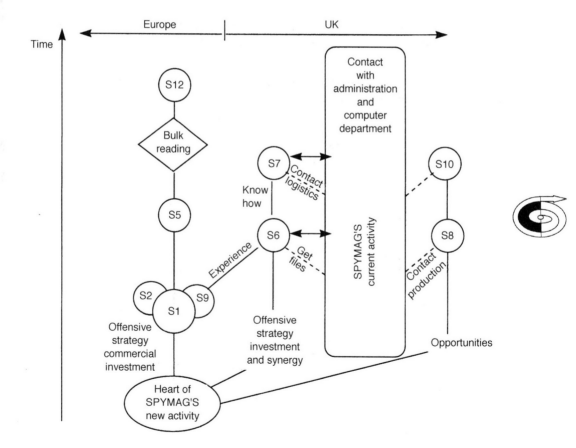

Figure 13.4 SPYMAG's global plan

Planning action at the segment level

Figure 13.4 illustrates the big picture of what SPYMAG intend to do at a global level, together with a definition of the commercial objectives they hope to fulfil. How can this be broken down into each segment? In order to do this there are two questions that need to be asked on a segment-by-segment basis. These are:

- What product offering is required to deliver the value each segment demands?
- How can the product offering be differentiated from those of competitors? (Figure 13.5.)

In addition to these overall requirements for each segment it is also extremely useful to be able to identify:

- prestigious, leading or influential clients whom you would like to work with as part of your segment entry strategy; clients who will appreciate the benefits of your product, and give you more insight into customer needs
- the critical success factors. For every segment that you deal with the detailed product offering can be summarised as shown in Figure 13.6 (Millier 1999b).

Figure 13.6 gives you a comprehensive list of requirements; you can also draw another chart with the critical success factors. This shows what really matters for each segment, and highlights aspects of differentiation. This enables you to differentiate not only between segments but also yourself from your competitors.

Critical success factors (Figure 13.7) are the actions that it is necessary to take or the elements required to be successful in a given market. These might include for example, reliable delivery, low running costs and, of course, more obvious things such as a

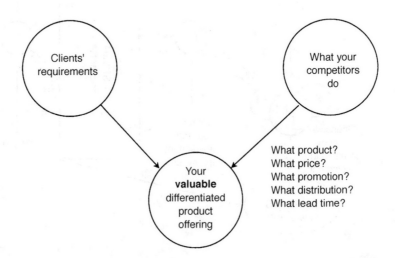

Figure 13.5 Differentiating your product offering

Segment	Objective	Still to clarify: uncertainties to remove	Still to do: barriers to raise, risks to reduce	Position vs competition

- Name and brief description of segment
- Size and commercial importance of segment
- Technical risk level ($\nearrow = \searrow$)
- Commercial risk ($\nearrow = \searrow$)

Technical part of offer
- Functional definition (functions, performance)
- Analytical definition (supply contents)
- Process and implementation

Non-technical part of offer
- Price and sales conditions
- Lead-times
- Service

Sales techniques
- Commercial information
- List of customers, competitors, advisors, norms or sales regulations in force
- Target customers to contact and lead-users to co-develop with
- Internal sales or buying centre
- Motivation
- Sales arguments
- Communications
- Organisation
- Choice of point of entry into the sector and partnership (type of entry and commercialisation)

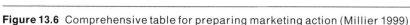

Figure 13.6 Comprehensive table for preparing marketing action (Millier 1999)

	Weight	You (0 to 10)		Competitor 1		Competitor 2	
		Score	Score x Weight	Score	Score x Weight	Score	Score x Weight
CSF 1	50	7	3.5	3	1.5	7	3.5
CSF 2	30	5	1.5	8	2.4	8	2.4
CSF 3	20	9	1.8	6	1.2	8	1.6
Total weighed score			6.8		5.1		7.5

Figure 13.7 Scoring your position on critical success factors

competitive price. Critical success factors by their nature are few as they are the primary criteria that really differentiate your product offering.

About critical success factors

Remember that the mind of the client, as well as your own, can take into account only 7±2 criteria at the same time in order to make a decision.

So: *be sure you have selected the appropriate critical success factors in order to compete.*

Do not attempt to address a multitude of factors. To do this is to oversell to the client and is ultimately counterproductive. The client is overwhelmed with information and most of it is useless. This confuses, obscures and paralyses the client's decision-making process.

To be consistent with one of the working principles we set out in Chapter 7, you must now write a plan for each segment. This is the layout in principle we recommend for such a document.

Let us use SPYMAG to illustrate how to write a segment plan.

Segment 1

Segment name: Taxi flow management in restricted areas

Potential market size: 80 sites in the UK estimate £4 million potential turnover
300 sites in Europe estimate £15 million potential turnover

Technical Risk: Low

Commercial Risk: Low, but beware of cost of access to overseas markets

Target Clients: Heathrow, Gatwick, Roissy, Frankfurt

Potential Partners: ABB, automotive control systems, barrier systems
New venture electronic chip manufacturers

Standard product offering

In segment one SPYMAG's offer encapsulates a control system for counting vehicles in order to regulate traffic, traffic flow and queues. The system is complex as the area to be covered is large and requires more than four monitoring units.

The monitors are fixed and magnetic tracers are mounted on board the vehicles. It is a 'hands free' type system with a reading distance of less than 1.5 metres. The magnetic tracers must be protected against shock and high temperatures, so the tracking device is placed behind the windscreen. The monitoring units are linked with shrouded cable. The technological competition in the segment consists of cameras and traffic lights.

Negotiation of the offer

If required, SPYMAG can provide clients with additional monitoring units, access control and passenger information (in the airport shuttle for instance). These are segments 2 and 9 respectively.

Commercial action

A series of activities will be undertaken with each major European airport:

- The pilot site will be established in France and potential clients invited to visit.
- Due to the importance of the segment the CEO of SPYMAG will visit the clients with a project engineer.
- SPYMAG will carry out a marketing survey in order fully to understand and classify European airports and railway stations in order to arrive at a better understanding of appropriate targets.

- SPYMAG will also work with manufacturers of barrier systems jointly in particular to develop prospects using, initially, direct mail.

By carrying out the exercise illustrated in Figure 13.8 for every segment that you have decided to deal with, by the end of the process you can conduct a 'sanity check' to ensure that your proposed courses of action and resources match.

Often in such circumstances it is the sales resource that can be limiting. It is not easy to

Segment 1	Year 1	Year 2	Year 3
Number of contracts	1	1	1
Number of sales visits	6	6	5
Turnover (£K)	50	60	60
Marketing budget	10	12	12

Figure 13.8 Commercial objectives in segment 1

	Year 1	Year 2	Year 3
Segment 1			
Number of contracts	1	1	1
Number of sales visits	6	6	5
Turnover (£K)	50	60	60
Budget	10	12	12
Segment 2			
Number of contracts	3	3	4
Number of sales visits	18	18	20
Turnover (£K)	150	150	2000
Budget			
Segment 3			
Number of contracts	4	3	4
Number of sales visits	20	15	20
Turnover (£K)	200	150	200
Budget			
Total number of contracts	8	11	11
Available sales visits	38	38	44
Expected turnover (£K)	270	390	390
Total budget			

Figure 13.9 Consolidating the objectives per segment

substitute for skilled salespeople or readily to obtain additional sales resources. Effective use of and targeting a salesperson's time is therefore essential.

Appropriate sales planning based on marketing activity by segments will enable you to match the resources with the available budget. For instance, in Figure 13.9 we can see (year 1) that the sum of the sales visits per segment is 44 for a total available of 38. Therefore, you should lower your sales visits objective in one segment (segment 3 for example) and adjust the turnover in consequence.

The product offering

14

KEY POINTS

- *The product offering encapsulates product technology, aspects of service and the price that we intend to sell at.*

- *There are other more intangible aspects of the product offering, which whilst intangible are intrinsic to marketing. These include elements such as the relationship we enjoy with our customer and our reputation for financial probity and innovation.*

- *The product offering also helps to define the market and vice versa. There is often a looped influence between these factors. The price at which we intend to sell determines demand, and demand in turn influences the price that we are able to achieve.*

- *Segmentation helps us to understand these relationships and decide on our course of action.*

A COMPOSITE PRODUCT OFFERING

So what is the 'product offering'? This is a phrase that you may have heard from time to time; perhaps you have wondered what the difference is between the product and the product offering. The product offering is really 'marketing speak' for the entire bundle of products and associated services the client buys from you to solve their problem. For example, an industrial product offering could include:

- the basic technology, product or core service which constitutes the basis of the business

- the service associated with the product in order to make it attractive to the clients (training, help desk, after-sales services, etc.)

- the price that we charge the clients for the product offer.

Yet, your clients do not buy just this well-defined bundle to resolve their problem. As previously stated (Chapter 5), industrial clients are influenced in their choice of a supplier by much more than that. For example:

- the way that the product is promoted and communicated to clients

- your company's image which includes your reliability (as seen by your reputation and

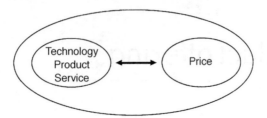

Figure 14.1 The bundle

the financial health of your accounts), your product quality as verified by ISO 9002 for example

- good relationships developed over many years of close and fruitful collaboration
- your capacity to innovate and therefore to help the client in their own development
- the way that the client can obtain the product, the distribution channel or route to market that is used.

The product offering (Figure 14.2) then is more than the product; it is that unique combination of the four Ps (see Chapter 4) that is designed for that customer or segment of customers together with all the intangible and perceptual issues surrounding your company.

Another problem in this area is the way the technology is incorporated or designed into the product. We should focus on producing complete products that meet clients' expectations, rather than elegant, technically complex expressions of the technology.

The complete product or product offering encapsulates the product itself, back-up documents (literature, manuals, etc.), service (e.g. maintenance, hot line support), technical support, the surrounding product range and accessories and the options and variations that are designed to help the product meet a wide range of needs. Think of a product in the way illustrated in Figure 14.3 (McDonald 1995).

The central core product incorporates the principal functionality; the product surround helps to deliver the value of the product. It is often said that the core product accounts for 80 per cent of the cost but only 20 per cent of the impact, whilst the product surround

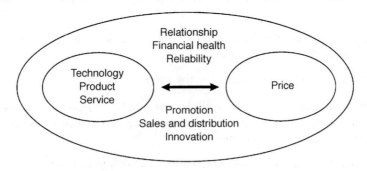

Figure 14.2 The product offering

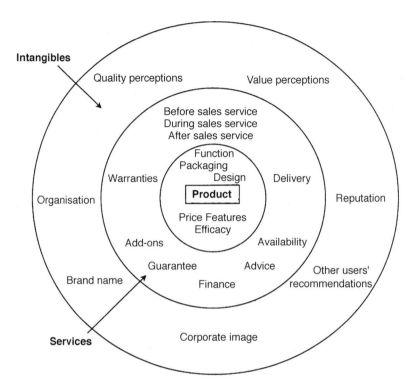

Figure 14.3 More than just a product

really helps to deliver benefits and generates 80 per cent of value but is only 20 per cent of the cost. Some others go still further saying that an industrial client does not buy a product as such but the entire company (Valla 1985), or more correctly what the entire company can do for them as Figure 14.4 illustrates.

To summarise, in industrial markets the product is actually the solution to the client's problem. Of course we sell products, but we also transfer solutions from our own

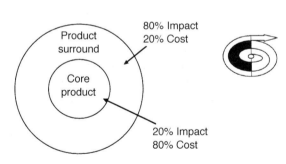

Figure 14.4 The client buys your company

organisation to the client by helping him through every stage of the process from installation to training to start up and through to after-sales service. Even after this stage we can continue to support our client by continually seeking ideas for change and development which will help our client to stay ahead of the competition. In this way we sell not just core, technology-based products but use the product as a vehicle for wider service delivery and the development of an ongoing relationship.

Designing the product offering is a difficult and challenging task. There are so many different elements that could be included in the product offer; some of them overlap or contradict each other or they could be interdependent in a looped process. So we never really know where to start and because of the interdependencies we can never fully understand the consequences of a decision taken about any one element of the product offering. In other words it is rather too simplistic to regard the elements of the bundle as separate, independent elements. Rather, we must also think about the way they work together and their relationship with competitors and the wider business environment.

Designing the product offering is not a linear activity. To give you a more comprehensive insight into the process we shall start from the situation where we have no history or background. In other words, we have to create a product offering from scratch. Obviously a difficult situation but once you have understood how this can be managed this will equip you to tackle other offering design issues. In any other case you will always have a starting point, for example, a current range of products, a highly competitive market where price is extremely sensitive or an established distribution channel in which to have invested a lot of time and money.

Which comes first – the product or the market? Simplistically we would say that we go out and investigate market needs and then set out to satisfy them. So, of course, the market comes first. In reality the answer is probably somewhere in between (Figure 14.5). This means that the market will influence your offer as much as your offer influences the market. If this is not clear then think about these examples:

- Can we think of who it was who first said that they wanted a CD player? Obviously no, the client had no conception of this particular technological application until it was brought to the market in the form of a product.

- Which client asked for a LAN (local area network) before it existed in the market? Again very difficult to say as the product helped to develop the market.

We could offer hundreds of examples like this where the offer has both influenced the market and vice versa. If we want to understand the process let us consider Figure 14.6 (Millier 1999).

Figure 14.5 What first, offer or market?

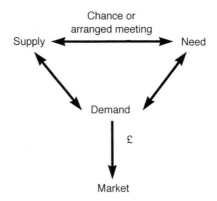

Figure 14.6 Schematic arrangement of market-producing concepts

From Figure 14.6 we can see that there has to be a demand before there is a market. This demand must be identified. However, there is an essential phase before the actual demand. This phase occurs by chance or concerted effort, where the market offer and market needs meet in terms of demand. The laser CD player, originally invented as a computer storage medium, coincided with the client's needs for better sound quality, a recording medium with no wearing parts and which offered easier and quicker access to the music tracks. It is unlikely that any one client could have envisaged this type of product before it actually existed. So the role of marketing in this situation will consist of revealing and creating the market by making the offer and the need coincide.

 A distinction must be made at this stage between needs and wants. Needs are real but wants are aspirational or even dreams. Ask me if I would like a Jaguar and of course the answer is yes. Do I need a Jaguar? Maybe not. I may only need a small, reliable, economical car to get me backwards and forwards to the office.

Market research helps us to explore these issues and differentiate between needs and wants. Needs help us to design the product, and often by understanding wants we can use this to design the advertising and communications programme.

Let us bear in mind that, due to their technical knowledge, industrial clients have a certain capability to express their needs in advance of the solution being offered. If we want to go one step further our clients may even suggest modifications and developments to our original product that we might not think of ourselves. As in the example of Figure 14.7 there are several iterations before the product and demand are matched.

 In the case illustrated in Figure 14.7 we would not say that the original product was wrong just because there was no demand for it so far. It is only when the product does not fit the existing demand that it can be called 'wrong'. In this example the product was not wrong compared to the demand, it was just in advance of it.

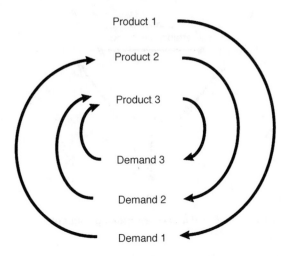

Figure 14.7 The table tennis effect

GROUND ZERO APPROACH

How do efficient marketers tackle the problem of designing a new product from a blank sheet of paper? An appropriate approach to use if you want to introduce a new range, develop a new product or reorganise or rationalise an activity is to sit down around the table with your internal stakeholders – sales, R&D, manufacturing, the boss – and start with three questions:

1. What are we able to do? What are we able to design, to manufacture, to deliver …?

2. What do we want to do? In which markets do we want to stay and towards what markets do we want to go?

3. What do the clients want? What do we know about the clients and the market expectations?

Then continue wrestling with these questions until they are argued through and some answers begin to emerge.

 It is highly likely that you will not get agreement at the first attempt. It takes time, perhaps a lot of time, far more time than you would expect. This is a case where the π (Pi) factor applies: three times longer, three times costlier, etc.

During the course of the interviews that we conducted, one of our interviewees called the starting process 'reset ground zero'. In all the cases that we have studied the process took between one and two years before people agreed on an answer and one more year to rationalise this first basis of understanding into a new activity development. It is crucial to involve a range of people in this activity. Not only are several people able to contribute more good ideas and input than just one; it is the best way to develop a shared vision of what is emerging. It is your assurance that the outcome will be agreement and 'buy-in' rather than lack of it, entailing a further round of discussion to sell the idea internally.

WHAT PRICE FOR WHICH PRODUCT?

A loop exists between the product and the price; this makes it difficult to design the product offering (Figure 14.8). A conversation could go something like this:

Marketer: What will it cost to make these parts?
Manufacturer: It depends on what the volume will be.
Marketer: But the volume we can move depends on the price at which we sell it! (Figure 14.9.)

The loop of Figure 14.9 is following the route that the lower the price the larger the demand, the larger the demand the bigger the volume of products that can be sold. The bigger the volume, the lower the cost per unit. Hence, if we can manufacture at low cost then we can afford to sell at a lower price. So it is impossible to decide either the price or the market size since they are influencing each other.

A good example exists in assessing the world's oil reserves. How big are the oil reserves? A rather difficult question if we do not also state the price that we are prepared to pay for the oil. At $15 per barrel the reserves are 135 billion tonnes, but at up to $50 per barrel they are 215 billion tonnes. If we are really prepared to incur more cost and dig more deeply and invest more to obtain more oil then at $100 per barrel the reserves are 400 billion tonnes.

Henry Ford had a good understanding of how many of his cars he could sell if only he could make them cheaply enough. The challenge for him was how to do so. In fact he developed the production line as a means of lowering costs in order to supply products at the price the client was prepared to pay. His decisions involved judgement and a degree of risk taking. Profit is the reward for risk, and Henry Ford had a shrewd understanding of the issues involved that encouraged him to invest and persist in introducing the Model T.

There are no simple and straightforward solutions to this problem. You need information about your cost levels and a projection of the relationships between volume and cost. From the marketing perspective you require a well-developed understanding of

Figure 14.8 What first, product or price?

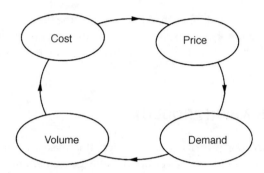

Figure 14.9 A loop between price and demand

the market expressed in terms of segmentation. That gives you a good understanding of what price is appropriate for clients in each segment. You can then draw the chart shown in Figure 14.10.

Consider that the segmentation reveals three markets of interest:

Segment 1 — 1,000 units/year at £20 per unit
Segment 2 — 10,000 units/year at £5 per unit
Segment 3 — 1,000,000 units/year £1 per unit

From Figure 14.10 you can see the production costs are respectively:

- £10/unit for 1000 units/year

- £7/unit for 10,000 units/year

- £80 p./unit for 1,000,000 units/year

Let us assume that our analysis demonstrates that you could make a sensible profit either in the first market of 1,000 units/year or the third market of 1,000,000 units/year. The

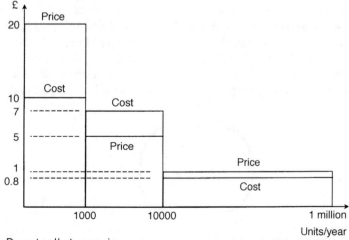

Figure 14.10 Do not sell at any price

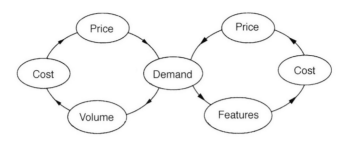

Figure 14.11 Opposite strengths affecting the price

analysis also shows that you should forget the second market initially, as this will demonstrate a loss if you focus primarily on this. To complete the looped analysis (Figure 14.11) we should also take into account the product features.

Clients may demand products with specific functions and performance – in other words features – but higher levels of functionality usually increase cost and hence price. This may well influence a client to review their requirements and reconsider the volume that they require. If we take the example of the Jaguar that we discussed earlier, having looked at all the desired features and taken a view of this against price, we may decide that the Ford Escort is perfectly adequate for our needs. As we can see this is an iterative process involving some spade work to develop a sound view of the market, understanding and insight into the real needs of our market and the ability to make judgements and take risks. Unfortunately, no amount of two-by-two matrices will help you to make that final judgement or take the decision for you.

In other words, demand for a given product will exist only at a certain price. We have now dealt with the difficult relationship between the components of your product offering, let us in the next chapter have a look at technology/product/service on the one hand and price on the other.

The product

15

KEY POINTS

- *The product is a solution to the client's problem.*
- *From a marketing viewpoint, products are 'made for' not 'made of'. It is necessary to adopt a customer-driven perspective.*
- *Good products are those that meet client needs, not those that incorporate superior technology. They meet client needs, not exceed them.*
- *Products can often be understood by use of the life-cycle analogy.*
- *A single product is often part of a wider product range.*
- *The marketer must manage the range as well as individual products.*

INTRODUCTION

You hardly need to buy a book on industrial marketing to appreciate that the product is one of the most important issues. We would say that failure to define the product properly is almost certainly not going to be compensated for by a cheap price or a high level of service. If the product is simply not suitable for the purpose then it is unlikely to be used by the client – even if you give it to them.

A comprehensive view of the product can be formed by thinking of it in these main ways:

- the product itself and its design and definition
- product life cycle
- the product range.

MARKETING VIEWPOINT OF A PRODUCT

From a marketing viewpoint the product is no more than the solution to the client's problems. In some respects, clients sometimes do not really bother about how the product is made and what it encapsulates, technology and components, as long as it provides them with a solution.

You should remember that the clients' concerns are about:

What your product is made for
not
What your product is made of

This idea was succinctly summarised by marketing guru Theodore Levitt, who said that what customers want when they buy ¼-inch drills is ¼-inch holes.

From a marketing viewpoint the best way to design the product is to start with the client's problem, which means that you have to know what it is, and follow the process illustrated in Figure 15.1.

As you can see the first part of this process is much more marketing orientated than the others and requires considerable focus. In effect, if you let technicians start with an inappropriate or too sophisticated product you will have some difficulty in rewinding the tape.

From this point of view an industrial product is both enhanced and endangered by technology. In industry, where the technologists are often the Kings, technology assumes almost mythical status, so highly is it revered, that we then forget other important aspects of the product. Also, a superior technology can sometimes be the critical weapon in the battle to beat the competition. However, technology alone is rarely enough of an argument to sell a product.

- Why should a builder buy your encrypted walkie-talkie to provide his workers on a construction site with the ability to communicate? A cheaper, analogue system is adequate for his needs.

- Why should a chemical company buy an expensive, state-of-the-art silicon-based pressure gauge when a cheaper, run of the mill mechanical pressure gauge is perfectly good enough?

To expect that the superior technology gives marketing advantage is insufficient. You must be able to demonstrate to your clients that this added element of technology gives additional benefits. In other words, it has to be useful and it cannot be useful if it does not at least meet the client's requirements (Figure 15.2).

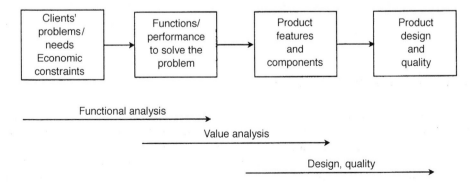

Figure 15.1 A process approach to understanding products

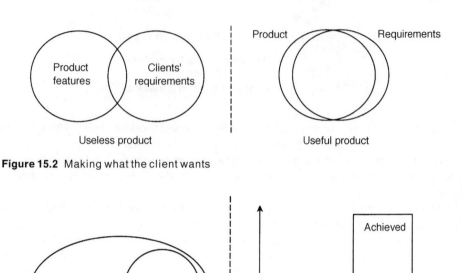

Figure 15.2 Making what the client wants

Figure 15.3 Exceeding client expectations

What lessons does the example of Figure 15.3 teach us? Not only does your product match the client's requirement but it also significantly exceeds them; in marketing terms this is incorrect. Why? Because the client feels as if he has paid for a lot of features that will never be used! Furthermore, there is also a risk that because additional features are not understood and not used this somewhat negative view will then reflect on the entire product. I have only to look at my video recorder and see a wide range of functions that are of no use to me. Perhaps when – or more likely if – I come to buy another then perhaps I shall look for one with just 'stop and go' buttons on it.

 Marketing is therefore in the realm of *just enough*. We should give the clients just what they want. No more, no less. Of course, this increases the need to know what the client wants and meet those expectations but *without over-selling* the product.

WHEN TOO MUCH IS ENOUGH

Nevertheless, there are two cases in which you cannot avoid giving the clients more than they want. The first is found for example with material. Some materials have sometimes twice or three times more functionality or performance than required by the clients. For instance, your material is tough, rustproof and a good heat conductor. What then about the clients who do not need rustproofing and heat conduction. Well, do not mention these properties and sell them only a tough material! The second case is found when you

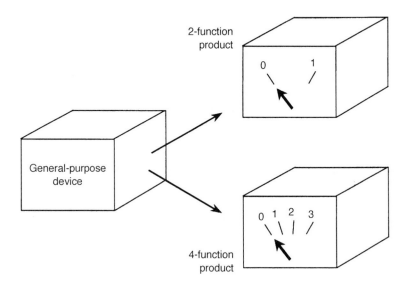

Figure 15.4 Late differentiation

have to manufacture in volume in order to produce at lower cost. You have to make the same product but not all clients want the same features. A solution in this case is 'late differentiation' (Figure 15.4). Make the same products and differentiate them afterwards on the main production line. Take for instance a device for determining the composition of different types of aluminium. Some clients needed to differentiate one type of aluminium from another. Other clients needed to sort ten types of aluminium.

The device inside the box is the same but the final product is different and the cost of doing this is as low as possible. There are usually two ways of proceeding. You can either upgrade a basic product by adding some other functions or downsize a complete product by masking or removing the useless functions (Figure 15.5).

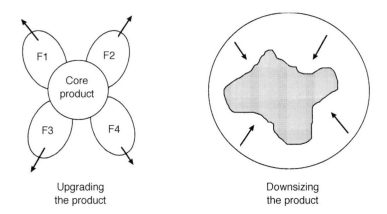

Figure 15.5 Upgrading or downsizing the product

LATE DIFFERENTIATION AND RIGHTSIZING

An example is that of a pharmaceutical manufacturer of over-the-counter products. These can be sold without a doctor's prescription. A new product was being introduced throughout Europe and being launched at various times as the registration procedures in each country were completed. By adopting a standard bottle size the manufacturer was able to produce economically in volume, and stockpile in anticipation of the launches. So called 'naked packs' were produced and then labelled in the appropriate language as required. The use of naked packs and late differentiation enabled costs to be lowered due to economies in production and reduction of local stock, whilst having the product available to meet peaks of demand in launch periods. A more comprehensive way of defining the product will be given in Chapter 25 (Technical analysis in marketing); nevertheless a small example will give you an overview of how to tackle the issue.

VALUE ANALYSIS

You are, for instance, an electric motor manufacturer. Some of these motors are used for powering machine-tools. The client's requirement is to drive a turning tool between 1,000 and 100,000 rpm with an ultra-compact spindle integrated to the machine tool's head with absolute safety (Figure 15.6). Taking into account these problems, the features required of the motor are to

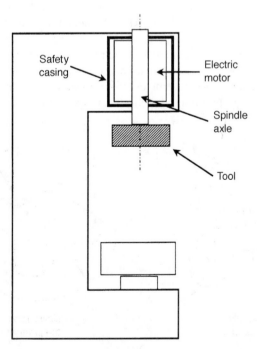

Figure 15.6 A motor application in a milling machine

- be able to rotate between 1,000 and 100,000 rpm
- be compact enough to fit inside the casing
- be powerful enough (50 kilowatt)
- avoid overheating in enclosed conditions
- be compatible with the machine tool's spindle.

To achieve these features, your electric motor system should include a number of components. To help you find which components are required you can draw a matrix as shown in Figure 15.7.

To avoid the pitfall of basing the product on technological features you should not start from statements such as 'our motor will have a flat, cold, high-voltage rotor' even if they are your product's distinctive features. They must be a marketing consequence not a starting point. This means that you should use them only if they are the best solution to satisfy your client's needs not your technicians' ego.

Components / Functions	Flat rotor	Cold rotor	Electronic power-supply system	Gas bearing	High-voltage rotor	Safety casing
Turning between 1000 and 100 000 rpm	★		★	★		
Size constraint	★					
Absence of overheating		★		★		
High power					★	
Working safely						★

Figure 15.7 Value analysis matrix

PRODUCT AND QUALITY

Is quality expensive? Delivering more quality than the customer is prepared to pay for is certainly expensive. Nevertheless, as a rule of thumb, quality certainly pays. Higher perceived quality is strongly related to profitability, market share and return on investment. Of course we should not necessarily conclude that this is a cause-and-effect relationship but if you are paying attention to quality then it is quite likely that you are also managing other aspects of your business to a high standard.

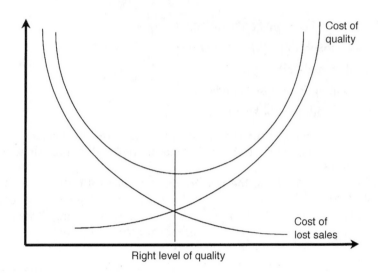

Right level of quality

Figure 15.8 The quality cost trade-off

Beware of excessive quality

Both quality and performance can suffer from overdelivery. 'Over' means that we exceed the client's requirements. It is sometimes depressing to see the number of corporate mission statements that say that their objective is to 'exceed the client's requirements'. In other words, what they are saying is they intend to overdeliver against the client's expectations but not be able to recover the cost involved.

We can summarise the quality issue in Figure 15.8. To confirm that poor quality has a negative impact let us take the example of a solar panel (Lilien 1981).

Impact of product quality on sales Case solar heating	
Type of success/failure	Impact on market
Damage to house	−50
Short MTBF (mean time between failure)	−10
Poor performance	−5
Runs perfectly	1

This real case demonstrates how poor quality detracts from the objectives of the organisation. What this demonstrates is that in terms of market impact one improperly installed solar panel requires 50 perfectly installed panels to counterbalance the loss of reputation. The chart clearly shows the strongly negative impact of poor product quality. You may think that these figures are unbelievable – but we suspect that you would be wrong particularly if you applied this technique to your own business. The real question is how will we measure relative perceived quality. The PIMS study suggests an appropriate tool. This is discussed further in the next chapter.

PRODUCT LIFE CYCLE

Despite an excellent definition and design, your product will not last forever. Due to technological evolution and other factors, change is always an issue. For instance, if your telecommunications clients switch from analogue to digital systems it makes your analogue components obsolete. You should also switch to digital components if you want to stay in, or even ahead of the race. In the same way, competitors' technology evolution can make your products out of date and the clients may be tempted to buy competitor products.

When a product is new, clients need to assess carefully the way the product works and become more familiar with its usage. They will require training and technical support. Once down the learning curve familiarity with your own and competitor products increases. Inevitably this greater client knowledge will lead to a focus on price. Therefore, your margin will be doubly affected. First, because the selling price drops. Second, as the competition is stronger you sell less and less and this has a knock-on effect to buying and manufacturing economies (Figure 15.9).

Eventually your margin reaches zero, or sometimes less, and you have to give up. Giving up means either withdrawing the product from the market or rejuvenating it by an improvement such as better performance, design or manufacturing innovation to reduce costs. This process is called commoditisation and is a real challenge for marketers who must constantly fight against it to restore their margins and maintain their market share.

You can identify commoditisation from the following clues.

- Fewer and fewer criteria are taken into account for the buying decision.

- More and more importance is given to the price. Bargaining becomes tougher.

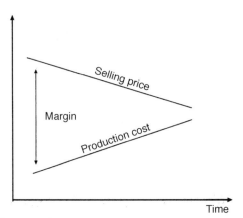

Figure 15.9 The plummeting margin

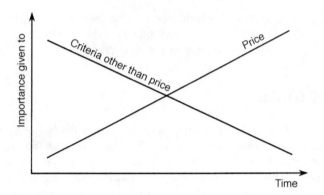

Figure 15.10 Commoditisation (Salle 1985)

- Stronger competition.
- Less differentiation between competitive products.
- Relationship confined to salesman and buyer.
- The client seeks a simpler and more routinised buying process.

We can summarise the commoditisation process in Figure 15.10. These principles are summarised in an important marketing concept, the product life cycle (PLC) illustrated in Figure 15.11.

There are four stages in the PLC:

1. Introduction stage – The product has just been introduced into a small market.

2. Growth stage – The market becomes larger yet under supplied; competitors are encouraged to enter.

3. Maturity stage – The numbers of competitors reaches a maximum. The market becomes oversupplied. Price increases in importance.

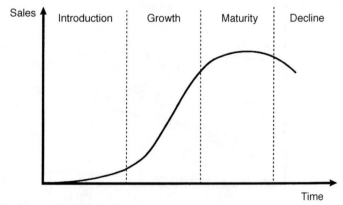

Figure 15.11 The product life cycle

4. Decline stage – There are few survivors in a market that continues to shrink; rationalisation takes place.

Typical strategies to adopt at each stage are the following:

- Introduction stage – Emphasise product's unique benefits, sell directly at a high price to pioneer clients, market education is important.

- Growth stage – Emphasise differentiation. A strong marketing emphasis is necessary with strong sales presence, distribution and communication. Maintain price as high as possible but balance this against market share.

- Maturity stage – Emphasise brand values and the quality of the relationship. Continue to market and differentiate the product but be cautious of long-term investment as the future becomes increasingly uncertain.

- Decline stage – Emphasis on costs as volume and margin declines. Rationalisation takes place.

Despite the considerable prominence given to the PLC, we regard it as a tool more clearly relevant to FMCG type products. The large volumes and frequency of purchase of such products allows the PLC to be more closely understood and even statistically modelled. A big disadvantage of the PLC is that it could become a self-fulfilling prophecy (Figure 15.12). What do we mean by this? There may be initial indications that sales are slowing. Costs get levered down, investment in innovation is cut and there is more focus on price. Lower prices force out competitors and the maturity stage has been entered. Nevertheless, by checking your sales level and price/margin achievement, the PLC can provide you with a good planning tool in the sense that you should not adopt the same strategy at every stage.

Lastly, the analysis of both the commoditisation process and life cycle should allow you to identify products on which you lose so much money that it should be more

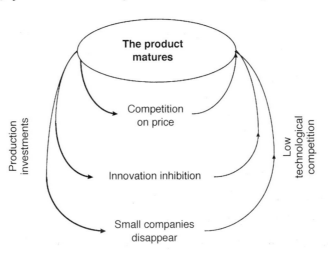

Figure 15.12 A self-fulfilling prophecy

profitable to withdraw them from the range. Adding and deleting products from the product range is part of what we call 'range management'.

PRODUCT RANGE MANAGEMENT

Managing just one product is one matter; managing a whole range of products is entirely another. In principle managing a product range means:

- Having a basic range of products to meet the requirements of clients in each market segment. In other words, there are clearly defined products appropriate to each segment. This is the principal criterion on which the product is justified.

- Supporting one product range with others. For instance, if you sell spanners, the clients might ask you to supply them with pliers and screwdrivers as well because they do not want to see ten salespersons for ten different types of tools. Furthermore, you will share your selling cost on a great number of items. The danger is to develop too many products than are sensibly required and to be tempted to diversify into related but unsuitable areas.

- Around the core range of products there can be a range of proliferating products and options which enable the product offering to be customised as far as possible to customer requirements at the lowest possible cost. For example, as a software house obviously you will not produce a separate software package for each client, but the core module may well be modified with additional modules and add-ons to meet specific needs.

- Launching new products to anticipate or create demand and maintain and improve competitive advantage.

- Deleting products that no longer justify their position in the product range.

To manage the product range or portfolio, we suggest the use of 'portfolio tools'. There are a range of portfolio tools that can be used to assess and manage the product range. These are discussed in more detail in Part VII, Chapter 27.

For typical marketing purposes we suggest the use of a simple matrix in which you find on the Y axis the products' potential and on the X axis the product's contribution to the current activity. Typically, on such matrices the size of the circle represents sales volume, value or contribution (Figure 15.13). You could foresee high product potential by using, for instance, the following criteria:

- potential for performance improvement
- potential for new applications or new markets (overseas for instance)
- potential to supersede an obsolete technology
- strong position in a fast growing market.

Conversely, the following criteria are likely to indicate low potential:

- obsolescent product or technology

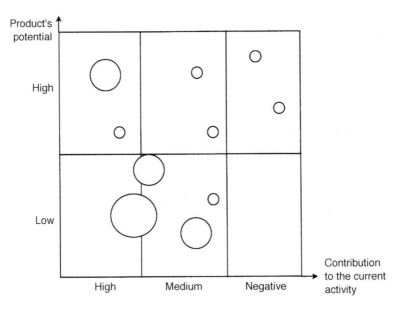

Figure 15.13 A product portfolio

- outdated product
- declining market
- occurrence of strong competition
- end of a patent.

In the other dimension of the portfolio each product in the range should be justified against a set of criteria such as:

- margin
- volume and growth
- consistency with the firm's overall strategy
- ability to utilise fixed assets such as production capability.

To understand fully how your products perform relative to others in the range their turnover can be represented graphically on the matrix (Figure 15.14). To expand on this further we can show for example the overall market volume and the volume of our product relative to the market in the form of a pie chart (Figure 15.14) which gives a good representation of market share.

An ideal portfolio would show several products in each box of the matrix. By balancing our portfolio like this we can manage the mix of products which are strong cash contributors, new products that need to be developed and products which need to be selectively deleted as they reach the end of their useful contribution (Figure 15.15).

By matching the position of products on the matrix this strongly visual tool demonstrates gaps in our portfolio which we should consider filling. This means that we

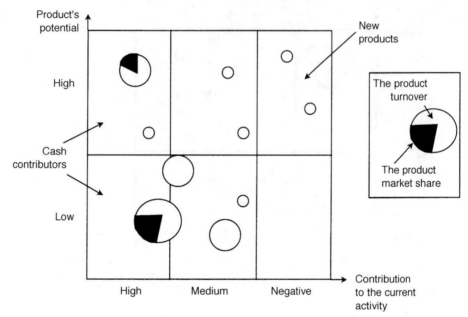

Figure 15.14 Enriching product portfolio analysis

can start to plan forward by identifying potential gaps and managing our product introductions and deletions accordingly. There are some common problems that managers have when trying to do this.

- Products do not really meet the requirements of specific clients as you try to sell the same products in every segment, therefore not meeting anybody's requirements particularly well.

- There are gaps in the product range, which means that there are missed opportunities.

- You may have a 'big burner' product, but lack additional products to support your major product.

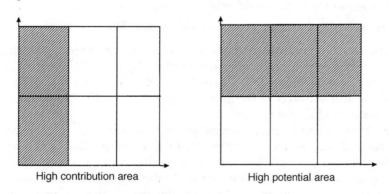

Figure 15.15 The product role in the portfolio

- The focus is on 'creative new product development' and a consequent focus on product introduction rather than product range management. It can be very difficult to support a larger number of products effectively within a range.

- The tendency can be to customise products to meet specific clients and requirements and make bespoke products. A smarter approach is to define the options within the range and look for a modular approach which will enable you to meet this and other clients' requirements. Otherwise the development cost of specific products needs to be borne by specific clients. When considered on this basis customisation may be only marginally profitable.

- Overhanging old products that soak up management resources and build inventory without significantly contributing to volume and margin.

- Alternatively failing to invest and develop new products, alternatively killing them off too quickly before they have realised their potential. When unprofitable products are eliminated they sometimes save only small amounts of direct costs, so the remaining products have to absorb high costs and become less profitable.

- One of the challenges for the marketer is to consider not just the volume and margin of products when making decisions about the range, but also to consider the underlying costs associated with maintaining products, for example, the costs of inventory maintenance, the complications of managing literature, promotion and salesforce briefing. Consider also that additional products could really be substitutes for the sale of other products in our range. How much volume would be lost by rationalising the product range? This should be considered against the opportunity for compensatory sales of other products and ease of overall management.

Valuing the product

16

KEY POINTS

- *Pricing a product is not enough. A marketer should value the product and position this in the mind of the client. In an ideal world cost should be ignored as this has no relationship to value.*

- *Understanding the reasons why clients buy and their cost base are important inputs to the pricing decision.*

- *Lowering price is the last option. The volume/margin relationship should be fully investigated before lowering prices.*

WHY VALUE RATHER THAN PRICE?

Perhaps one of the most difficult subjects in marketing is that of how to determine the price of the product. In reality nobody is very clear on how this should be done, yet price is critical since it determines your positioning, market share and profitability. In other words, price is both a strategic and dangerous tool.

From a marketing point of view the price is just the tip of the iceberg (Figure 16.1). The real marketing groundwork consists of valuing the product rather than pricing it, pricing is more a short-term and sometimes opportunistic sales matter.

We can more effectively value the product if we understand:

- The benefits that the client obtains from the use of the product, and how great the benefit actually is. In other words, why our clients buy our product rather than a close substitute.

- How our client's costs are made up.

- The elements that influence the setting of the price.

What we are really suggesting here is that the price is the means whereby we realise the value, value for the clients but also value for us (Figure 16.2).

Unfortunately many industrial companies make the mistake of setting the price on the basis of their costs. From a truly market-driven perspective there is no relationship between cost and price. The basis for price should be on the value that customers obtain in terms of benefit for a product; the difference between the price and the cost is of course

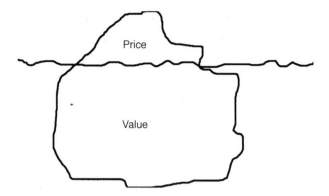

Figure 16.1 The price as the tip of the iceberg

our margin. However, all is not rational and open to calculation in marketing, especially when thinking about price. As a matter of fact, though less psychologically based than in FMCG, price in industrial markets is an indicator of quality and positioning. For instance, why are some industrial robots, trucks and more utilitarian and mundane products more expensive than others?

From the optimal way of setting price shown in Figure 16.3, we start with the selling price and deduct cost to find the margin. Ideally a good marketer should ignore cost before setting the price. This would suggest that cost does not influence the way the price is fixed. Of course, we have to consider not just the price but the linkage between price/cost/value. The first reason is obviously that you cannot price the product lower than cost, although this might be the case in exceptional circumstances. The second is that in marketing, price is often just the basis for starting the negotiation. Despite all our

Figure 16.2 Play winner-winner

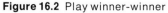

Sub-optimal way of setting price
Price = Cost + Margin

Optimal way of setting price
Price − Cost = Margin

Figure 16.3 Two ways of setting the price

market-place work in understanding segmentation, how the product is used and the way that clients' costs are made up, the reality is that price is always likely to fluctuate around the price points that you would like to achieve. Several factors can play a role in this (Webster 1974, pp. 198–9), for example:

- The salesperson may choose to accept a lower price when negotiating the deal if there is evidence that a key competitor could win the deal instead.

- Where 'switching costs' are relatively low then this is an incentive for the client to negotiate on price.

- If working through the distribution chain, the distributor may decide to cut prices in order to stimulate demand and reach sales objectives, to 'bundle' your product with another product on which they can achieve a much higher, compensatory margin or to clear stocks to avoid finance charges.

- Local price wars may break out for a wide range of reasons. A competitor may choose to dump a product in your area of market strength, but away from their own. Often price can be a way of breaking into a new market, perhaps by geographical expansion where a low price is traded off against the opportunity to get into the market and perhaps lever prices up once established.

VALUE ORIENTATED WAY OF SETTING THE PRICE

Let us now look at some examples of how to value the product correctly. In this first case, large industrial clients buy commodity-like chemical products from you, priced according to your price list. As these are commodity-like products then competition tends to be both high and focused on price. The natural tendency is to use cost-based pricing, particularly as the cost of raw materials is widely known within the industry.

Would you charge the same price to a client who buys the same product but also asks us to hold a safety stock of products immediately available for delivery to them should they need it? In this case you are selling not just the chemical commodity but also the ready availability of the product. How much is the client prepared to pay for this additional availability? It will depend for instance on how much it would cost them to stock the product and what it will cost them in lost production if the chemical is not available (Figure 16.4).

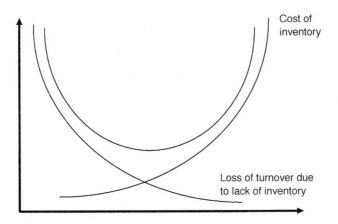

Cost of inventory

Loss of turnover due to lack of inventory

Figure 16.4 The availability/cost of inventory trade-off

A manufacturer of diesel engines supplies stand-by equipment for emergency power generation. Many organisations – hospitals, supermarkets, hotels – have such equipment in the unlikely event that the electricity supply should fail. For virtually all their life these diesel engines stand idle, just in case. As the manufacturer would you be inclined to offer the same bundle of products and services at the same price for, say, a North Sea oil rig application. Here an investment of several billion pounds works continuously to drill for and pump oil. The supply of electrical power is critical to the safe and continuing operation of this enormous investment. Is the purchaser likely to worry about a few thousand pounds on initial capital cost and maintenance support, providing that operational standards are maintained? The following example shows how difficult it is to fix the price of an industrial product.

'Control Online' has developed software for productivity management in high-output packaging machines. Originally Control Online determined prices on the basis of the complexity of the machine. The more complex the machine, the longer the analysis took in terms of analytical time, therefore the more it cost. Eventually Control Online found that, particularly with the simple machines, they were charging too low a price to achieve a profit and were competing with less sophisticated and cheaper software. With larger and more complex machines the higher prices discouraged clients, who were constantly focused on price. Control Online had a problem, neither the large or small users particularly valued the service.

In order to overcome this problem Control Online worked closely with the manufacturer of the packaging machines. In conjunction with an interested customer this revealed that the benefits for the customer were largely dependent on the machine's initial productivity, utilisation and reserve capacity. The machine's complexity was in fact influencing the cost but not the price they could charge and Control Online had mistaken one for the other. We could summarise the situation with the segmentation matrix shown in Figure 16.5, very typical of industrial marketing situations, in which the column represents the applications (the technical problem to be solved) and the rows the behaviour of the customer (based on perceived risk and motivation).

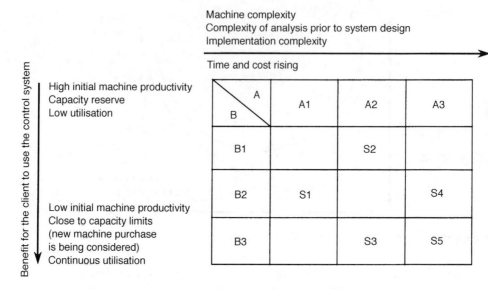

Figure 16.5 Distinction between cost and price (A = application; B = benefit; S = segment)

From a marketing perspective, it is clear from this matrix that Control Online's original marketing error was to mistake the application for the segment. In other words, they had taken into account the technical dimension of the problem (the columns) and ignored the marketing one (the rows).

What do these examples tell us? The first and main lesson is that:

 A good market segmentation that clearly helps us to understand why our clients buy is the key to understanding and helps us correctly to address the value/price problem.

This would suggest that to value the product this should be done segment by segment and sometimes on a client-by-client basis. Two different clients can value our product completely differently. Take on the one hand the client who uses your non-destructive controller on a production line with the aim of improving productivity. On the other hand another client checks aircraft wings for passenger security purposes. How can you compare the way that these two clients value the product?

In the first example what may be important to the client is the lowest cost per unit for each of the tests conducted on line. In the second example the test equipment is fundamental to the safety of the aircraft, for which the company could be liable in the event of a failure going undetected by the equipment and causing an accident. A much higher price is appropriate here.

As we can see, valuing a product is not easy. It is yet more challenging if clients cannot understand or recognise the value. An intrinsic part of the sales process is the presentation of the price and helping the client to recognise the value that the product offers. Take for example two helicopters that may be particularly appropriate to a client's needs. One is much cheaper than the other but requires nearly twice as much maintenance. A potential purchaser needs to understand that over the lifetime of a helicopter the maintenance cost can be four times as much as the initial purchase price. Simply comparing these two competing products on the basis of price would be very short sighted. Selling to the clients in this case will involve explaining the value offered by your product but which may be unfamiliar or not obvious to them.

UNDERSTANDING THE CLIENT'S COST

In order to set the price we should also take into account the downstream price, in other words that of our customer's customer, in order to understand the influence of your product price on the client's ability to market his (and your) product to his customers. A first and simple way of doing this is to draw the following chart. This helps us to understand how significant the price of our product is when compared to the price of our customer's product. The higher the price of our product relative to that of our client's, then the more price sensitive they will be. This is best done at two or three levels in the industrial chain downstream of your client as Figure 16.6 illustrates.

You could probably achieve a better margin if you manufacture air-conditioning systems for motor cars rather than gearboxes. An air-conditioning system is a desirable and valuable extra as perceived by the ultimate purchaser, who will therefore pay proportionately more for this feature. That same purchaser is unlikely to be even mildly enthusiastic about your gearbox, an item taken for granted as part of the overall package. In this case, the value is at the consumer level, yet you must be aware of this in order to negotiate with the car manufacturer. This is quite a simple example; more complex situations will require a more detailed type of analysis. What follows is a more challenging example.

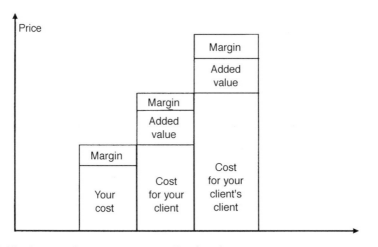

Figure 16.6 The impact of your price on the client's price

'Electric Solutions' had invented smart electrical components that enabled machine manufacturers to save 10 per cent of their wiring costs. Electric Solutions decided to sell the components at a price some 15 per cent above the cost of standard products, trying to take into account the added value for customers. Unfortunately, they overlooked the fact that the cost of wiring when compared to the overall cost of the machine was less than 10 per cent. Hard-nosed buyers were not motivated to make a saving of something like 10 per cent of 10 per cent particularly as this involved the additional risk of using untried technology whilst the components they currently used were perfectly satisfactory. In other words the client was simply not motivated to purchase the product. So how can this problem be resolved?

In order to understand more about how clients used and valued their products, Electric Solutions set up a client laboratory. Working with customer co-operators they broke down their costs in order to understand the cost structure. In this way they found that the smart components could enable the machine manufacturers to save 30 per cent on the cost of the basic design and 60 per cent on non-quality costs due to wiring imperfections. Now Electric Solutions have developed worthwhile interest in the market for their components despite a price that is now 30 per cent above the cost of the components they replace. However, it took more than a year of effort working with three customers to achieve this result.

It is not in every case that a cost-based price decision is relevant. Clients may have a range of other and stronger motivations to buy your product. Working with a company manufacturing equipment for noise analysis for use in milling and turning machine shops, we surprised our clients by telling them that one of the factors important in the purchase of the product was the Production Director's age! Why should this be so? Our findings were that a young or recently appointed Production Director was looking for every opportunity to demonstrate his prowess. Our client's system, although costly, performed extremely well whilst at the same time enhancing the prowess of the young and ambitious Production Director. Perhaps there was an opportunity to make the product even more expensive and the sale even easier? What this demonstrates is that the rational analysis of costs and prices does not necessarily answer all the questions that we ask about pricing.

When thinking about value you should also bear in mind that there can be potential negative value for the client. Whatever the price of your product you must estimate how much it will cost the clients to use your product instead of one that is currently in use. Take for instance a centralised grease-distribution system that is used in workshops in order to provide grease at any appropriate point (Banting 1978). There will be worthwhile economies in grease alone, as every time the grease reservoir is changed in any one of the perhaps hundreds of manual grease pumps, 30 per cent gets wasted. Despite this the client may still not buy as the advantage of the centralised system is outweighed by the more pressing issue in the client's mind – what to do with a hundred or more surplus, expensive grease pumps?

GUIDELINES FOR PRICE SETTING: FACTORS THAT INFLUENCE PRICE

There are many factors that complicate the decision concerning the setting of the price. Even if all the factors are understood, no two situations are alike and a greater weight could be given to each of these factors depending on circumstances. It is therefore impossible to set out a list of rules for defining the price. However, we can list the main factors that influence price, some or all of which may be important price drivers depending on the context.

As previously stated there are some client-related factors that should be taken into account:

- benefits delivered and value gained

- the significance of your products in terms of the client's overall product cost

- switching costs (disposing of old products, staff training, changes in procedure, installation costs, etc.).

These are 'hard' factors surrounding the pricing decisions; there are also those that are more difficult to quantify:

- Competition – many industries are very sensitive to price, and the price expectations set by competitors cannot be ignored. Your price should also consider the price premium or discount that should apply with respect to the industry leader's product.

- Industry profitability – if the industry is suffering pressure on sales or margins, then clients are much more likely to be price focused. This also offers an opportunity to demonstrate ways in which your company or your product can contribute to your client's profitability or the extent to which it offers advantages over competitors. This becomes much more complex when selling overseas to clients in different economic circumstances.

- The legal framework in many countries regulates pricing issues and the extent to which prices can be managed without collusion taking place.

- The distribution channel – what are the margin expectations of your distributors and what are your distributor's costs relative to alternative routes to market? In effect you pay the distributor through the margin they achieve to distribute your product. If there is a cheaper route to market then this should be considered.

- Your own costs – this will help to determine your minimum price expectations.

- The price of your product relative to other products in the range and in the product portfolio – the degree to which your products within a range are differentiated in terms of performance will have a strong effect on your ability to realise price. Price may also be used as a tool quickly to dispose of end-of-line or out-of-date products in order that you can achieve more consistent pricing without the drag on the market caused by old products being available.

When considering the pricing of products it is often suggested that 'bundling' products and services together can help you to achieve more consistent and higher margins. This may well be the case, but you need to consider carefully the service element of the product as this is often much more difficult to cost. It may well be that, after careful analysis, you should consider separating the products from the associated service. This may well lead to higher overall levels of profitability for a number of reasons:

- The core product can be sold at a lower price. This may well result in higher margins due to savings on the disproportionately high cost of service.

- If it is not specifically charged for then service may not be valued highly by the client and indeed could be perceived as free and hence valueless.

- There are a number of legal constraints on the extent to which you can charge different prices for the same product to different clients. Because service by its very nature is not tangible, it is much easier to charge different prices for the element of service.

VICIOUS OR VIRTUOUS CIRCLE?

There is a well-established concept that has become almost axiomatic, repeated by managers and gurus alike, but without qualification of the limits and dangers. Essentially what this says is that the lower the price, the more you can sell and therefore the lower your production costs. The so-called 'learning curve' effect means that you can continue to drive production costs down, lower costs further, and lower prices further and increase volumes yet again. There is some truth in this bigger-is-beautiful argument, particularly for capital-intensive businesses, but this is not always the case. However, this argument is so well established that everyone tries to get into this virtuous or perhaps vicious circle (Figure 16.7).

The reason why this is perhaps more appropriate to capital-intensive industries is that it is possible to spread those higher fixed costs over more units of output, but this concept has limits in industries in which price leadership is not the critical success factor. Other studies (Webster 1974, p. 191) have shown that the most profitable firms are those that have high-quality products, a strong market position and high – not low – prices. Rather than hampering the ability of these firms to penetrate the market and gain market share, high prices support the strong market position. The issue here is really about product quality rather than low price. The quality of the product is important in the market-place and of course is supported by and interacts with a relatively high price. All of which leads to a profitable position in the market.

Where price leadership is not critical, you should think very carefully before competing primarily on price and starting a price war. This may give a boost to market share in the

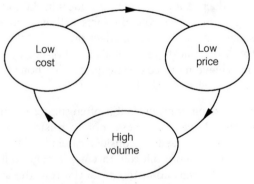

Figure 16.7 Price–volume relationship

$$\textbf{Quantity increase} = \frac{\textbf{5}\%}{\textbf{25}\% - \textbf{5}\%} = \textbf{20}\%$$

Figure 16.8 Is it really worth lowering your price?

short term, but ultimately acts to reduce margin to the disadvantage of all players in the industry as margin trickles down through the supply chain. The price and volume effect is one that should be considered very carefully. Supposing the actual margin on a product is 25 per cent. Let us further assume that you lower the price by 5 per cent. To maintain the same level of profitability it is necessary to increase the volume by 20 per cent to compensate for the loss of margin (Figure 16.8).

At the lower end of the price spectrum, if you are keen to start a price war then make sure that you have advantages over your competition; for example, lower production costs or a more efficient distribution system. Equally, if one of your competitors appears to have an abnormal pricing policy, work hard to understand how this can be. However extraordinary their actions may seem, remember that from their perspective they are acting rationally. What is the basis for this?

PERCEIVED VALUE MEASURMENT

To measure the perceived value, following the PIMS suggestion for measuring perceived quality, we can sort the criteria used by the clients of a given segment into three categories:

1. Product related criteria.

2. Service and related criteria.

3. Image related criteria.

Finally when all these characteristics have been rated they are then compared against price (Figure 16.9).

Each criterion is weighed as 'vital', 'important' and 'secondary'. The criteria are scored by the clients both for yourself and your competitors. By making a weighted mean you can appraise your competitive position.

In principle this method is a reasonable one for measuring perceived value. Take care not to have too many criteria on the list; generally speaking clients can really only take around seven criteria into account at the time of purchase (Miller 1956). This is a case where more is not better and it is more important to decide on the criteria that are really important.

A thread that runs throughout this discussion on price is that it is a composite of many factors and therefore complex. In particular, when your product is new to the client or represents a significant change from the status quo then price will need skilful handling. On some sales training programmes it is said that you should never disclose the price without first having every opportunity to understand customer needs and explain the benefits of the product. This chapter helps to give some background to this sensible advice.

Figure 16.9 Perceived value measurement (after Buzzell and Gale 1987)

Buying criteria (except price)	Relative weight %	Relative perceived value measurement (1st part) Performance judgement								
		You		Competitor 1		Competitor 2		Competitor 3		
		N	%	N	%	N	%	N	%	
Product related										
1 Performance										
2 Size										
3 Benefit in use										
4 Benefit/maintenance										
5 Additional factors										
6										
7										
Sub-total										
Service related										
1 Presales										
2 Postsales										
3 Innovation										
4 Telephone support										
5 Training										
6 Additional factors										
7										
Sub-total										
Image related										
1 Market leader										
2 Recommendation										
Sub-total										
Total perceived value	100%									

Relative perceived value measurement (2nd part)

	Your value	C1 value	C2 value	C3 value
Value	100%	100%	100%	100%
Price				

Dealing with clients

17

KEY POINTS

- *As a marketing person your role is not to sell to the client but to maintain the appropriate level of relationship with them.*

- *From this perspective two overarching categories of factors are important. Those needed to build relationships, and those to maintain them.*

- *As a marketer you may be involved in supporting the salesperson perhaps in difficult or important circumstances with the client, for example, if there is a risk of losing a large client.*

- *Dealing with clients starts by recognising that they have different characteristics requiring a different response from the company, managed by the marketer.*

CLIENT INTERFACE

Clients are the reason why all of us have a job, so it is not unreasonable to think that you will have to spend at least some time with them. When you do so though, you should be aware that you are not the salesperson and your job is not necessarily to sell the product. This is why this chapter discusses what a marketing person is likely to do when with clients.

Once again, not all clients are alike and you may well need to treat different clients in different ways. Nevertheless there are some common points which would apply to most industrial clients. That is why this chapter will be divided into two parts:

- Common points that apply generally

- How to deal with specific types of clients.

THE GENERALITIES OF DEALING WITH INDUSTRIAL CLIENTS

From a marketing point of view, one of the most common points which applies to virtually all industrial clients is that you have a relationship with them. This is very much the concern of marketing and someone, you, must have an overview of what happens between your company and your client's company. Of course relationships exist at the

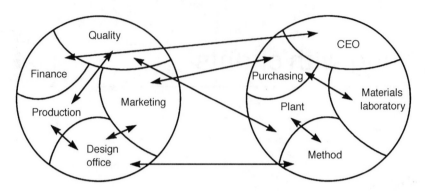

Figure 17.1 Supplier–client relationship (from Hakansson 1982)

individual level, between the buyer and the salesperson for example, but the overview must look at all levels of relationships between the two companies. As shown in Figure 17.1, contacts can be many; an average of ten from the client side have contact with seven from the supplier (Michel 1997).

Because you too will have relationships with clients, it is sometimes difficult to be both a participant and an observer. This is one of the reasons why, if you want to develop this more comprehensive view of the relationships, you do not play the part of the salesperson when with clients.

As a marketing person you should seek to maintain the longest relationship possible with your clients. It is one of the characteristics of industrial markets that relationships stretch over many years. Generally speaking, clients tend to be relatively few but relatively large and we can optimise our profitability by retaining these clients for as long as possible. Our competitors will be doing the same and any clients that we lose will have every reason to go to them and not come back to us. In effect, in some industries it is sometimes said that competitors do not win new customers but that established suppliers drive them away. One of the reasons for long-term profitability of retained clients is that we can offset the very substantial cost of winning new business over the lifetime of the customer. Some very interesting work demonstrates that a small increase in customer retention, and hence the lifetime of the customer, can yield disproportionately large benefits in terms of profitability.

By developing this comprehensive overview you should be able to avoid a common pitfall. In order to retain clients there is every temptation to provide that little extra support that helps to retain them. As this continues, the initiative for managing the relationship gradually passes to the client. There is an insidious and creeping loss of control and as it happens over a relatively long time it can be difficult to identify and avoid. Salespeople often do not notice this as they are dealing with the client on a day-by-day basis and this is generally an issue that needs to be looked at more objectively and over a longer period of time. In other words, you should not always say yes to the client if it is not in the best interests of your company. You must actively manage the client relationship and decide what both parties need from the relationship rather than passively allowing the client to occupy the driving seat.

A French company – now disappeared – was famous for saying 'we may lose a little on every article that we sell, but thank goodness, we sell an awful lot!'

 As a marketing person you should closely monitor relationships with the major clients. Profitability is often calculated on a product basis or on a geographical or sales team basis. If you can understand the profitability of your clients by matching the returns against the costs of generating those returns this insight will give you a valuable management tool.

In order to understand better the costs involved in servicing clients, particularly major clients, it is essential to know the relationship between inputs, often sales and technical resources, and outputs – the volumes and margins generated. In other words we need to know who does what in order to sell how much and at what margin.

This kind of information will allow you, for example, to develop a strategy by clients rather than by product. Rather than selling the same product at the same price to everybody, for our most important clients it may be more appropriate to decide on an appropriate package of products and services which are relevant to them and for which we know that we will be appropriately rewarded.

Another challenging issue is managing the different stages of the relationship. The factors which are important in gaining new clients are not necessarily the factors which will be important in retaining them and these factors should not be confused. The critical success factors in gaining a new client may be for example (Salle 1989):

- price and cost
- technical
- innovation and adaptation
- established secondary supplier.

However, the factors which will ensure that we retain clients having now won them could well be:

- availability
- reliability
- short lead time
- quality of relationship
- ability to work on co-development projects
- high and consistent quality standards
- high service standards
- partnership.

Bringing this down to a personal level, the skills required in selecting an appropriate marriage partner are somewhat different from those required to sustain a relationship for perhaps 50 years or more!

As the list implies, service is actually a very important part of customer satisfaction, from the time the order is placed until the product is delivered to the customer. A whole series of factors can be considered as components of customer service (McDonald 1995):

- the frequency of delivery
- time from order to delivery
- reliability of delivery
- stock availability
- convenience of place order
- accuracy of invoices
- quality of sales representation
- credit terms offered
- customer query handling
- quality of packaging
- consultation on new products development
- reviewing product range regularly.

We could add to this list further and you will note that none of these issues is specifically product related; they are all factors which enhance and support the product we actually sell to our customer.

- innovation
- pre-sales and post-sales technical support
- maintenance
- start-up and implementation support
- training
- support of user groups.

Providing service to customers requires that we are appropriately organised and can co-ordinate our various functions such as production, distribution and marketing to ensure that we offer a smooth and seamless service.

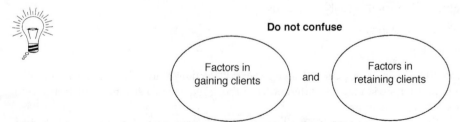

Sales support, 'think relationship'

The salesperson's role is obviously to sell. But there is more to the job than that. The salesperson should also be aware that many other people from both supplier and clients may be involved. The salesperson's natural focus is to the purchasing/selling interface, but you should consider whether it is appropriate to help them to think more widely about the influences involved in the relationship.

Once the decider, a 'godfather' in the eyes of the salesperson gives the order then the salesperson may feel much more comfortable in discussing this client with you. After all, the salesperson has done what they are paid to do and has generated success and justified their existence. However, it is not always easy for salespersons to meet people other than their usual contact. The decision-maker's hierarchical position can be too high or perhaps they will not understand why anybody should wish to visit and talk to them. In this situation the responsibility passes to you as the marketer, perhaps to go with the salesperson to support the relationship. By visiting in this way you demonstrate your commitment to the clients and enhance the relationship. If your visit is suitably 'sold in' then the status of the salesperson and yourself is enhanced, and this will enable you to meet contacts who otherwise might not be available and give you access to information about the client.

For example, with one very large client, in fact the largest single purchaser of the company's products, one of us was working as a marketing director. It was vital to develop a special relationship with the managing director of the client company. The company was located some way from head office and a visit entailed several days out of the office and substantial travelling. A relationship developed whereby an annual visit took place over several days during which time market research information and sensitive company details were exchanged. Each visit was carefully arranged with a full prior briefing from the senior management team and the local sales contacts. This was supplemented by further contact and meetings at trade shows and industry events. The client had historically sourced its products from two competing suppliers. The strength of the relationship built between the two organisations eventually encouraged the client to source from the one supplier. This more than justified the investment made by many of the suppliers' staff over the years.

Difficult negotiations

As previously stated, salespeople should be supported not just when things are going well but also when the going gets tough. This is particularly important with large clients that you do not want to lose. If you are asked to become involved then be prepared for a difficult negotiation and accept that you have a direct responsibility here to retain the client. Before going in to see a client we can never really know what the issue may be but as the above example demonstrates, preparation is essential. Far better to be prepared than surprised.

Here are some guidelines that can be of value in a difficult negotiation (Keiser 1989):

- Avoid negotiation by telephone. If the case is really important go and visit the client. A face-to-face conversation is always better and demonstrates commitment.
- Do not overlook one of the interpersonal skills mentioned in Part IV and particularly talk to the clients about what they are interested in; themselves! Focus on them rather than yourself.
- Bear in mind the following sales rule. To be successful with a client you must talk about
  - money: how much it will save you to work with me
  - ease of doing business: how comfortable it will be to work with me
  - reputation: what your clients will think of you if you work with me
  - future: how we commit to each other if we do business and can work together on future initiatives.
- Prepare in detail for your meeting. What is the problem? Why have I come? What do I want to get from the client? What are the questions to ask?
- When in the client's office
  - If possible, try to avoid sitting down between the client and the door (Figure 17.2a). They must subconsciously feel free to walk out if things go wrong.
  - Do not sit with your back to the window.
  - Do not sit on the opposite side of the table which is confrontational. Sit across the corner (Figure 17.2b).
- With aggressive clients, allow them to express their views and listen carefully to what they say. By allowing them to sound off the emotional temperature can be lowered. Agreement will often quickly de-fuse anger.
- Avoid a confrontation but do not allow your clients to benefit from the use of bullying tactics.
- Keep the options open and seek to develop more options for resolution.
- Avoid 'take it or leave it' statements.

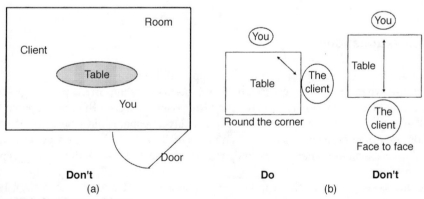

Figure 17.2 Seating positions

- Listen carefully to what is being said, collect as much information as possible. Consider how this may open up new courses of discussion perhaps in line with options that you have previously prepared. Be careful that you do not concede anything and that silence is not taken as agreement.

- Recapitulate frequently to show that you have understood what is being said and to demonstrate that you are listening.

- Remember that anything that you concede at this stage is likely to be permanently lost.

- Accept any concessions made by the clients.

- If a concession is required then seek a concession in return.

- Develop a view of what the client wants and how much this is likely to cost you. Concede those things that they value highest and you value the least.

- Try resolving some of the small issues first before addressing the larger ones. In doing so you may generate a route to solving the intractable problem.

- Start high and concede slowly.

- Take your time and do not be afraid to ask for a break when you can discuss the issue and options privately with your colleagues.

- If tempers start to flare then remain calm. Simply state that this is not helping to resolve the problem and that you would like to move to a more constructive position. This is difficult to do but in the end you will win respect for this approach.

MANAGING SPECIFIC TYPES OF INDUSTRIAL CLIENTS

What we have discussed so far could be applied to a 'typical' industrial client, perhaps a medium to large company with established requirements buying either consumables or small capital items. In addition to this case there are five other trading circumstances that we can identify and these are illustrated in Figure 17.3.

The chameleon

The first tier of clients is the so-called 'chameleon' client, since their behaviour changes depending on their circumstances. We can all identify this type of behaviour because if

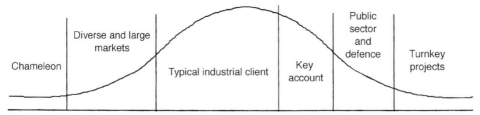

Figure 17.3 Different types of clients

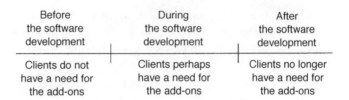

Before the software development	During the software development	After the software development
Clients do not have a need for the add-ons	Clients perhaps have a need for the add-ons	Clients no longer have a need for the add-ons

Figure 17.4 One client in different situations

we ask the question 'so what product do you need?', we tend to get the reply 'it all depends'. Let us take the example of a company making software 'add-ons'. An add-on is a small software program that you can add to a larger one to improve it incrementally. In this case the add-ons could enable the client to develop software more quickly and easily. Would the client be interested? Well it all depends, but on what? (Figure 17.4.)

As Figure 17.4 illustrates, before the client actually starts the software development process, for example developing an invoicing system, they perhaps do not anticipate that it will be as long and difficult as it actually is. Therefore they have no need for the product. Once the software is written and the problem is behind them, albeit at a high cost, they no longer have a need for your add-on. It is only during the development phase as they are struggling to write software that they would be ready to pay, and perhaps an attractive price, for the benefits that the software offers. In the circumstances you actually have very little opportunity to be in front of the client as the need emerges. So how do you deal with this? In this case there are perhaps three things that could be suggested:

1. Develop a communication message which is very 'situation' orientated. This communicates to the clients the specific circumstances and the appropriate solution relevant to those circumstances.
2. Develop a training package which is situation orientated, and raise awareness of the potential need.
3. Rely on third parties who visit these clients regularly. Perhaps the company who supplies their basic software requirements would be in a good position to act as a distributor for your product.

Diverse and large markets – the role of distributors

The second case describes circumstances where there are many diverse clients in a large and undifferentiated market. In this case it will be almost impossible to visit all the clients and one obvious solution would be to sell through distributors or retailers. The relationship switches then from the client to the distributor. However, the product is obviously still designed around the client's requirements. In this case catalogues and direct distribution may be used in the case of small items and consumables – welding rods, safety equipment, nuts and bolts, etc. Distributors have a strong role to play where products are bulkier or have particular handling characteristics related to safety or conditions of storage or supply, for example, agrochemicals, pharmaceuticals, perishable food products, etc. Where products are seasonal in use then distributors also add value by holding stocks and supplying according to demand peaks.

Key account

The key account client is exceptionally important. So important in fact that you should manage it almost as an individual market with a specific and individual approach. The so-called key account manager will be the champion for the client within your organisation. The rationale for this degree of specialisation is to provide this valuable client with a high level of bespoke service.

 Ideally the company, even the very large one, should not have more than four to six key accounts. Not all your clients can be key accounts, as paradoxically if they are then they are not key accounts!

A key account should be chosen after you have made a ranking of your clients relative to your client base (Figure 17.5). The key account will be in the top right-hand box of the client portfolio matrix.

The key account manager is more than a salesperson. He or she will almost certainly have direct accountability for sales revenue or contribution but the distinctive feature of this role is the responsibility for managing the interface and relationship between your own and the client's organisation. The key account manager role is a critical one requiring technical skills and product knowledge, sales skills and also exceptional interpersonal skills which will enable the manager to work effectively with a wide range of people. Not

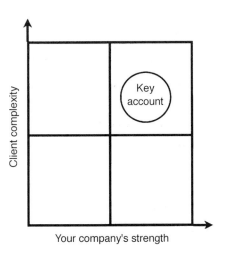

Figure 17.5 Determining your key accounts

everybody will share the same level of burning commitment to the interests of the clients as the key account manager.

Public sector and defence

This is a rather special type of client and due to the nature of the requirement and the degree of specialisation required on your behalf, they may in fact be your main or indeed only client. This is not an ideal situation as it breaks the 'eggs in one basket' rule. However, sometimes the situation is such and there is little alternative other than to make it work.

The critical success factor in this case is groundwork and preparation. The decision-making process on behalf of the buyer is long, complex, involved and with many people with differing points of view responsible for the outcome. This requires a huge investment of time in the relationship in order to develop proposals and contracts.

This type of client could be considered as a type of key account; it is not unusual that large companies seek particular types of skills, for example former senior army officers, who have developed relationships and understand the complexities involved. One distinctive characteristic of this market is that purchasing is usually by competitive tendering. The tendering process can be very complicated and the evaluation of bids protracted and complex with many criteria for evaluation involved.

In general, characteristics of marketing to the public sector are:

- less hospitality and entertainment
- very strict purchasing procedures
- lengthy time scales
- tenders on a European rather than national basis
- political involvement and overtones
- large contracts, with a win/lose outcome.

In addition in the defence sector some additional characteristics also apply:

- very international markets with the requirements to travel and build relationships overseas
- strong involvement of the account manager
- extensive preparation and development required to build trust and create the selling environment
- frequent joint bidding required in order to sell a complete package to the clients
- networks are very important in order to identify appropriate alliance partners
- an even longer time between the initiation and award of a contract
- need to understand and manage not just the client relationship but the network of relationships involved in concluding the deal as illustrated in Figure 17.6.

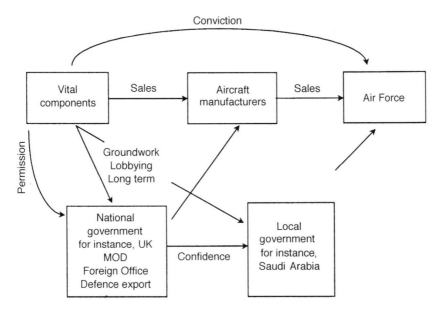

Figure 17.6 Networking in the aircraft industry

- decreasing budgets and increasing drive for value for money
- extremely competitive.

Turnkey projects

The characteristic of the turnkey project is that there is no or little relationship between the supplier and the client. Take for example a construction project, a dam in Venezuela. You do not tend to sell many dams to Venezuela each year or even each decade or century. Therefore you cannot forecast that the next big project will follow on from the previous one, as you might with another type of client. Yet it is absolutely vital to forecast as it has been demonstrated on many occasions that you are doomed to failure if you start to prepare your bid only when you find out about the tender. By then it is too late. How can this be done?

Let us take the example of the Bedfordshire building company wishing to build a factory for an overseas company relocating to the UK. The builder cannot be in contact with every international company to find out who wishes to set up a plant in Bedfordshire. The solution to this is, once again, to understand the network. This means keeping in touch with all the UK institutions and departments likely to be contacted by a prospective client. A company wishing to set up a plant in Bedfordshire might need to speak to:

- the County Council
- utility suppliers

- the local Chamber of Commerce
- appropriate trade associations
- government departments, for example the Department of Trade and Industry
- industry consultants
- professional advisers such as architects, surveyors and estate agents.

Once you are aware that the company is considering a move such as this, the next step is to start to utilise the power of the network. In this way discussions can take place with possible partners and appropriate preparations, for example, ideas about design can be prepared. At this point it would be appropriate to contact proactively the company concerned and make initial inquiries as to what is 'open' and what is 'closed' on the tender. In this way it is possible to influence the format of the tender so that what eventually emerges matches your capabilities. Once the client commits the tender to print then it will be extremely difficult if not impossible to bring about change. Once the tender is issued opportunities to vary the terms are very few. In this case the appropriate course of action would be to submit a bid which conforms as closely as possible to the requirements of the tender.

Dealing with partners

18

KEY POINTS

- *It is quite typical for marketing managers to spend a significant amount of time dealing with external partners.*

- *Such partners take two forms. Those who provide a service, in the sense of being a supplier to the business. Secondly, others whose motivation to work with you is other than as a supplier.*

- *Dealing with service suppliers requires care in their initial selection and in defining your requirements of them. Both parties need actively to seek the best way to work together for mutual benefit.*

- *The other main group marketing managers work with are distributors. A close relationship exists but this can often be more competitive and based around the agreed terms of business. Significant effort may be required to support and motivate them.*

- *If your company wants to be a big player, then you will need to partner with big players.*

EXTERNAL LIAISON

If we are to believe the many marketing managers that we have interviewed, they spend a significant part of their time working with partners of the organisation. We use the term partner in the general sense of the network of alliances that companies build. These alliances can include:

- distributors and retailers
- industrial partners and co-suppliers
- logistics service providers
- consultants and agencies
- legal advisers
- members of the wider social community.

Whilst these organisations are all external to the company they may need to be managed in different ways. To simplify matters we can classify external partners into two main categories:

- those who provide a product or service to the company and where a client–supplier relationship exists
- others who must be motivated other than by financial means. This group will also include distributors despite the fact that they are rewarded by the margin that you allow them.

Why is it necessary to make this distinction? Because the behaviour of each of these groups is very different, and will therefore require different strategies and levels of involvement from you. In effect the first group are suppliers and the others, if not clients, are at least downstream partners.

To deal with the first group you are the client, defining your requirements and perhaps going to the extent of signing a formal contract with respect to the product or service provided. Theoretically at least things are clear cut, you know what you have asked them to provide and how much you will pay. The rights and duties of each partner are relatively clear.

In the case of the second group of partners things are often not as clear or as certain. Experience shows that even if a contract exists, partners may not fulfil their commitment and may even break their word. In other words, with this group of partners trust, your trust in them and likewise their trust in you, is much more reliable as a basis for a relationship than a written contract.

SERVICE SUPPLIERS

We can include in this group different types of consultants and agencies such as

- market research
- public relations
- advertising agency
- designers
- legal services
- training providers
- students and contract staff.

Dealing with many of these consultants is often quite difficult as they supply a service rather than a product. The intangible nature of a product means that you often have to experience it before you can develop a full understanding of the service and its quality. In other words, you need to work with people to know how they work and if there is mutual compatibility. Your early experience will often guide your view of their value.

Choosing service providers such as those we have listed requires particular care. Many of these types of businesses are not regulated or necessarily operated to high professional standards. Most are good and reliable but unfortunately others are little more than snake-oil salesmen, and how could you tell the difference? The first piece of advice would be to follow up some references. A reputable company will be happy to provide you with details of previous users with whom you can discuss the quality of their work. Word of mouth is a very powerful tool in choosing suppliers of this type.

Having identified a suitable provider you should be consistently clear in your requirements. It is often good practice when dealing with outside service providers to minute formally the details of the meeting, sometimes known as a contact report, which lists the points that were discussed and the agreements and action items resulting. By doing this there is clarity about what has been agreed and as a consequence what will have to be paid for. In any event your initial brief should include clear and measurable objectives which have been agreed as deliverable in advance. It is on this basis that you would judge whether or not a service provider has actually achieved that for which they will eventually ask to be paid. For example if you are hiring market research consultants you might want to set objectives around a number of issues, which could include:

- an analysis of your market share compared to your competitors

- potential applications for a new product under development

- investigating and identifying potential distributors in overseas markets

- researching your competitors' position in the market

- segmenting your own market.

The limits to the research project should also be defined in terms of the geographical area or country to be investigated, the industries to be researched or the type of clients. The nature of the report-back required to the company will also affect the cost. It could take the form of a written report either small or large, perhaps with detailed appendices of additional information, a presentation or involvement to the extent of implementing the outcome of the report. A good market research company will also discuss with you the research techniques that they will use and give you an idea of the number of respondents that would be involved.

In all cases there is a degree of trial and error tempered by experience. The more you work with outside agencies the more you will get to know how they work and the types of things that are possible for them to do. As your experience builds so it is likely that you can be more precise in your use of service providers, hence your own level of satisfaction with the work should also improve.

Of course a mitigating factor in this potentially pleasant relationship is that consultancy services can be expensive. Some companies, particularly smaller companies with less formal business procedures, can be intimidated by consultants and outside agencies and perhaps have a distorted view of what they can do and what they might cost. You could well hear comments such as:

'Consultants just borrow your watch and then tell you the time'
'The reason we use consultants is to justify the decisions that we have already taken'
'They are outsiders and will never know the business as well as we do'
'It is all very well for them coming along to tell us what to do, but they don't actually have to do it'

An interim solution to reduce costs whilst still gaining an external view and additional resource whilst developing your own experience of working with consultants, is to build a relationship with a local university or business school. Students are often extremely enthusiastic to be involved in business problems and issues and this adds significantly to their experience. In return you benefit from their developing expertise supported by the faculty of the university or business school who will have a fund of experience and a strong interest in producing a satisfactory result.

DEALING WITH DISTRIBUTORS

Distributors become a necessity when the number of clients is too high for you to service yourself or perhaps when the turnover per client is not sufficiently great to support a direct-calling salesforce. Distributors come in all shapes and sizes ranging from small to large, and from the general to the specialist. Of course there are also good and bad distributors. Distributors should be chosen as an integral part of the product offering that is made to the customer. For example, if your product requires a high level of demonstration or after-sales service then a technically proficient and aware distributor is necessary. Should you sell small, consumable items in large volumes then a distributor with good sales coverage and market penetration would be appropriate. Distributors can be classified according to the kind of service they provide (Morin 1980):

- the after-sales specialist
- the technical service specialist who provides clients with comprehensive technical support
- the 'logisticians' will ensure a high level of product availability
- the 'commercials' are characterised by their persistent sales activity.

Choosing and managing distributors is a difficult but very important task in industrial markets. The 'ideal' distributor is often quite obvious but may not wish to work with you for a number of reasons. They may, for example, already be dealing with a direct competitor, perhaps they lack certain skills or the margin may simply be unattractive. By the time you have identified those that do not wish to trade with you or you would not wish to trade with yourself, then the choice may be somewhat limited.

Having chosen a distributor there is a need for an initial investment of time and energy to establish the relationship. A continual flow of support is required thereafter, as you should never forget that the distributor is your first client in the distribution chain (Figure 18.1). As a general rule of thumb the closer the relationship the better the commercial result. Distributors will require consistent motivation and support and ways in which this can be provided would include:

- regular contact at all levels in their organisation
- technical and commercial support when required
- regular training on product information and market developments. Distributors value the market research and information that their suppliers can provide them.

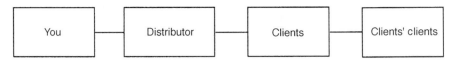

Figure 18.1 The distributor as your first client

- resolve problems and complaints as quickly as possible
- help to promote your distributors through your own promotional activities
- fulfil your commitments
- develop a sense of belonging. For example, Toshiba Carrier Air Conditioning Systems promote a 'distributor club'. This goes so far as to run fun days and children's parties as well as the more conventional newsletters and social events.
- the opportunity to achieve suitable margins will always be an incentive, and our experience would suggest that enhanced levels of margin can often produce a disproportionately high response in terms of sales from a committed distributor.

CO-SUPPLIERS

Another example of a mutually trusting relationship would be when two companies co-operate on a joint bid for a contract. For example, a manufacturer of engines working with a generator manufacturer to provide a comprehensive power plant solution.

All managers that we interviewed said that they had concerns about the management of co-supply relationships. They often had problems in finding and then managing suitable partners. In particular they had concerns about:

- brand equity and the way the company's reputation was managed
- patents and intellectual property
- joint communications
- joint exhibitions and trade shows
- ensuring satisfactory levels of client support
- exclusivity.

They also fear that by not working with the partner company there was the risk that the partner might work with a competitor.

In some instances the co-supply arrangement develops into an industrial partnership. The company you work with adds value to your product either by further processing or by incorporating it into other products. For example, a fibre manufacturer will work with a manufacturer of electrical insulation to gain access to the electric motor market. The fibre manufacturer will also work with a weaver to gain access to the fabrics market (Figure 18.2). The relationship in these circumstances can be so close that an exclusive supply and purchase arrangement exists. Companies are dependent on each other to market their products to the ultimate customer. In this case the commitment and hence

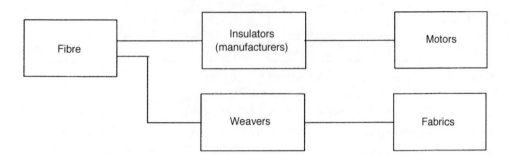

Figure 18.2 Gaining access to the market

trust is much greater as each company is dependent for its future on the actions of its partner. The mutual balance of power is important for the long-term maintenance of the relationship. Just as with distributors, working closely with co-suppliers to develop a shared vision of the market is important. A word of caution, however. Linking your future to that of another company could ultimately limit your potential. If you have ambitions to be a big player in the industry then you will eventually need to identify and work with other big players.

PART VI

Dealing with your internal environment

INTRODUCTION

As you have perhaps noticed it can sometimes be a lonely life as a marketing person and yet you cannot do your job without strong contact with those who design and manufacture the products and provide all the sales and service resources. So, sooner or later you will have to work with all of these people if you want to achieve your objectives.

Furthermore, a large part of your marketing job consists of initiating and driving through change within the company. Change means all sorts of things to different people. Changes in the way of working, in the way of doing things, a change of role and responsibility, more or less power and influence. Change therefore is not necessarily something that people will welcome, and in order to drive this process of change, care and diplomacy are required. Of course not all change is actively resisted. A salary rise is invariably welcomed, so it is much more likely that colleagues will resist change which they perceive as holding drawbacks or disadvantages for them. In fact, as some research shows (Morin 1980), they resist things that particularly affect

- the level of effort required
- things that require their time
- organisational threats, changes to procedures, schedules, timetables, etc.
- hierarchical threats, changes to levels of authority, constraints to judgement and freedom to act.

Conversely these drawbacks can be offset by

- an increase in rewards
- more congenial working relationships, which increase esteem and prestige
- more interesting work, with a higher intellectual content and more direct responsibility.

In other words, people will be more likely to accept change if they feel that they personally will gain something from it. Which of course means they have to understand the nature of the change and the consequences for them. Yet, as the consequences are sometimes unpredictable, people usually imagine the worst rather than the best.

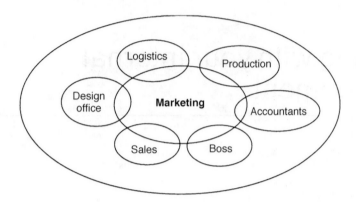

Figure VI.1 Your sphere of contacts

Dealing with people, especially when trying to bring about change, is very challenging. Things never really work out as the textbooks imply. What seems simple and straightforward when sketched out on an organogram can be much more complex to implement. People are accustomed to working in groups and form informal bonds and relationships which are supported by habit and routine. It is difficult to make any sort of change until you really understand these invisible but actually very important characteristics of the organisation. Who gets on well with whom, who really has influence in the organisation, how work is actually organised and tacitly shared between roles and who actually does what in an organisation is difficult to understand. Job descriptions are all very well but the actual way the organisation works is fuzzy and unclear. You really need to understand who does the job and how it is done alongside the rule book and organisation structure chart.

Basically marketing has to deal with (Figure VI.1):

- Salespeople and the sales back office (sales order processing, invoicing, etc.)
- R&D, design office, quality. All the people responsible for bringing products to the market
- Accountants for pricing information, margin, management reports, etc.
- Production and logistics, responsible for manufacturing and order fulfilment dealing with issues such as lead times, forecasts, etc.
- The board or senior management team.

Developing a good understanding with the board, and particularly the boss, is especially important if marketing is a new function within the company. As we have discussed, change is intrinsic to the job and you will need the support of senior management if you are to achieve this. This should not be a problem as if you have been recently appointed to the job then presumably the ground rules have been discussed and agreed as part of the appointment process, indeed the rationale for the appointment is to bring about change.

If you are considering a marketing position then this is a point to clarify as part of your

Figure VI.2 Iteration with your boss

entry strategy. The tacit approval and buy-in of your boss will help you through the difficult stages as although marketers generally do not have a high level of direct or line management responsibility, this is counterbalanced by having some powerful friends.

Secondly, it is vital to understand the company's strategy and how this will influence the marketing objectives, strategy and tactics, issues such as the design of the product offering and communications strategy. Unfortunately many marketing managers find that it is quite difficult to get this sort of clarity from the boss. The reason for this is, unfortunately, that the boss himself is sometimes not very clear about the company's strategy.

This understanding can be developed little by little; you should seek the opportunity to discuss the strategy as often as you can with the boss. These discussions will help you to understand how the boss is thinking and by feeding this back and checking understanding the key components of what the company wants to achieve will become clearer (Figure VI.2).

You: If I understand this correctly, we are in competition with Hewlett Packard in the Middle East?

Boss: Not really because this market is peanuts for Hewlett Packard in the Middle East and they won't really pull out all the stops. Conversely, IBM has a plant in the Middle East which they consider as strategic.

You: I suppose we cannot count on the MOD to help us to sell our aircraft engines to Eastern Europe?

Boss: No, the MOD will not commit itself officially but Mr Jones from the MOD has shown in the past that he tacitly supports us.

By asking questions, listening to the answers and then feeding back your understanding of this to check that it is correct you can help your boss to deliver the strategy to you by putting the words around his thoughts. This does not necessarily have to be done in a formal meeting; take the opportunity over lunch or on a car journey to raise the subject. Making a formal appointment to talk about the company strategy may not be a good idea. If the boss is not clear about strategy and you confront this too directly the meeting could be counterproductive. You could end up with the sort of useless banalities that he is likely to say at the annual meeting 'our strategy is to be the technological leader in the rare-earth magnets industry' or 'our aim is to maintain double digit growth for the next ten years'. Worthy statements in themselves, these are not objectives and provide little guidance to you on how you should organise and manage the company's marketing resources.

ADDITIONAL BENEFITS

These discussions with your boss will have a number of benefits. You will get to know with greater clarity what he is really expecting from you. Believe it or not, this is far from being the case in many companies. This gives you a big advantage in making sure that marketing makes a useful contribution to support the aims of the company and your boss.

In one of our client companies the boss literally grabbed the output of the market research project we had conducted in conjunction with the marketing manager. The reason for this apparently overwhelming interest in the research was an imminent and important annual meeting with the shareholders. The research, in this case a segmentation study, gave him an excellent way of demonstrating how clearly he understood his market as a basis for his future strategy. He was able to interpret this into a range of alternative investment strategies to which his shareholders could relate. This little story should remind you that your boss is a human being who acts in view of what he thinks he will be judged on. Once again, know what is driving your boss, you will understand what he is expecting from you.

Apart from the boss your two main relationships in the company will be with the salespeople and the technicians. As your relationship with them will sometimes make you feel – more often than you wished – between the hammer and the anvil (Figure VI.3), we shall dedicate the next two chapters to dealing with them.

Figure VI.3 Between the hammer and the anvil

Selling and marketing within the company

19

KEY POINTS

- *As marketing is not well understood and often held in low regard in industrial companies you will have to sell the idea of marketing within the company.*
- *In the short term you must be careful to preserve your credibility and gain acceptance.*
- *Be prepared to justify your actions at any time and avoid half measures.*
- *Maintain a record or 'black book' of your activities and successes.*
- *In the longer term, marketing should assist the rest of the company by developing the marketing skills of colleagues and involving them in the projects and activities you undertake.*

WHY DO YOU NEED TO SELL THE IDEA OF MARKETING IN THE COMPANY?

Do you not feel sometimes that you have to constantly sell marketing as well as yourself to the rest of the company? If so, do not worry; you are not alone, as everybody else we interviewed found the same thing!

Because marketing is usually poorly regarded in industrial companies, it lacks prestige compared to FMCG companies where marketers are kings. In circumstances where marketing has recently been introduced into the organisation, that poor regard can even turn to suspicion, with some members of the organisation not wanting even to hear about marketing or to listen to what marketers are saying. Let us ask ourselves why marketing is generally badly perceived in industry.

REASONS FOR MARKETING'S POOR IMAGE

Of course there are many possible explanations as to why marketing has such a poor image in industrial companies and these will vary from one organisation to another. Nevertheless our survey revealed some common points in both large and small companies. One of the most ubiquitous is largely due to history. Marketing is a more recent innovation in industrial compared to FMCG companies, and quite a few industrial organisations are still organised around sales and production. In most of them the culture is still very technical, engineers are kings, and marketing is in turn considered as

- sales recipes
- mass-market techniques
- advertising
- public relations
- cynical manipulation of customers
- sales forecasting.

It almost goes without saying that the existence or otherwise of the marketing department in a company does not greatly influence this deeply held conviction.

What this is really saying is that marketing has a fuzzy image of what it is and what it does. Furthermore, this feeling of irrelevance is reinforced by personal convictions such as 'we've managed without marketing so far' and by the fact that the industrial client is much more present, real and tangible than the consumer in FMCG organisations. In your company, many people know the client very well and may well meet them personally, sometimes quite frequently. So where is marketing's added value?

Conversely, in FMCG companies the consumer is much more a concept, the mythical figure that everyone understands in abstract terms and never sees. The role of marketing in the FMCG companies is to bring deep insight and understanding and in that sense to make the client tangible, a much more direct and obvious role.

Another common reason for the poor perception of marketing is that it is often not seen as a line function, perhaps more a head office service function. Perhaps if marketing has been introduced recently it is located on the organogram as a wart, belonging to nobody and just another hobby horse of the boss, his latest whim (Figure 19.1).

Typically marketing is chronically short of funds. It is quite legitimate in the organisation for engineers to spend £200,000 on an R&D programme, but spending just

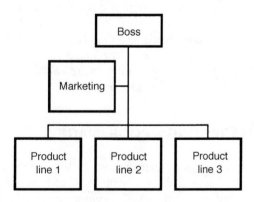

Figure 19.1 Where are you located in the organogram?

a tenth of that on a marketing study is regarded as a criminal waste of money, even if this marketing study can demonstrably add value.

Of course, budgets have psychological properties related to their absolute values. The size of your budget reflects the power that you have in the organisation. In other words, the bigger your budget the more you matter. Should the marketing budget be peanuts compared to the R&D spend then the strong implication is that marketing does not matter. Pursuing the issue about budgets, another argument held up against marketing is that it is a cost to the organisation, as this quotation demonstrates:

> '...profits were restrained by promotional costs'.
> (Comment made by the Chairman of a FTSE 100 company in the Annual
> Report.)

In companies that are very financially driven, where projects are tightly managed and profits, payback and cash flow are critical factors then it can sometimes be difficult for marketers to justify their expenditure.

We are prepared to stick our necks out and forecast, on the basis of our background survey work, that marketing will in fact be subject to more scrutiny in the future. There is an emerging need for marketers to develop more sophisticated tools to measure their results and demonstrate their efficiency and effectiveness. If this emerging gap is not filled by marketers then there is a big danger that marketing will be judged on the basis of the financial tools that are used in the rest of the organisation. Supposing you were asked the question: 'How much extra has the marketing function contributed to sales revenue this year?' This is a seductive trap, since hundreds of factors can influence turnover, and this is why we need more specific tools for measuring marketing performance in order that we can be more specific about what we can actually deliver.

SELLING MARKETING WITHIN THE COMPANY

As you may imagine, the critical time for you is when you first take up your marketing position, particularly if this is a new role within the company. We should distinguish between what needs to be done as you enter the job and develop trust and understanding around you (the short term), compared with what needs to be done to maintain that trust in the long term.

The short term

How can you generate trust and understanding as you enter your new job? We can summarise what needs to be done in these three points:

1. be accepted

2. be careful

3. be credible.

Be accepted

The entry period in a new job, which can range from some months to perhaps a year, can be particularly frustrating for a marketing person who can become a victim of distrust. Obviously what you want to achieve at this stage is to be accepted within the organisation and to avoid circumstances which could lead to rejection. We interviewed managers who have experienced this situation for themselves. They reported that they had to spend a significant amount of time, perhaps even too much time, providing effective and prompt responses to those of their colleagues who asked for help and assistance; dozens of small but tangible demonstrations of your value, dozens of small but worthwhile answers to questions and solutions to problems. So the first step is to listen to the needs of those who do ask for help, and then to frame an effective response.

Examples that we found were:

- preparing a summary and analysis of the product range because 'we don't really understand what we make'

- help with writing product literature

- obtaining information about competitors

- outlining ways in which additional markets can be penetrated

- explaining to the boss precisely what a SWOT analysis is and how it should be conducted

- developing an instruction manual and user's guide for the company's latest product and having it translated into various European languages in time for the launch.

 Nevertheless, pleasing your colleagues is a good thing – as long as you do not go too far from your marketing mission. Bear in mind the example given in Chapter 2 and do not transform your job into an enquiry service.

In fact any of the numerous small problems can interfere with the company's smooth operation. From these snapshots of what managers have been doing in their new jobs you could say that they are acting as firemen with a continual succession of fires that need to be extinguished. They perform a useful role, but this is not going to change the world. The good thing is that these are tangible contributions to the company, and have avoided a common mistake that marketers make of talking in jargon and introducing theory.

To start to bring about a greater acceptance of your role it is useful to introduce the client perspective. In this way you can demonstrate the contrast with the previous situation and start to make people think. For example, how many people in industrial companies talk about their products being 'made of' rather than 'made for', or think about features instead of applications and benefits. It is very common in technology-driven companies for managers to be very proud of their unique technology rather than performance and application, the things that customers buy.

A good start here would be to write a 'client glossary' to demonstrate that the client does not use the same words or units that are common within the company. For example, the client does not necessarily want foam of a certain 'density', what they refer to is 'foam hardness'.

 In other words, help your colleagues to switch from technical jargon to a client language. The glossary will help to break the client code.

Be careful

Nobody will ask much of you as long as things are going well. But when things start going wrong you will never have enough arguments to justify your position. This is why we would advise that you keep a record of things that you do, particularly your successes. It is often at unexpected times that you will be asked for comments or opinion about some point. It is useful to keep a 'black book' of general market information and get into the habit of carrying this around with you so that you are never without an authoritative source of information. Make sure that the information is updated and in a variety of formats – hard copy, electronic presentation, OHP acetate, etc. This means that you can always deliver when called upon in the 'public' and therefore visible arena. The sort of things you ought to think about keeping in your 'black book' are:

- a record of success for quotes and tenders
- examples of new client gains, contracts won, new product successes
- repeat business from new client gains
- general market-place information, market and segment volume/value/trend
- product performance and market share.

Quantify marketing activities where you sensibly can. For example, keep a note of the contacts that have been made at trade shows and exhibitions. You can do this by producing a simple checklist that can be used quickly by those manning the stand to note name, address and nature of the inquiry, or just staple a business card to the form. Even advertisements can to some extent be measured. For example, how many potential clients read each journal and what is the cost for each 'opportunity to see'? Does the journal have a reply-paid inquiry coupon and can you check and follow up on the responses you get?

It is extremely desirable that at an early stage you try to identify those who could be your allies, and indeed those who may well be indifferent or even hostile. In this way you can plot your course as part of your entry strategy. Ask yourself some questions as part of this entry strategy:

- How does my boss feel about marketing?
- Who performed these tasks that I'm doing before I arrived?
- Are there any signs of jealousy or discomfort with my presence here?

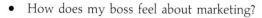

You will inevitably get questions such as 'so you're the marketing person, how do we sell more?' Or even 'you're so clever, so what do we do now?' These are fairly acid and direct questions and you will need quickly to develop credibility with the sorts of people who ask questions of this type.

Be credible

Bear in mind that in the early stages of your new job you will be under close observation. Do your utmost to deliver what you promise. It is far better to make a modest promise and deliver, rather than attempt to change the world and fail. Once you have developed a reputation as a loser it will be a difficult hurdle to overcome. Think how you can demonstrate your successes in a concrete and tangible way. By publicly committing to targets which are measurable, then you can be seen to achieve. This is the key to your success.

There is no substitute here for rigour and robustness. Avoid the 'it'll do' approach and if you are going to present figures or analysis make sure that it has been carefully conducted and that you understand all the details. At least in this way you will avoid somebody destroying your credibility by finding an obvious error in the information. At this stage there is very little that you can do other than to make sure that your information is as accurate as possible.

However, you do have a number of tools at your disposal and one of the most valuable of these is segmentation. This helps to present a customer-based overview of the market that you can share with others and provides justification and argument for an alternative, customer-driven view. However, you must not just *state* but you must *demonstrate*. You must explain the marketing ideas in contrast to the preconceived views that will surround you, but you must avoid imposing these ideas on others. Marketers have to gain respect by the power of their arguments and not by any authority they may have.

The long term

In the long term, having successfully entered the organisation and established a degree of trust and credibility, you now have to work to sustain and improve this. Our work showed that marketing managers basically needed four things to achieve this:

1. Disseminating marketing information – regular communication throughout the company to update colleagues on marketing activities. Short, regular briefings containing relevant and interesting information about, for example, your clients, big contracts, sales updates, recent marketing activities such as exhibitions and other events, new product introductions, etc.

2. Undertake things that everybody in the organisation can be proud of – a major sponsorship programme perhaps or involvement with the local community or environmental issues.

3. Teach colleagues or arrange training for them – perhaps you could offer to attend internal meetings to update them on what you are doing and what you hope to achieve. If the message is a little more difficult to get across, for example, training in the principles of marketing, then use a third party who understands you and your company to provide this service. It is sometimes said that the definition of an expert is somebody who comes from more than 20 miles away. An outsider can sometimes say the same things that you would say but for this reason they are more credible and believable.

4. Involve colleagues – by involving colleagues in projects you are undertaking you gain their commitment and involvement and of course their good ideas. If they have been part of solving the problem then almost by definition they will own the solution. We all know it is the kiss of death for somebody from the ivory tower of head office to descend with the tablets of stone providing the solution to their problems. So, you do not have any other choice than working closely WITH your colleagues to make them want to share your view and projects

A CAUSE FOR OPTIMISM

You may feel that we have painted a somewhat depressing picture of what it is like to engage with the job of marketing in an industrial organisation. Despite the admittedly low status of marketing in organisations there is a strong view that the situation must change in the future. An extensive survey (Palmer and Meldrum 1998) demonstrated very clearly the reasons why we can be more optimistic about the role of marketing in the future. These drivers of change can be summarised as:

- External pressures – increasingly competitive markets, shorter product life cycles, more demanding customer requirements.

- Increased awareness of what marketing can do for the business, promoted and supported by people such as yourself.

- Organisational change – with a switch from functional structures to customer process-driven organisations.

- Marketing professionals – the increasing requirement for professional, industrial marketers that can understand the specific issues organisations face and take a leading role in contributing to the company's success.

- Emerging organisational priority – recognising that marketing can deliver innovative solutions means that the role of marketing is now being much more seriously considered.

So, keep your fingers crossed, your head down and grit your teeth. Remember that in marketing there are no such things as problems, only opportunities!

Dealing with sales

20

KEY POINTS

- *The salesforce is one of your greatest assets within the company. They generate revenue and gather information about clients and competitors.*
- *The relationship with the salesforce can sometimes be strained due to differences in timescale, position in the hierarchy and the difficulty of communication.*
- *Sales staff need your support in a number of ways – consideration and understanding, sales support material, co-ordinating sales with marketing activity and training.*

THE SALESFORCE AS A PARTNER TO MARKETING

It has to be said at the outset, no salesforce, no marketing. The salesforce is one of your major partners and tools in the marketing process, your route through to the world of the client. Salespeople implement the strategy that you design, they are the means whereby you can realise your ambitions. Salespeople are essential for several reasons:

- Firstly they sell and generate revenue; nothing happens unless we make money!

- Secondly, they know the market and the clients as nobody else in the company does. As most of their time is spent in the field they offer an exceptional means for collecting data and keeping your information up to date. This is not acknowledged as the case in every organisation. It may be that you have to agree this with the sales team and develop the appropriate processes in order that this can take place.

- Thirdly, they know the competition. They meet the competitors in the market-place, they probably chat freely and perhaps have a beer with them as well at trade exhibitions and so on. Also, when with clients, they see the competitors' products working, and can collect feedback from clients about performance. In many cases it is just not possible to acquire a competitor's products and monitor their performance, but this is one way in which you can get very good feedback. Clients also interact with the salesforce and they have a good 'feel' for what is happening in the market-place.

- Fourthly, the salesforce is an excellent means of communication especially in industrial markets where our clients are fewer but larger and advertising is less effective and worthwhile than in FMCG markets. In these circumstances the relationship with the supplier can make all the difference in terms of commercial success.

In summary, if you think about it, the salesforce is actually the first client that you have to convince in the industrial chain (Figure 20.1). The salesforce is the launching pad for everything that you do. If the salesforce is not convinced about the effectiveness of the products then we can hardly expect them to convince our clients.

Our involvement with many new product launches demonstrates that products often start well and then sales slow for a while (Figure 20.2). This is explained by the fact that with any new product there is a degree of interest from those who are always looking to test new products – the innovators. Sales then hang for a while as clients develop an opinion of the product and this is discussed with the sales team. From this point, if the feedback is favourable, then this gives the salesforce some powerful ammunition to increase sales. If the feedback is poor then unsurprisingly they will not be motivated to sell.

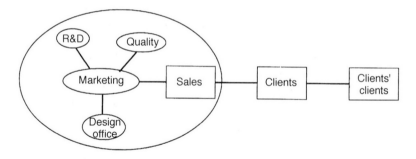

Figure 20.1 Selling to the salesforce

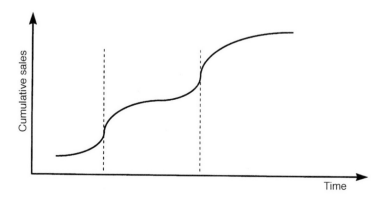

Figure 20.2 A step model of growth (Millier 1999)

SOME RELATIONSHIP CHALLENGES

We must take nothing for granted with regard to the marketing and sales relationship and it is one that requires your investment of time and energy. There are a number of common problems that exist between marketing and the salesforce:

- *Timescale.* A traditional problem is the trade-off between the short term and the long term. Salespeople measure their time horizons in terms of weeks and months, the marketer looks to months and years. This difference in perspective leads to differences in emphasis (Figure 20.3).

- *Power.* Another problem occurs when marketing has been recently introduced as a discipline to the company. Prior to this point the salesforce were entirely responsible for managing the relationship with clients and no doubt this led them to think that they were also involved in marketing. We can understand how it is, that when marketing is introduced and starts to take a different perspective concerning client relationships, that this can lead to problems. The salesforce, for example, might feel that there is no need for marketing, marketing is taking power and influence away from them. This can lead to the emergence of company politics and an unhelpful atmosphere. You can address this by clearly defining the roles of marketing on the one hand and sales on the other. Whilst written rules are unsatisfactory, it is probably better than nothing. This difficulty with sales is reinforced by the fact that they also had control of all budgets. Now they have to share some of this with you, again a perceived loss of power. Finally, if you are handicapped by youth and have to deal with some of the very wily, old foxes in the salesforce, life can be even more difficult. They could even derive a certain amount of pleasure at your naïvety as you struggle to get to grips with the company, its products and markets. This can be a lonely and isolating experience.

- *Rewards.* Related to the issue of perspective and emphasis is that of rewards. The salesforce is not necessarily motivated to achieve marketing objectives. They are usually rewarded on turnover or contribution and these are short-term and very concrete measures. If we are taking a long-term marketing perspective it may well be very difficult to ask the salesperson to visit a new client and present a new product, as we know that it will take some time to generate results. Indeed, it may take years

Sales will emphasise	Marketing will emphasise
Price	Value
Sale	Relationship
Purchaser	Buying centre
Product	Company
Feature	Service
Client	Market
Contract	

Figure 20.3 Different emphasis between marketing and sales

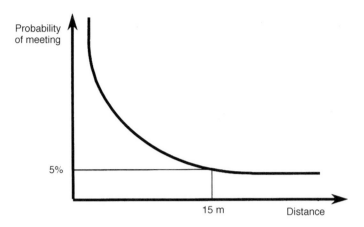

Figure 20.4 Chance of meeting drops dramatically with distance (Allen 1977)

before this effort is rewarded. This begs the question of how we can motivate sales to achieve marketing objectives. One way round this is to involve the sales team from the start in developing projects so that they are both involved and enthused, and a formal procedure can be developed to compensate for this issue of reward. If this cannot be done, then you (or someone from your team) may just as well do the job yourself – visiting clients, developing contacts and marketing new products.

- *Communication.* There is also the issue of distance, both metaphorical and physical, between you and the salesforce which makes communication difficult. You may feel that in this electronic age, with mobile phones and e-mail, communication is much easier. Some of our recent research has shown that there may well be a substantial increase in correspondence due to new technology tools, but sadly this does not necessarily mean increased communication. An intranet can undoubtedly be useful to provide your salespersons with a lot of essential information, yet the functional aspect of the tool should not replace human communication. And furthermore, how much distance do you reckon is enough to stop communication between people? 150 km, 15 km, 1.5 km? Surprisingly 15 metres is enough, the probability that two people meet drops to below 5 per cent! (Figure 20.4.)

- *Status.* It is unusual for a marketing person to have a hierarchically superior position with respect to sales. It is unlikely that you will be responsible, for example, for their annual appraisals, defining objectives and reviewing salaries. For this reason you will need to establish a very good working relationship as soon as possible with the sales or commercial manager. This relationship should focus on three main points:

  - linking sales information with the marketing information system
  - forecasting sales
  - co-ordinating the commercial and marketing activity. This means deciding actions and priorities for the planning period. For example, there is nothing worse than marketing instituting a direct-mail campaign, than for the salesperson to know nothing about it on the next client visit.

Not everything will be channelled through the sales manager and certainly in the initial stages of your marketing job it is quite likely that you will have personally to commit your enthusiasm and energy to building a relationship with the sales team in order to gain their commitment to your projects.

SALES SUPPORT – WHAT DO THEY NEED FROM YOU?

There are four main ways in which sales can be supported by marketing.

1. consideration
2. sales support material
3. training
4. co-ordinating sales activity.

Consideration

Demonstrate your sympathy and understanding for the difficult job that sales have to do. If you are seen as an 'ivory tower' manager, sitting behind your computer for hours on end, then the impression built up by salespeople will be very poor. Demonstrate a commitment by, for example, going out on field visits and meeting clients. Set yourself a target of carrying out field visits perhaps one day every two weeks. Not only can you meet clients but you can also get to know salespeople and understand their problems and concerns. In this way you can get to understand what their requirements are and what can be done to help them. You can even start to develop a relationship by picking up one or two points from each visit and making sure that you follow up and respond to them. Of course getting out into the market-place is an excellent way of learning about clients and markets; until you stand toe to toe with clients they are just a 'concept', and concepts do not spend money. Furthermore, you will not get a feel for clients and a first-hand impression and understanding of what their needs are.

You could well be surprised to learn how big the gap is between the image that you think the company has, and the image the clients reflect. By accompanying salespeople on client visits you would certainly not wish to give them the impression that you are assessing them in some way. To overcome this potential barrier explain that you regularly make field visits to develop a view of the market-place, take advantage of some special event such as a new product launch, new clients or maybe a complaint where a visit to the clients by you would be appropriate.

Sales support material

This is a very important issue with a high symbolic significance. For salespeople literature is part of the tools of their trade. If you can provide them with sales support material that is genuinely useful and helpful to them this will be very positively received. Of course, these sales documents should relate to the marketing analysis and, in particular, segmentation. The type of things that they would value could include product leaflets, corporate brochures, sales presenter material, computer software for sales purposes, etc. If you can supply novel and different sales aids, particularly computer based, then marketing will really be seen to support sales. The lap-top computer carries a high symbolic significance alongside the mobile phone and company car. Of course this should not be a one-way process and the opportunity for dialogue with the sales team gives you an opportunity to collect information about the clients on a regular basis.

Training

It would be nice to think that our professional sales team is fully skilled in sales techniques. This may not always be the case and a good, early, quick fix could be to check the training records and put in place appropriate sales training. It is likely that this will be highly valued by the sales team. Training is often perceived as a mark of professional expertise or sometimes even a reward for success. With respect to training, marketing comes to the fore in a number of areas.

Products

Sound product knowledge is an absolute requirement of a salesperson. Not just of our own products, but of the relative advantages and disadvantages compared to those of competitors.

Markets

Whilst the salesforce spend most of their time in the market-place it is unlikely that they have analysed it in the structured sort of way that a marketer would. Explaining the ins and outs of the market-place leads to insight and understanding.

The clients

Developing an understanding of the buying cycle can help in applying salesforce time and effort where it is likely to yield best results. This could also encourage salespeople to call on clients at a much earlier stage. Often the reason why it is difficult to sell new products is that before the client will buy your product, they have to buy you. This is also an excellent opportunity to discuss segmentation and how segmentation can be used as a sales tool.

Co-ordinating sales activity

It is a common misbelief that salespeople are independent, self-determined and make individual choices. But we all like to know what the grand plan is, we all like to know that there is a sense of direction and that the organisation is co-ordinating its activities in order to make progress. Like many other people, the sales team enjoy belonging to a group and feeling that they are motivated and committed to the same ends. Unless you make the effort to communicate the strategy and work with the sales manager and sales team to develop direction, then just as nature abhors a vacuum, that gap will be filled by what is sometimes perceived as the independent, uncontrolled actions of the salesforce. The sales plan is the appropriate vehicle for co-ordination and is likely to be broken down into monthly activities. This is a useful focus for regular discussions between you and the sales manager. By working with the sales manager you can discreetly help to resolve some of his/her problems, for example, by helping him or her to decide priorities, identify problems, decide how to allocate resources and then to deliver and share the plan with the sales team at the monthly or quarterly meetings. It is vital that the salesforce buy in to the plan. We expect the salesforce to go out and face the clients on behalf of the company. Sales activity cannot be legislated into a salesforce.

One of us found this out when organising a direct-mail campaign. The campaign was aimed at customers who had not previously traded with the organisation and a worthwhile number of very useful potential leads were generated. The salesforce were targeted with following up the leads, and were asked to report back on a monthly basis. All sorts of excuses were received to explain why some of these leads were not pursued — bad debt risks, they have always refused to trade with us, etc. When this was addressed in more detail it was found that some of the salesforce were actually very uncomfortable approaching prospects in this way. The real issue was to provide training and support that gave them the confidence to talk to new prospects. So unless you think through clearly the marketing and subsequent sales plans, there can sometimes be some time bombs that will take you by surprise.

Working with technicians 21

KEY POINTS

- *Of equal importance to the salespeople that you have contact with, are the technical staff. They design and maintain the products that you market.*
- *Marketing should lead the technicians to develop appropriate products designed with client needs as an imperative.*
- *It is the job of marketing to manage the product range in conjunction with the technicians.*
- *Technical staff will also provide new product ideas, test and demonstration results and technical arguments to support the products.*
- *Good relationships can be encouraged by involvement, dialogue and recognition.*

TECHNICIANS

This chapter concerns your relationship with people involved in the design and development of new products before they are brought to the market. Typically these people are found in

- research laboratories
- development centres
- design offices
- quality departments.

Not included in this list are those we would associate with the production and logistics areas. Just as with sales, your relationship with the technical departments of the company is a double-headed coin, good on one side, bad on the other.

THE GOOD SIDE

The positive aspect of your collaboration with the technicians is that if you can work arm in arm with them, you have really laid the foundations for a very positive future in the organisation. R&D and development centres will help you to understand tomorrow's products and keep ahead of the competition. They will help you to update your product range in order not just to respond to, but to lead to your client's requirements.

In return you will guide them in the right direction and avoid costly failures, not just in terms of money but that other valuable commodity, time. Of course, the technical staff will be fully aware of the developments in their area which will enable you to forecast some of the future trends. In some industries, this close relationship between the scientists and marketing is the critical success factor. For example, in the microchip manufacturing and telecommunications industries that are moving very rapidly; this will be extremely important.

THE BAD SIDE

As with sales, there can also be some relationship problems that arise with technical and scientific colleagues. This is especially the case, for example, when marketing is perhaps a new concept to the company that has previously been driven by engineers. Before marketing was introduced into the company, the engineers were taking their own decisions concerning new technologies that they wanted to develop into products. This can be a long way from the marketing perspective; we found this to be a very real issue with some of the marketing managers we interviewed as background to this book as these representative quotations illustrate:

> 'One of the problems with technical people is that when a client comes across a problem or question, the technicians are immediately interested and excited by the problem and rush around spraying resource over too many lost causes without focus or co-ordination.'

> 'Before I arrived we had too few engineers for too many projects. When you have to cope with ten projects that means you spend less than half a day per week on each one. You never reach critical mass, you are just inefficient.'

This can help to explain why technical colleagues may be reluctant to help you when you ask for a simulation, bench test or whatever. Likewise it also suggests why you have constantly to justify the technical choices that you make. Therefore you need to prepare some sound arguments based on market and customer information to support your point of view.

Broadly, R&D managers divide into two camps when thinking about marketing (Gupta and Wilemon 1988). They admit that marketing provides them with updated information that identifies issues unforeseen at the beginning of the projects. They also believe that R&D/marketing co-operation is essential for innovation and help R&D understand marketing and business aspects of product development. Yet they find that marketing lacks an understanding of technology and of customer and market needs. They are reluctant to use marketing information that they believe to be incomplete, inaccurate, and biased by the short-term interests of marketing. Finally, R&D people perceive marketers as rather more interested in promoting their own interests. They see them as salesmen or MBA types. In summary, marketers lack credibility in the opinion of R&D people.

A very common complaint made by marketing managers is that technicians and scientists often have a distorted or selective view of the market. Therefore they guess what kind of products they think the market needs and then set out to develop them. In fact, quite often they develop a product that performs extremely well and then genuinely cannot understand why the client will not buy it. One manager that we interviewed on the subject was quite passionate and said:

> 'They know everything! We can't tell them anything about the client's requirements, they know it already. In fact they know what the clients need before asking!'

An interesting point is it not? In those circumstances perhaps a natural reaction of the marketer would be to say 'well, why don't we ask them anyway'. Such an apparently simple and innocuous remark can inflame a discussion and lead to scarred relationships.

In a technically driven company there is a tendency to be almost secretive about the features of the product. For example, the technology employed, manufacturing methods, etc., on the basis that the less we let a customer know about our leading-edge work the less the competitors can find out. The technicians then work away behind closed doors and develop 'devices' rather than 'products'. As another manager that we interviewed said of his technical colleagues: 'We are geniuses. The clients must come to us to buy.'

Of course there are circumstances when we should be discreet about our products and the features and technology underlying them. Yet, in a brilliant article entitled 'Trading Trade Secrets' von Hippel (1988) showed that at the end of the day you can be better off exchanging information than hiding it on the basis that you get as much as you give, and yet you do not disclose your core knowledge when in discussion. He says that even exchanging information with your competitors should be helpful as long as you do not reveal the essential, core information. Once you help a competitor, who could be a colleague from university perhaps, the next time he may help you and so on (Figure 21.1). What this amounts to is that asking the technician to go and visit the client comes as a cultural shock, almost a sacrilege! 'What! What's the matter, are you really asking an eagle to scratch the ground with chickens!'

As a consequence of the previous points new products can often develop in a haphazard way and we eventually arrive at a situation where there are so many products that they do not respond in any logical way to clients' needs or competitors' actions. When interviewing the production manager of a plastics company he was asked the question 'how many products do you make?' The answer was '8,000'. And how many of those are specials rather than inventory items? 'All of them' was the rueful reply.

The creative instincts of those concerned more with technology than with customer needs can lead to some of these very practical problems arising. Of course it is personally rewarding, exciting and glamorous to, for example, develop a new program code for use in a pocket calculator which will then display a hyperbolic cosine. Unfortunately, the vast majority of us are completely indifferent to hyperbolic cosines and can barely spell it let

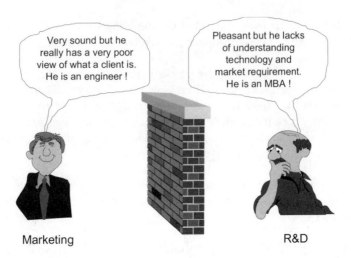

Figure 21.1 A polite but distant relationship

alone understand it. In this instance the feature does not add value for which we might be prepared to pay more.

In other words, it is quite easy to design creative new products and although you might think this is a paradox, part of your marketing job may well be to slow down the pace of innovation. This seems almost counter-intuitive and can certainly lead to frustration on behalf of colleagues. There is a snowball effect with this flow of new products. With some of the companies we spoke to, new products were introduced at the rate of one every month; it is very difficult to manage and sustain them all. The result is that the products are sold without appropriate supporting literature, after-sales service etc., and there are enormous complications to production and inventory management.

Another difference between the technical and client fields is the language that is used. Technical jargon is perceived as complicated by clients, who often use jargon of their own. But language frames the way that we think and the way that ideas develop. Hence technicians do not naturally put themselves in the shoes of the client. When discussing their microwave oven, they would rather talk about 'temperature gradients' and 'Magnetron generated waves' than 'drying plaster tiles slowly to avoid cracks'. In other words they take the view that 'my product is made of' instead of 'my product is made for'.

And that is how the world has happily continued until the time you were appointed to a marketing job. The technicians were kings and quite free to do whatever they wanted as long as the company could afford it. But now you are here and whilst they may have to work with you, there may well be an air of reserve or even mistrust.

A CHALLENGING COLLABORATION

As you can see from the points previously discussed one of your jobs may well be to intervene with the technicians and prevent them from doing things that they have been doing and are quite happy to do. Fundamental to this is the product design process that should start from the list of requirements drawn up on a customer-driven basis and provided by you. At some stage you will also have to consider how to manage both the process and speed of new developments. It is quite likely that you will have to slow down the pace of innovation. It is quite apparent that the technicians will not appreciate this intervention as they see their power and freedom to act diminish. And no doubt they will express their point of view.

So your new job already has plenty of challenges and, because you must at some stage start to bring about change in this process, it will involve a challenge to the kings. At the same time you must keep them engaged and moving in the new direction. You also want all their creativity and innovation but to channel this in a different and quite probably slower way. Handled badly this could even raise concerns in the minds of the technicians that they could end up reporting to you, or at least having to submit their budget for your approval as they become a form of internal sub-contractor.

You will also need their contribution in other areas. They will need to be involved in preparing technical documentation and contributing to sales and marketing literature. Maybe they will also need to be involved in setting up demonstrations, and other promotional activities. They may then eventually see themselves more as commercial rather than technical staff, accepting responsibility and being judged on commercial outcomes rather than on research results, technical publications and patents (Gupta and Rogers 1981).

SOME SOLUTIONS

All these pitfalls sound very daunting, and indeed more than a few potential marketers have found this to be a really intractable problem. Fortunately there are some useful solutions that we can apply when working with technically orientated colleagues.

The first of these solutions is unlikely to surprise anybody, but that does not mean that it does not work or indeed that it is easy to do. The issue here is involvement. Involve the technicians in the decision-making process around the issues concerning products, innovations, new technology trends and the new markets that can be served by differentiated technology. Conversely, involve marketing people in R&D tasks such as new product development. In other words, work together as much as you can. If possible try to have one of the team who has special responsibility to work with the technicians. The so-called 'upstream' manager. Equally it can be useful to have a 'downstream' manager responsible for relationships with the salesforce (Figure 21.2).

The second potential solution will also not come as too much of a surprise, particularly if you have read Chapter 8. Technicians are human beings as well; they like to be recognised and appreciated for the skills and abilities and the good work that they undoubtedly do. So consult them and involve them before taking a decision, make them feel that they have been part of the decision and accept their opinion in the areas where they have competence. They can provide the technical creativity but you can provide feedback to them of the client's technical requirements. In effect this is an internal marketing job and you will demonstrate your competence by arriving at a win-win

Figure 21.2 Marketing as a link between R&D and sales

solution. Let them feel and understand that you cannot do your job without them, but that should be no great surprise to you either – because it honestly is true.

A manufacturer of plastic laminate products provides an example of this. The production process involves the joining together of two different types of plastic using an adhesive medium. There were persistent but occasional quality problems reported back by customers, which involved the delamination of the product as the two plastic sheets separated. Rigorous and persistent quality checks failed to find the cause. It was only when in casual conversation with one of the production managers that the cause of the problem became apparent. Due to lack of storage space it was occasionally necessary to store incoming materials outside. Drums of adhesive used in the manufacturing process were from time to time subject to the prevailing weather conditions and particularly temperature. This led to a change in the characteristics of the adhesive and ultimately the delamination problem. It was only by discussing the problem with the manager concerned that the cause eventually came to light.

Another useful way of solving this problem is to define clearly everyone's role when they are expected to work together. What are the tasks that we have to achieve on our own and what do we have to do together? (Figure 21.3).

One way of achieving burden sharing would be to spell out what marketing will help R&D to do (Gupta and Wilemon 1985), in effect a job description. For example:

- define new product objectives and priorities
- generate and prioritise new ideas
- develop new applications for established and new products
- help in managing the project timetable

Figure 21.3 Share the burden

- provide information about client needs
- provide regular feedback on the marketing activity
- provide regular updates on market and competitor developments.

Conversely, R&D could commit to marketing by:

- regularly testing and assessing new products and competitor products
- modifying and updating current products to sustain them over the life cycle
- developing new products
- preparing technical documentation for new products
- preparing user manuals
- providing training
- analysing client requirements in terms of a technical response.

An excellent way of bringing the market to the technician, rather than the other way round, is to develop what we might call a 'client laboratory'. In this laboratory your engineers or technical specialists work with selected users from clients. The direct dialogue helps technicians to really understand clients' requirements but without the necessity to visit them. Clients also see this as a very useful service. In this way the relationships can be built at different levels in the organisation. This and other means help to provide technicians with useful and accurate information about the clients' requirements and about the real benefit delivered by the products to the clients.

Finally, we would also suggest that it is extremely useful to share these concerns and potential solutions with your boss. By anticipating issues that may arise and demonstrating that you have thought them through and not only understand the problems but also the solutions, you are much more likely to be supported when the environment becomes a little more challenging. This helps to build confidence in your abilities and also provides the boss with an argument to put forward should the discussion escalate. In effect you are marketing the issue to your boss, and incorporating him or her as part of the solution.

DIFFERENT ROLES IN DIFFERENT CIRCUMSTANCES

No two situations are alike but nevertheless, as previously pointed out, there are two main types of projects.

- Projects originating from R&D. We refer to these as 'push' projects.
- Projects originating from an analysis of clients' needs. We refer to these as 'pull' projects.

Both types of projects have a role to play. Push projects build on the technological assets of the business and help to secure the long-term future by continually reinventing and developing our products. Of course you need to be aware that you are investing with no

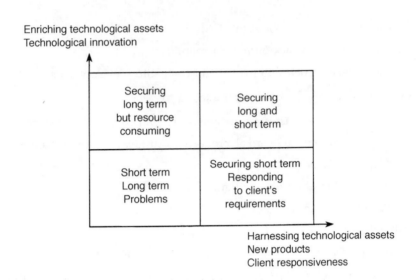

Figure 21.4 Role of new products and technological innovation

guarantee of success. At some stage invoices need to be generated by selling products to customers (Figure 21.4).

Pull projects are valuable in helping us to keep ahead of the competition by responding to our clients' requirements, but this can lead to a short-term view. With technology-led products progress is often, but not always, incremental. By really understanding our client's needs, pull-type projects, then we have the opportunity to set the pace for our competitors by looking for step-wise change. These two types of projects do not require the same involvement from marketing or R&D. In considering the differences perhaps the first issue is who should lead these projects, R&D or marketing? The answer is not so clear since the roles will vary through the development process.

Let us first take the push project. As the product is coming from a scientific or technical source it is not surprising that technicians start leading the project. Furthermore, as no assurance can be given at this stage that the products will work, there is possibly no application that has been identified at this stage. The role of marketing in this project is, in the first instance, to be aware of its existence, the first stage in Figure 21.5.

In the second stage some applications start to be identified. Marketing can then help to quantify or 'scope' the market potential for this application. It may be that the clients have a problem in reinforcing car bumpers, your composite material has a possible application but would the clients be prepared to buy? Marketing can also step back a stage and help in choosing the application, and therefore the market segments on which developments can be focused. This is extremely important because development can be ten times more costly than the initial research. It is very important not to choose just one segment at random.

The third stage involves the development of the product to the point at which it can be tested with the client and fine-tuned to meet their requirements. This is largely an

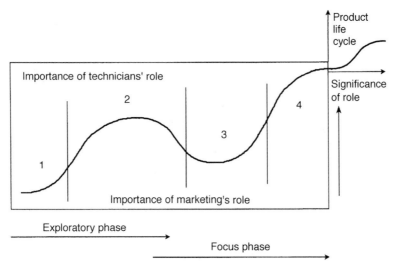

Figure 21.5 Relative importance of marketing and technicians in the technological innovation process

R&D rather than marketing role, providing that the protocol for the test procedures has been agreed in advance.

In the fourth stage marketing becomes increasingly involved as the product nears launch and the technical aspects are largely resolved. There are two reasons for an increasing involvement of marketing at this stage. First we are closer and closer to the launch day, a very important marketing issue. Secondly, we cannot afford to make a mistake and choose the wrong market and thus the wrong products, as we are on the eve of investing in production capability that can cost ten times more than the cost of development (Figure 21.6). For a more detailed discussion of how to manage roles and tasks as the project unfolds see the next chapter concerning co-ordination.

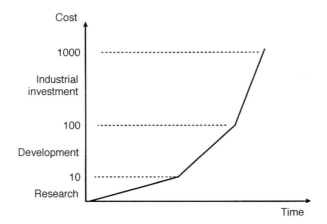

Figure 21.6 Escalating costs as commercialisation approaches

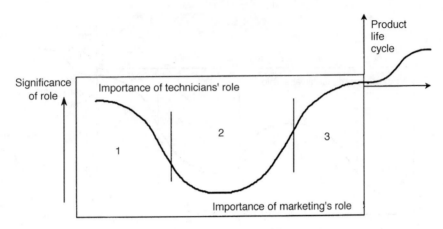

Figure 21.7 Relative importance of marketing and technical roles in the new product process

Moving to a pull project, as they are formed on the basis of a perceived market need it is not surprising that marketing is primarily responsible in the early stages (Figure 21.7). After discussion with the technicians to ensure that it is technically possible to do something (stage one), and fixing a timetable for this to happen, the role of marketing subsides for a period (stage two). Having given the brief to R&D this is the period in which development work is carried out. Nevertheless marketing will still participate in the review and management process to ensure that the project keeps on track. Then again, as the product approaches market launch stage, marketing will take the initiative.

The advantage of this type of approach is that both the technicians and marketing are continuously involved in the project. There is continuous dialogue within the overall framework we have discussed but with a change in emphasis from either side as the project progresses.

Co-ordination with other departments

22

KEY POINTS

- *Co-ordinating projects and activities is a critical marketing function.*

- *Do not be overly concerned at taking a lead role in co-ordination. Apart from being an important part of your job, it is often surprising how many of your colleagues seek direction and a goal.*

- *Visual tools help in explaining the inter-relationships between different elements of a project and help everybody involved to get the big picture.*

- *A Gantt chart is a useful project-management tool.*

PROJECT MANAGEMENT

The proverb says 'he who organises is king', and this is also true in companies. So a little co-ordination can go a long way towards achieving and completing your projects. There are many ways to manage and co-ordinate projects. Experience shows that one of the most useful is the Gantt method. It is useful because it is efficient and easy to use and understand.

Basically a Gantt chart is the same as the one suggested for organising your own timetable. A Gantt chart is a two-dimensional chart. For instance for building your house you could draw the chart illustrated by Figure 22.1. For marketing projects you might want to use several different Gantt charts that are adapted to the particular situation you find yourself in or to your own style of working. To illustrate how to use this chart let us take the example of new product development.

PLANNING A NEW PRODUCT PROJECT

In this instance the marketing department has initiated a new product. The product let us say, is a particular type of oscilloscope, an extension of your product range into the markets you are currently working with. To simplify we shall assume that it does not require any new technology. It is simply a variant on your current product range to satisfy the requirements of a particular range of clients and to follow the market trends. In other words, this is a fairly run-of-the-mill new product development activity.

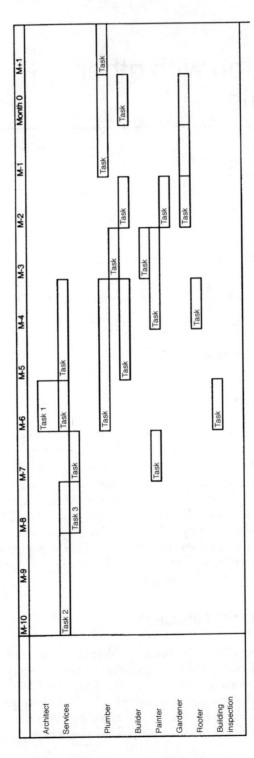

Figure 22.1 A Gantt chart

First step – the tasks list

The first step is to draw up a complete list of things that need to be done when launching a new product. For instance, you might be considering the following:

- understand customer needs
- select target segment(s)
- define needs by segment
- product feasibility; does the state of the art allow us to expect that we can reach the required performance (e.g. a 1GHz sampling speed instead of 500MHz for the current products)
- prototype definition; the list of requirements, functional analysis, technical design
- product adaptation; perhaps to meet different legislative and usage requirements in various markets
- prototype qualification; otherwise known as Beta testing, where prototype products are tested by users
- further client-based trials and development work
- feedback; go–no–go decision
- ensuring patents and intellectual property are properly safeguarded
- develop an appropriate training programme
- user guide and manual
- maintenance procedures need to be defined and appropriate after-sales service put in place
- product literature
- entering the products in the catalogue
- setting the price
- developing sales propositions
- domestic promotion
- export promotion
- sales literature translations
- sales staff and distributor training
- fill supply chain, put in place launch product, inventory within the distribution chain and supply of demonstration products
- presentations to major clients
- back office administration
- sales forecasts
- production build-up

- launch event
- initial sales, order fulfilment and invoicing
- sustaining of all of these activities on an ongoing basis.

Second step – task grouping

Some people or departments in your company will probably carry out several of these tasks. Therefore they can be grouped together as a subset of activities to be carried out by, for example:

- marketing
- sales
- accounts
- production
- design
- after sales.

If we take the marketing department as an example, the types of activities that would fall within their remit, taken from our previous list of activities, would include:

- product literature
- setting the price
- domestic promotion
- export promotion
- developing sales propositions
- launch events
- etc.

Third step – preparing the Gantt chart

This involves taking our allocated tasks by department and then prioritising them by date using the Gantt chart. In Figure 22.2 we can see how the period prior to product launch is divided into months and each work element is allocated by department along this timescale. The value of the Gantt chart is that it helps us to understand the sequence of events and get a much better idea of the timescales involved. These can sometimes be surprisingly long so planning early in the project will avoid embarrassment when it comes to fruition. The chart also helps us to understand where one activity is dependent upon another. In this way we can plan that the events follow each other logically without conflict. As the chart is a visual tool it is also a very good way of encouraging others to put forward their ideas and suggestions to ensure that no critical steps are omitted.

	M-10	M-9	M-8	M-7	M-6	M-5	M-4	M-3	M-2	M-1	Month 0	M+1
Project manager					BETA TEST							
Design office	Feasibility	Proto definition	Writing user's and maintenance manual									
Quality control			Proto qualification									
MARKETING					Preparing product leaflet, catalogue				Sales propositions		Promotion campaign	Publicity
Sales						Price setting / Information to key clients		Arguments	Video tape		Launch event	
Production				Pilot run			Production starting	Training				
Logistics									Inventories			
Maintenance							Training		Inventories	Supplying retailers		
Clients					BETA TEST							
Outsiders												
PR									Campaign design		Launch event	
Design				Product design								
Writers				Product leaflets, catalogues				Technical slips				
Translators									Translation			

Figure 22.2 Compiling the Gantt chart

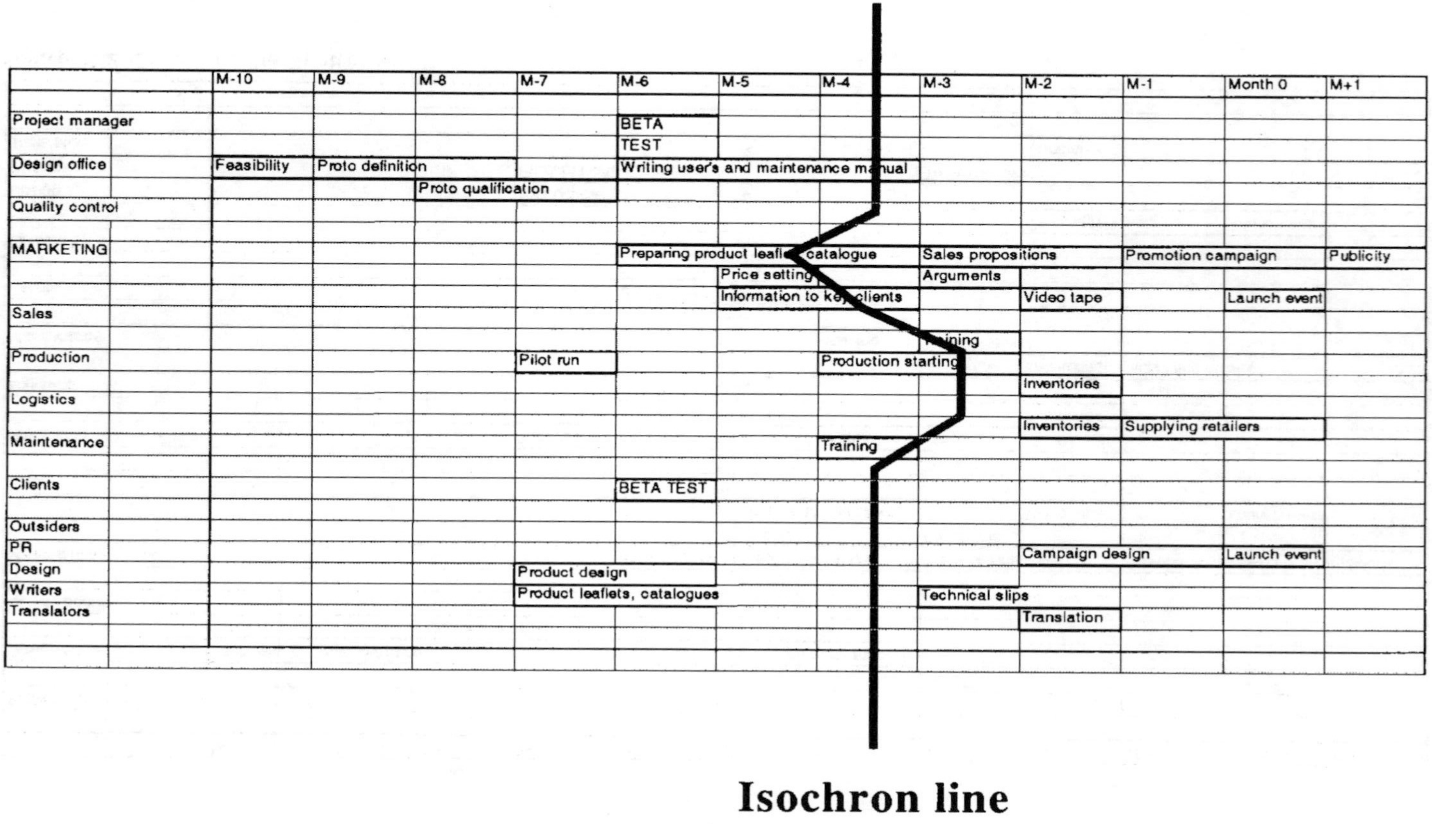

Isochron line

	M-10	M-9	M-8	M-7	M-6	M-5	M-4	M-3	M-2	M-1	Month 0	M+1
Project manager												
Design office		Feasibility	Proto definition		BETA TEST / Writing user's and maintenance manual							
Quality control			Proto qualification									
MARKETING						Preparing product leaflet, catalogue		Sales propositions		Promotion campaign		Publicity
Sales							Price setting / Information to key clients	Arguments	Video tape		Launch event	
Production				Pilot run				Production starting				
Logistics									Inventories			
Maintenance							Training		Inventories	Supplying retailers		
Clients					BETA TEST							
Outsiders												
PR									Campaign design		Launch event	
Design				Product design				Technical slips				
Writers				Product leaflets, catalogues								
Translators									Translation			

Figure 22.3 Monitoring the project

Fourth step – monitoring the project

From this point on, monitoring the project becomes if not easy then at least routine. At each project meeting the Gantt chart can be used as a control mechanism to ensure that activities are co-ordinated across departments, functions or process, in line with how the Gantt chart is structured.

 An excellent way of using the Gantt chant in practice is to use a large display board in the main meeting room. Before every meeting draw an 'isochron' line (Figure 22.3) on the chart to highlight which tasks are on schedule and which are behind or ahead. This has a big impact as it really demonstrates very well the parts of the project that are proceeding satisfactorily and those that require more attention or resources.

There is a range of simple-to-use software packages which make the preparation of Gantt charts simple and straightforward. Packages such as these also have a range of 'whistles and bells' which elaborate on management and also aid presentation. When using such a package it is advisable that one member of staff, usually the project manager, is nominated as an 'owner' of the package and is responsible for updating information and circulating printouts to those concerned.

ROLE OF THE PROJECT MANAGER

The project manager has a vital role in the project process. This role is to centralise the information and decisions. In one of the projects that we worked on, we conducted a sound marketing study with a clear segmentation and recommendations. Surprisingly, despite intense research, nothing had really been achieved by the end of the year. An audit of the situation revealed that the 15 team members had carried out their research in exactly the same way as before the marketing study. No one had taken the initiative to drive the project from a marketing perspective, following the recommendation. Therefore, the 15 researchers were carrying out 15 inconsistent research projects, at least from a marketing viewpoint. For each of these 15 persons, channelling the energy towards market requirements was someone else's business. If everybody decides, the project is not managed. There are too many chiefs and not enough indians, or perhaps in the case illustrated too many indians and no chief at all.

A difficult balancing act is to consult and involve the project team members on the one hand and to centralise and take the decision on the other hand. Involving the team maintains motivation for the project, but nonetheless the project needs to be steered by one or very few decision-makers. Massimo d'Alema (the Italian Council President) said during the Kosovo crisis, that he consulted everybody but at the end of the day he decided.

PART VII

The marketing expert's toolbox

INTRODUCTION: FROM INFORMATION TO ACTION

As your knowledge of industrial marketing develops it is likely that you will require some more sophisticated tools in order to:

- describe comprehensively and analyse the market and business environment
- analyse and understand your current market position
- develop an informed view of your future marketing options.

That is why the last part of this book will deal with:

- market research
- market segmentation
- market analysis
- diagnosis of your current situation.

Furthermore, as you have developed your understanding of some of the big issues and in particular the nature of industrial marketing, you will appreciate the consistency between the expert tools presented in Part VII and the principles developed in the previous chapters. You will note how the marketing analysis is consistent with 'thinking about your marketing strategy' and how segmentation is relevant to a market in which the technical issues are important.

Marketing analysis will provide you with the building blocks for strategy – segmentation, product specification, supply-chain analysis, client buying behaviour, etc. The method for segmentation we discuss here differs from other models in that we place more emphasis on the technical nature of the product.

From a general perspective, we can overview the different steps of the analysis as follows. This takes us from the problem to action (Figure VII.1). This general framework can be cast in a marketing perspective as illustrated in Figure VII.2. To increase the relevance to your work in industrial markets where technical issues are integral to marketing solutions and in which markets are structured as a chain, we should carry out an analysis in three sections (Figure VII.3).

Segmentation is the critical part of the analysis. We discussed above the emphasis given to the technical nature of the product. This is complemented by the commercial analysis to give a comprehensive understanding of the structure of the market. Taking

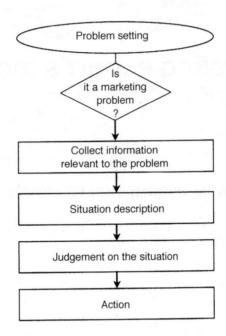

Figure VII.1 The problem-setting process

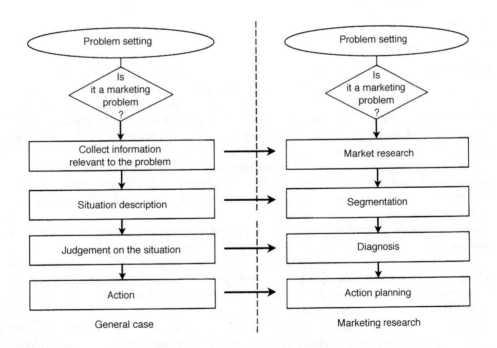

Figure VII.2 The marketing problem-setting process

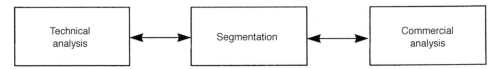

Figure VII.3 A comprehensive segmentation method

into account the previous elements, the marketing process can be displayed as shown in Figure VII.4.

The first three chapters of Part VII will discuss the tools appropriate for Figure VII.4, that is to say:

- market research
- segmentation
- technical analysis
- commercial analysis
- diagnosis.

The last chapter will be dedicated to a well developed method of carrying out and presenting a marketing plan.

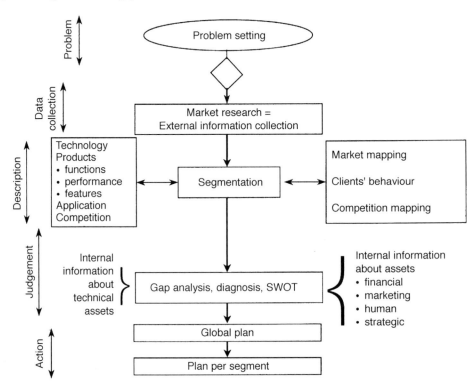

Figure VII.4 The marketing research process (Millier 1999)

An important point should be mentioned. In Part VII we give some marketing tools which should be considered as no more than frameworks or templates to be adapted, modified or adjusted to your needs. The marketing tools are not that rigid. Not only can you, but you must, adapt the list of criteria if the given list does not suit you. You must not be the slave of the tool. YOU MUST WORK WITH WHAT MAKES SENSE.

Marketing research and marketing information   **23**

KEY POINTS

- *A clear distinction must be made between data and information. Data is material from which you may obtain information.*
- *The objective of any market research activity must be clear before starting work.*
- *Data and information can be collected from both internal and external sources.*
- *If you are not sufficiently selective it is easy to be overwhelmed with information.*
- *Market research can be conducted for both exploratory and confirmatory purposes.*

TOO MUCH – YET NOT ENOUGH

A paradox with information is that you can easily be overwhelmed with too much, yet on the other hand not have the precise piece of information that you require. In fact you are overwhelmed with data but lack information. Data is the mountain of raw material from which to extract nuggets of information by processing the data (Figure 23.1). It is very common for companies to collect a multiplicity of data, but this is actually useless for marketing purposes until it is processed in order to answer a question.

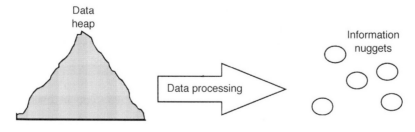

Figure 23.1 From data to information

It is no exaggeration to say that it is a crime that some companies regard the collection and storage of information as an end in itself. Such information is often useless for any purpose, let alone marketing.

The information system must be a means not an end. It must be built to support the role of marketing. Similarly marketing strategy and segmentation, the marketing diagnosis, must not be built as a function of the information system.

A second paradox with information is that it is obsolete as soon as you get it, since markets and technology are in a continual state of flux. Therefore information once it has been collected needs to be maintained. So when gathering data we have to think not just about its relevance to the question that we want to answer, but also the way that we structure the data to give us information will also determine how easy it is to maintain the relevance of the information.

When?

The role of market research is to provide you with additional information and explanation about any aspect of the nature of your market, customers or the business environment in which you operate. It should be used when it is not possible to obtain information from other sources such as desk research or published information but which is critical to the decisions that you will make about future marketing activities. If we regard information as the raw material for marketing then market research has a very important role to play in helping us to develop a complete and unique picture of our customers and market. Common issues that are researched for marketing purposes include the nature of the market – the size, rate of growth, structure, issues concerning clients' needs – what they want, do they know what they want, and of course segmentation. Finally, we often want to know about our competitors and how they are perceived in the market-place and how we are perceived relative to them.

What?

Before we know what type of information we want to collect the first step is to define the nature of the problem. This is an extremely important part of the process. The type of question that we want to answer will determine the market research techniques that we use. Unless we are clear about the question that we want to answer it is a great temptation simply to collect more and more information in the hope that dazzling insights will emerge from it. There are a wide range of marketing questions that we can address. These might include:

- You are being attacked by competitors yet do not know why you are losing business.

- You want to diversify from one industry to another and need to gain greater understanding of your target market.

- You want to introduce a new product but need to define clearly the features and benefits needed.
- Sales are plummeting yet the reason is not apparent.
- Your distributors are not meeting expectations and you need to know why.
- Your product portfolio is too large but which products should or could you remove.
- Your most recent product launch has failed and you want to know why.

These are just some of the problems that marketers can come up against. With such diverse issues it is therefore very difficult to define what information to collect. However, it is possible to give you a framework as a guideline.

In order to increase the chances that you can identify how the framework can help you with your problem we have chosen the framework that is appropriate for one of the most difficult situations you are likely to find. The situation occurs when you know nothing about the market, the product definition, the clients, the competition and so on. So this somewhat complicated issue provides a comprehensive view on which something more straightforward can be based.

If we come back to the global marketing research framework we shall concentrate in this chapter on the upper part of the model (Figure 23.2). In other words, we shall deal

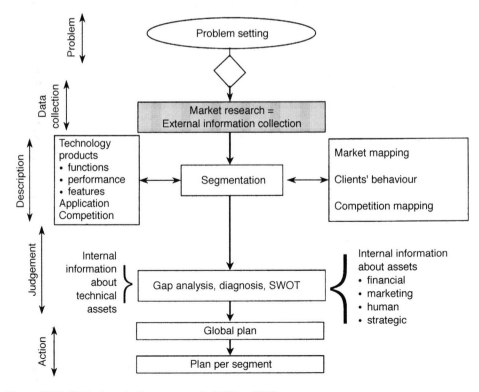

Figure 23.2 Global marketing research (Millier 1989)

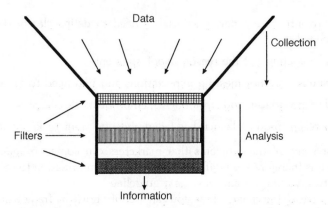

Figure 23.3 Reducing the data

with what data to collect and what to do with it in the first stage of analysis. Data analysis is a funnelling process in which our data is filtered through a series of grids or analytical tools that will transform the data into information (Figure 23.3).

INFORMATION COLLECTION

There are many ways of collecting marketing information. We can summarise these as shown in Figure 23.4.

Internal information

This should always be your starting point when considering marketing information, for two reasons. Firstly, you are very likely to have within the organisation some or all of the information that you are looking for. Secondly, it is cheaper and easier to use this readily available source of information. By way of contrast, bear in mind that one face-to-face

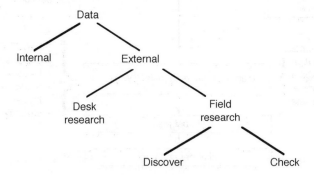

Figure 23.4 Different sources of market information

interview could cost you anywhere from £100 to £500 depending in which country you conduct the interview. There are many sources of internal information:

- company reference material, documentation and report libraries
- previous marketing studies
- sales statistics, representative reports, client files
- R&D records
- quality control and customer complaints
- after sales and service history records
- exhibition reports and visitor statistics.

One of the problems with internal information is that there tends to be rather a lot of it and it is by nature heterogeneous, scattered all over the company. It is almost a research project in itself to find out where the information is. In fact, in some cases it might be easier to give up and commission a new research project. In this sense

over information = under information

The second problem is that sometimes you do not know what information exists within your company and you can unwittingly take the long way round to obtain information that you in fact already have. Finally, internal information can often be short term in nature and may be unsuitable for your purpose.

The reasons for the ephemeral nature of internal information is that people tend to be selective in the information they keep and as they move from one job to another so the information is disseminated. Furthermore, lots of small pieces of information are never appropriately recorded and are simply thrown away. As we move much more into the age of electronic information the failure properly to record and store information could lead to a waste of potentially valuable material.

External information

Desk research

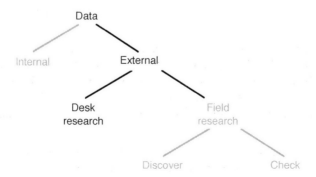

As we noted, we must distinguish between desk research and field research. Desk research is essentially a search of existing data sources, sometimes called secondary data, carried out 'from your desk'. Secondary data can be found from:

- technical centres and laboratories
- databases
- directories
- statistics
- trade magazines
- economic studies and industry reports
- competitor promotional material
- the Internet is a prime source of secondary data.

Desk research should be conducted before considering field research as it is relatively cheap and helps us to focus on the really critical issues that we might need to investigate with a formal market research study. In other words, it helps us to formulate a research question.

Before conducting field research always thoroughly investigate information available within the company and from the company.

Field Research

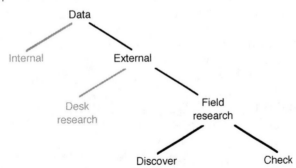

Field research involves obtaining primary or unique data directly from the market or clients. A carefully defined and conducted study will yield information that is not obtainable by other means. However, it is not often used as costs can be very high; perhaps between £20,000–£100,000 for a marketing study. Before setting out to conduct a research project you should clearly distinguish between three different types of research.

1. Confirmatory or explanatory research – whereby you want to flesh out and confirm your initial views and understanding and generate supporting information.

2. Descriptive research – to give a profile of, usually, a market or market segment, client base or industry competitors.

3. Exploratory research – a much higher level of uncertainty as you are not clear about the nature of the information you seek.

The nature of your question and the type of research will give you pointers to the most appropriate method to use. 'What' type questions may best be answered using questionnaires or surveys, but 'why' questions could be better approached by using focus groups and face-to-face or in-depth interviews.

I keep six honest serving-men
(they taught me all I knew);
Their names are What and Why and When
and How and Where and Who.

Rudyard Kipling, *Just So Stories*, 1902

Kipling describes perfectly the ways in which we can ask questions using his 'six honest serving-men'. Each different type of question suggests an appropriate method of research. When commissioning research with an agency, challenge them to demonstrate how the method they propose to use is consistent with the type of question. Generally research methods fall into two types, qualitative and quantitative. Whilst it is difficult and sometimes dangerous to generalise in these cases we can see that quantitative methods such as surveys and questionnaires are appropriate for 'what' and 'how' questions and focus groups and face-to-face or in-depth interviews for 'why' questions.

Questionnaires are very popular for confirmatory research as they are relatively cheap to conduct and give a wealth of information. Of course they are much more appropriate for this type of research, as otherwise how would we know what questions to ask without some prior knowledge? They can give very good results in industry and you can increase the chances of success if

*   the questionnaire is simple and well structured

*   you briefly described to your respondents the reason for the research so that they understand what is required

*   you are recommended to the respondent by a colleague

*   you are able to address respondents personally by name

*   it is inconvenient to speak; perhaps you can make an appointment to call back

*   you complete the questionnaire within the time stated.

In the case of exploratory research different techniques would be used. With exploratory research we are much more interested in understanding the respondent's point of view. In this case we ask open questions in order to allow them to discuss the issue. Here we are concerned not so much with statistical validity, but much more with really understanding issues. In this case we might use face-to-face interviews and ask questions that help us to explore attitudes, perceptions and opinions in depth. By asking open questions and listening to the answers interviewees give, their answers can be very insightful. Great care needs to be taken not to suggest or precondition the answer, and for this reason this type of research is usually conducted anonymously and by skilled researchers.

To increase the value of qualitative research we should take care that

- interviewees are allowed to express their real opinions and views
- the company commissioning the research remains anonymous until it is appropriate to disclose the sponsor's name
- the interviewee is representative of our target market and has been carefully pre-selected
- the interviewee feels relaxed and at ease and confident to express their views
- the conversations are carefully noted, taped or videoed for later analysis
- confirmatory research is conducted to ensure that the views and opinions are representative.

Qualitative research can be very insightful by opening up new areas of understanding. Perhaps by helping us to understand emerging needs or to understand that whilst we may have a technologically superior product it is actually our poor reputation for after-sales service and maintenance that inhibits more sales. Significant issues in obtaining this kind of information is undoubtedly time and money. Typically, for a difficult case such as technological innovation, for which you know nothing at the outset, it takes roughly six months, requires 50 to 60 face-to-face interviews and will cost at least £30,000. For less demanding needs, telephone interviews offer cheaper and quicker respondent access.

When the product is quite new to clients you can also use experiments. You let the clients 'play' with your product and obtain their feedback. One step further in the involvement and cost is – as seen in Chapter 6 – co-development which is an extreme form of experiment. A variant of the experiment can be carried out by yourself with competitors' products. For an effective benchmarking, you can buy (when possible) and test your competitors' products, or have them tested by a third party if appropriate.

An important qualitative technique is the focus group. A focus group consists of six to twelve like-minded people gathered in a relaxing environment to discuss a topic or range of topics. It is useful for characterising a problem and gathering opinions, exploring attitudes and discovering emerging trends. It is more dynamic than a face-to-face interview due to the group effect but does requires a skilled facilitator to manage the group but without leading the answers or superimposing questions important to the company but not the client.

MARKET MONITORING

Up until now we have assumed that you have been seeking information in order to address a specific problem. Yet you will also need to monitor your market and understand the trends. For monitoring we commonly use a range of 'continuous' research techniques. Research is conducted at regular intervals to enable us to monitor trends over time.

There are a range of techniques that are used, for example we could use a representative panel of our clients or distributors. Perhaps we might purchase industry-wide research which is syndicated among key players in the industry. Such research often offers you the opportunity to 'buy' specific questions to be included on the survey.

Think carefully about the role of desk research in establishing and monitoring the key drivers in the industry. Understanding the drivers and monitoring them carefully may enable you to predict how the market will behave in the future.

 Be careful not to rely too much on continuous data. Whilst this is good for monitoring trends within the industry, be careful to ask yourself what specific use and value you derive from this research. It can be quite expensive and in some industries is just treated as a routine, the original purpose having been forgotten. Remember that with syndicated or industry-wide research your competitors will also be buying the same information. This means that it will be difficult to gain significant competitive advantage from the research.

By questioning the value of continuous research you may be able to release funds which enable you to address more specific and relevant questions.

Marketing segmentation   **24**

KEY POINTS

- *Segmentation is the most important step in the marketing process and is fundamental to many marketing challenges.*

- *In many industrial markets technology has an important role to play, and segmentation can usefully include techniques that help to define applications.*

- *Segmentation also encompasses aspects of behaviour that help us to understand how clients buy and what they get from our products.*

- *Mapping these two aspects of segmentation, application and behaviour, gives a segmentation matrix that allows an actionable description of the market.*

- *Segmentation enables marketing strategy to be developed appropriate to each segment as well as the overall market.*

WHAT IS MARKET SEGMENTATION?

Segmentation means describing the market as simply as possible whilst doing our best to emphasise its variety. This is achieved by using explanatory criteria (or descriptors) to classify homogeneous groups of customers; the so-called market segments to which we refer.

Market segmentation (Millier 1995, 1999) means having a representative picture of the market and being able to visualise it. As technology is of prime importance when you are analysing the situation for innovative products, we will explicitly introduce a technical dimension into the segmentation here. The term 'technical segmentation' will designate our procedure to identify all potential applications for the new product; that is to say, the technical needs the product can meet. But it does not just take unsolved technical problems to make markets, so we need to add a second dimension to the segmentation. In this case we shall talk of 'behavioural segmentation', which designates what we do to identify groups of customers with similar attitudes to innovation.

Once you have obtained your technical and behavioural segmentation, you make a segmentation chart (Figure 24.1) by intersecting them. Wherever the intersections between columns and rows have been identified, they correspond to market segments – homogeneous customer groups. We can illustrate this with an example from a non-

	Application 1	Application 2	Application 3	Application 4
Behaviour 1		Segment 2		Segment 6
Behaviour 2	Segment 1		Segment 4	
Behaviour 3		Segment 3		
Behaviour 4			Segment 5	

Figure 24.1 Segmentation chart

destructive ultrasonic laser project, where they pinpointed the two segments shown in Figure 24.2.

What gives these two segments their internal homogeneity and what makes them different?

- In Segment 1 the customers work in a research laboratory with very proficient people who are oblivious to price and spend their time trying to describe the shape of flaws inside composite parts.

- In Segment 2 the customers want to install the new product on a high-throughput production line, in order to locate defects in steel parts at a cost of less than 3p per measurement.

First of all you will note that segment uniformity does not depend on the industry customers belong to. So in fact there are aircraft companies and automotive companies together in the first segment. On the other hand, only automotive companies exist in both segments.

On the strength of this description of the segments you can see you will not be serving them the same way. You will send your best technicians to meet the researchers from Segment 1 and offer them highly sophisticated, high-performance equipment. In

1st Segment	2nd Segment
British Aerospace shopfloor Dassault shopfloor Rover Group laboratory	Vauxhall shopfloor Rover Group shopfloor

Figure 24.2 Example of two market segments

contrast, you will be sending a salesperson to see the buyers in Segment 2 to negotiate the sale of a fast, productive, reliable control system that operates at less than 3p per unit, very much a rational, economics-based sale. From the marketing perspective, you can clearly see that there are two market segments here.

TECHNICAL SEGMENTATION

Technical segmentation begins by identifying what use the customers are going to make of your product. For instance, what we mean by 'use' is

- products which are partly composed of the material or components you are developing
- measurement, manufacturing, maintenance, calculation operations or others that customers will carry out with the machines or equipment you are developing.

Hence, potential uses for a non-destructive ultrasonic laser control system could be controlling and monitoring

- water pipelines in mountains
- defects in metal blanks emerging from a high-speed rolling mill
- primary circuit pipes in nuclear power stations
- fighter plane wings in composite material
- outdoor piping in refineries
- cable-car cables whilst in operation
- nuclear fuel quality
- gas pipelines
- railway tracks
- controls during development of fissile material
- pipes in conventional fuel power stations
- etc.

Once you have compiled the list of uses, you need to use your intuition to subdivide it into smaller groups that each represent a specific type of technical problem. The intuitive approach works remarkably quickly and efficiently in processing all the information collected beforehand. Either consciously by enquiries conducted along specific interview guidelines, for instance, or subconsciously by observing details that seem insignificant but ultimately reveal deep-seated problems. For instance, if you use your intuition to subdivide the applications list for the ultrasonic laser project, you might get the results shown in Figure 24.3.

Of course, intuitive thinking can easily be discredited by others who propose that their own intuition is as valid as yours, but different. So it is necessary to rationalise this initial step by carrying out four logical tests on the groups of applications. The first and simple

Applications	Defect detection in the field	Defect detection in fast-moving parts	Defect detection in hostile environment
Products	• Pressure pipelines in mountains • Gas pipelines • Pipe in power stations • Outdoor piping in refineries	• Metal blanks out of high-speed rolling mill • Railway lines • Cable-car cables when in operation	• Primary circuit pipes in nuclear power stations • Nuclear fuel quality • Development of fissile material

Figure 24.3 Examples of applications for non-destructive laser control

one consists of giving a name to the applications and identifying the common technical problem solved in this particular application. If you are unable to find this common denominator, it means that the application is likely to be heterogeneous and you should continue to work on the problem.

The second tests whether your applications and your list of functions are coherent. This is summarised in the form of a matrix (Figure 24.4). This matrix lists every function that is needed to meet the technical requirements common to all the applications and is a valid test for your list; each application (or specific technical case) is met by a single innovative product that is defined according to its function. If the same product can be used for two applications as denoted by the two asterisks in line with 'Remote contact-free measurement'

Applications	Defect detection in the field	Defect detection in fast-moving parts	Defect detection in hostile environment
Uses / Functions	• Pressure pipelines in mountains • Gas pipelines • Pipe in power stations • Outdoor piping in refineries	• Metal blanks out of high-speed rolling mill • Railway lines • Cable-car cables when in operation	• Primary circuit pipes in nuclear power stations • Nuclear fuel quality • Development of fissile material
Remote contact-free measurement		⋆	⋆
Instantaneous measurement		⋆	
Portable	⋆		
In-depth penetration of material			⋆

Figure 24.4 Function/application matrix

Applications	Defect detection in the field	Defect detection in fast-moving parts	Defect detection in hostile environment
Uses / Technologies	• Pressure pipelines in mountains • Gas pipelines • Pipe in power stations • Outdoor piping in refineries	• Metal blanks out of high-speed rolling mill • Railway lines • Cable-car cables when in operation	• Primary circuit pipes in nuclear power stations • Nuclear fuel quality • Development of fissile material
EMA Probe	*		
Scrubbing shoes		*	
X-rays			*
Gamma-rays			*

Figure 24.5 Technology/applications matrix for non-destructive laser control

in Figure 24.4, you must amalgamate the applications and classify them as one. When the same solution applies to two cases, these cases can be considered identical.

The third test checks the coherence of your list in relation to competitor products. You need to construct a technology/applications matrix (see page 273) that includes technologies competing with your innovation. Then you show which technologies currently meet each application, for example by using asterisks as in Figure 24.5. If by chance there are two identical competitor techniques for two different applications, you may find they are similar enough to amalgamate.

The fourth test consists of discovering and combining criteria or descriptors that can explain the differences between the various types of technical need you have identified. Pinning down these criteria is a valid testing process, because if you fail to justify these differences then you must go back to square one and redefine your applications all over again according to use.

When looking for criteria for your technical segmentation you should begin by describing

- the new product manufactured or new operation carried out

- constraints regarding its use, implementation or manufacturing

- its environment

- the problem you seek to overcome by switching technologies

- problems encountered with competitor technology

- functions customers demand, basic functions, functions competitor techniques fail to offer, additional functions necessary to make the innovation fit customer needs.

Analysed material	Metal				Composites	
System configuration	Portable	Stationary			Stationary	
Measurement input mode	Static	Static	Relative motion	Scanning	Scanning	
Task required	Detection	Detection	Detection	Detection	Detection	Description
Applications	Outdoor defect detection	Defect detection in hostile environment	Defect detection in parts when in continuous motion	Defect detection in very large metal structures	Defect detection in composite material	Defect description in composite material

Figure 24.6 Applications for non-destructive ultrasonic laser control

Afterwards, you identify everything in this description that can explain or justify the difference between one application, or group of applications, and another. It is particularly important to root out criteria that explain the difference in terms of technical offer, implementation or the technical needs the innovation has to address. Once you find the criteria, you should work out which combination of these descriptors gives you the most complete picture of all the applications. Compiling a list of different types of criteria makes it easier to find your combination.

For example, in the case of the non-destructive ultrasonic laser project, you could list criteria that concern respectively,

- whether the material to be analysed is metal or composite

- whether the equipment is portable or stationary

- whether measurement data input is taken with

  - the parts for checking stationary in relation to the laser
  - the parts for checking and the laser in related movement
  - the parts for checking scanned by the laser beam

- whether the task in hand is to detect, or to describe, defects.

This would give $2 \times 2 \times 3 \times 2 = 24$ possible combinations. Not all combinations are appropriate here. We found six applications. The next step is to exclude all combinations with no apparent applicability in this particular field. You thus obtain the combination shown in Figure 24.6.

BEHAVIOURAL SEGMENTATION

The procedure for behavioural and technical segmentation is similar. You make a list of your possible clients, then you use your intuition to narrow this down to clients who seem to have similar attitudes to or interest in the innovation. This all depends on your perception of them. Their attitude may have been positive or negative. They may have

	C1	C2	C3	C4
Price	★			★
Lead time	★	★	★	
Training		★	★	
Image		★		★

Figure 24.7 Chart of key commercial success/behaviour factors

shown various degrees of enthusiasm. Perhaps they seemed more worried about the technology than commercial aspects. It could have been the head of research who talked to you, or the marketing manager, the person in charge of environmental affairs, the head of the purchasing department, etc. Each particular case gives a different impression that you will try to express in some sort of manageable form, by grouping together customers with comparable attitudes.

Next, you use four logical tests to give a rational basis to your intuitive classifications. The first and simplest consists of giving a name to the groups of clients. You should give as a name the common attitude adopted by all the clients to your offer. If you are unable to find this common denominator, it means that the group of clients is likely to be heterogeneous from a behavioural point of view and you should reconsider.

The second check tests the coherence of your grouping in relation to key commercial success factors. You then build a key commercial success factor/behaviour chart (Figure 24.7). This chart contains two behaviourally different customer groups that each suggest different success factors.

The third test checks the coherence of your list with regard to competition. With a competitor/behaviour chart, you should be able to show that two customer groups working with different suppliers have different behaviour (Figure 24.8). This supports the previous test, since customers presumably choose the suppliers who deliver the success factors they seek.

The fourth test checks the accuracy of your behavioural segmentation. It consists of discovering and combining behavioural segmentation criteria that make it possible to

	C1	C2	C3	C4
HP	★			★
IBM	★	★	★	
DEC		★	★	
Apple		★		★

Figure 24.8 Competitor/behaviour chart

Data acquisition	Offline	Laboratory
Increased productivity	Online	Production unit
	Offline	Servicing
Buying motivation	*Problem location*	*Behaviour*

Figure 24.9 Behavioural segmentation of non-destructive laser control market

explain behaviour differences between one group of customers and another. The process for eliciting descriptors for behavioural segmentation is similar to that used for technical segmentation. First, describe the behaviour characteristics of each customer group and possible causes. Then single out and retain only the criteria that best explain differences or similarities between the types of behaviour. Combining either behavioural or technical segmentation criteria requires exactly the same approach. You compile a list of descriptors of behaviour variables, but you only retain combinations that correspond with your perception of the attitudes you have observed.

In the non-destructive ultrasonic laser project, we identified three groups of customers with quite different attitudes:

1. 'Research Laboratory' behaviour – composed of scientists who were committed to increasing their knowledge and eager to acquire sophisticated high-performance equipment, however expensive and complex.

2. 'Production Unit' behaviour – the customers here were a purchasing department. They compared the new product with current products from the point of view of cost and reliability in an industrial environment.

3. 'Maintenance' behaviour – the customers were maintenance specialists who were going to choose products that simplified their job and made it less demanding, even if it cost a little more than conventional equipment.

You can explain these three types of behaviour by the following criteria:

- equipment-related motives – gain data via the measurements and increase productivity
- problem location – online or offline testing.

If you single out relevant combinations only, the results will be as shown in Figure 24.9.

SEGMENTATION CHART

The segmentation chart is obtained by intersecting technical and behavioural segmentation. You will find market segments wherever the intersections between

Analysed material		Metal				Composites	
System configuration		Portable	Stationary			Stationary	
Measurement input mode		Static	Static	Relative motion	Scanning	Scanning	
Task required		Detection	Detection	Detection	Detection	Detection	Description
Applications		Outdoor defect detection	Defect detection in hostile environment	Defect detection in parts when in continuous motion	Defect detection in very large metal structures	Defect detection in composite material	Defect description in composite material
Data acquisition — Offline	Laboratory			S1		S6	S2	S8
Increased productivity — Online	Manufacturing unit			S4		S7	
Increased productivity — Offline	Servicing	S5	S3	S10			S9

Buying   Problem location   Behaviour

Figure 24.10 Segmentation chart of non-destructive laser control market

columns and rows have been identified. We can illustrate this with a further example from the ultrasonic laser project (Figure 24.10). Once the chart has been constructed, you can then name the segments. To do this, you need a list of the characteristics of the clients in each segment. Then label each segment consistent with the characteristics these clients have in common.

In this particular case, segments can be defined as follows:

S1: Control department for irradiated equipment.
S2: Research laboratory for composites in cars.
S3: Maintenance in the nuclear energy sector.
S4: Control of long-length, continuous process products.
S5: High-pressure pipeline control by field teams.
S6: Measurement laboratory for nuclear energy sector and ship industry.
S7: Control of composite-part production.
S8: Aeronautic research laboratory.
S9: Modern fighter-plane maintenance.
S10: Continuous safety control on long-length installations.

Naming the segments helps in characterising the market as a basis for identifying similar potential clients and possibly going on to estimate segment size and potential.

The list below is an indication of the kind of descriptive criteria you can use:

- the size of the client
- what the company does
- the industrial sector it is in
- where it is located

- its production methods
- the department concerned (e.g. R&D, production)
- where the company is in the value chain
- its legal status.

In the case described below, for instance, you will note that customer nationality did not exert much influence on segmentation. There were English, French and German customers in the same segment.

Sifting through all this descriptive data makes you aware of one fundamental issue – you cannot quantify these markets until you have defined them. It is only through a qualitative definition of market segments that you can assess total volumes or income for each one, and quantify the market.

USING THE SEGMENTATION CHART

When you have built the segmentation chart, you will be able to

- define the offer to fit each segment; the offer is partly technical, partly non-technical
- establish the sales strategy and determine targets and sales arguments
- determine the range of products that best fits all market segments.

Establishing the technical content of the offer

Your initial step here is to specify what your product does by drawing up a specification or list of functions to suit the requirements of a particular target segment. For example, the application for segments 1 and 3 of Figure 24.10 is defect detection in hostile environments. This application has already been clearly defined by technical segmentation criteria. Now these will provide the broad guidelines for product definition. Therefore in S1 and S3 your offer needs to be a permanent fixture that can detect defects in irradiated, stationary metal parts.

As you will discover in more detail in the next chapter, developing a functions/applications chart provides a good tool for drawing up product specifications. This chart is obtained by adding together all the use functions and functional constraints required to meet your client's technical needs. Similarly, the technology/applications chart will provide you with all the elements necessary to design a really competitive product.

Establishing the non-technical element of the offer

You should set about establishing the non-technical part of the offer, e.g. price, service, lead-times, and your sales tactics by using customer behaviour data. Things such as price, service and lead-times are determined on the strength of information gleaned from Figure

24.7. For example, in S1, S2, S6, S8, customers will pay a high price for the product if accompanied by good technical service to assist with implementation and knowledge transfer on ultrasonic lasers. Your analysis is then cross-checked and confirmed against the competitor/behaviour chart. You can fine tune your offer and develop a more than competitive product in this way.

Developing sales approaches

Your sales approach should consist of targeting one or more people within the customer company and then developing specific arguments appropriate to each. Behavioural segmentation is helpful here, too, as customers' behaviour is determined by the risks they perceive as well as their personal motivation. It is not difficult to devise arguments for each target and then elaborate them. You must consolidate your position by emphasising everything that supports the customer's motives and reduces their perceived risk. To sum up, specific, multidimensional definition of the segments helps you to plan sales action as shown in Figure 24.11.

Co-ordinating your range of products

The work done so far will help you plan your sales approach to a given market segment. When you have reviewed all accessible market segments, you will be able to co-ordinate the range of products you are going to offer. Segmentation centres on a core product or technology, and your range of products will stem from this. Each product in the range is

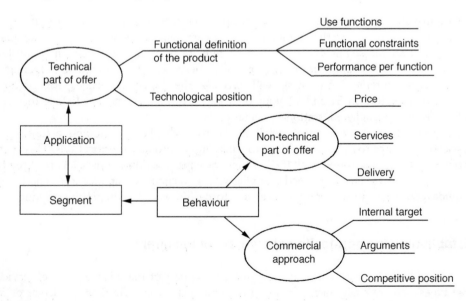

Figure 24.11 Utilising the segmentation

made to specifications by fitting core products to customer needs and removing or masking superfluous functions.

We could develop the following range of products based on ultrasonic laser technology:

- a detector of flaw characteristics: complex, sophisticated, hard to regulate, but sensitive and highly efficient in controlling composite material
- a detector of defects in parts as they move past online in harsh industrial environments (e.g. dust, heat, vibrations)
- an onboard, travelling railway line defect detector
- a self-powered, field backpack detector for defects in high-pressure pipelines
- a detector of flaw characteristics for very large, thick, metal structures.

UPDATING SEGMENTATION

Segmentation has a limited lifetime. It is only a snapshot of your situation in the market-place. The environment is constantly changing due to your actions and those of your competitors. Consequently, you need to update your segmentation so that you lead rather than follow the market. Basically, what you must do is re-segment the market as soon as there is any significant change in the market-place or in your environment.

KEY POINTS

- *This consists of defining products to match client's requirements in a competitive environment.*
- *Product definition is built on the basis of segmentation and the definition of features required to solve the client's problem.*
- *This analysis helps to define the product specification.*
- *The final step involves a comparison with competing technologies and solutions.*

PURPOSE OF TECHNICAL ANALYSIS

As previously stated, technical issues are of primary importance in industrial marketing. If you want to relate to the technicians and be able to interact with them, or even more than that, to be trusted by them, then you must be able to mix a healthy dose of technical understanding and analysis into your job of marketing.

The analysis of technical issues that we shall discuss here is strongly relevant to the issue of segmentation, since the starting point for this technical analysis is the *application*. In other words, we start from the perspective of the client. This of course is a true market-led approach.

The first purpose is to supply the client with a product offering that matches their requirements. Secondly, we aim to design a technologically differentiated offer, which means that our offering is more highly perceived by our clients than the technologies or products of the competition. Therefore a framework for a technical analysis could be considered in the way shown in Figure 25.1 (Millier 1993).

The technical analysis can be carried out and in a series of steps by defining:

- The product's application(s). The applications are the technical problems that the clients wish to solve. This is derived from segmentation (see Chapter 24).

- The functional needs; the functions that the client requires to solve their problem.

- The analytical requirements; the components that are necessary to be brought together to provide a function.

- The technical competitive positioning.

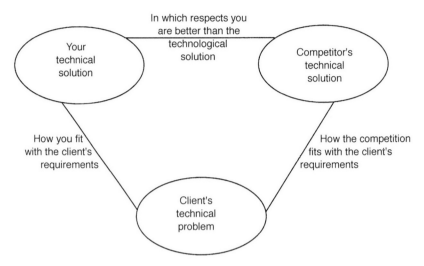

Figure 25.1 Framework for a technical analysis

APPLICATION(S)

Providing the segmentation has been conducted previously, defining the product's application(s) simply involves taking the applications from the segmentation matrix. They are the columns of the matrix.

THE FUNCTIONAL LIST OF REQUIREMENTS

'My product is made for' – ask yourself this and you will go a long way towards determining the function of the product. The easiest way to draw up the list of requirements is to build a function/application matrix as shown in Figure 25.2. The applications are taken from those that you have previously determined for segmentation. The functions are defined as 'what provides the client with a solution' or 'what the clients rely on to solve a technical problem'. In other words, what the product is made for. We can distinguish between several types of functions (Figure 25.3). The 'constrained' functions are compulsory. The product must have these or clients will simply not consider your product. For example, you would not buy a family car which had room for the driver only, yet you do not explicitly ask the car dealer for a car that has seats for all the family; this is something that you take for granted. This is a constrained function; it is a reason for rejecting the product rather than a reason for buying it. The 'service' functions are the real solutions that the client actually requires of your product.

'Esteem' functions are related to the client's behaviour; why they buy rather than what they buy. For instance, when you buy a watch it is to tell you the time. This is the problem to be solved. But why do some people spend more than £1000 or even £10,000 on a watch? Certainly not because they tell the time better, but because it is a statement of wealth or status. We shall expand mainly 'use' functions in this chapter because they

Applications / Functions	Cliff reinforcement	Reinforcement of poured concrete	Reinforcement of heated runway	Reinforcement of sprayed concrete
Improves tensile strength	*	*	*	*
Improves rust proofing	*			*
Improves heat conduction			*	
Ability to be sucked into a venturi	*			*

Figure 25.2 Completing a functional/application matrix

are more common in industry than in FMCG. But you should not entirely dismiss the esteem function in industry. Why do you think people buy highly sophisticated oscilloscopes when they use perhaps 10 per cent of their functions? Because they want to impress their clients (or competitors) when they visit their premises.

The use functions refer to the utilitarian aspect of the product, to its 'reason for being'. For instance, clients buying an ultrasonic detector using pulse laser will in fact buy the ability to

- detect internal flaws
- detect irregularities in moving parts
- detect faults in very hot components.

To differentiate between a constrained function and a use function, let us come back to the previous example. The main thing that the client requires of a non-destructive control device is 'detecting flaws inside parts without needing to cut them into pieces'. But if you work on composite material, your process must not hydrolyse the material when detecting flaws, which is the main problem with traditional ways of detecting flaws by

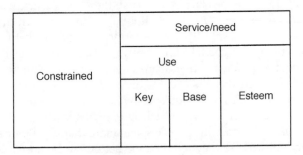

Figure 25.3 Several types of functions

Applications / Functions	Outdoor defect detection	Defect detection in hostile environment	Defect detection in parts when in continuous motion	Defect detection in large metal structures	Defect detection in composite material	Defect description in composite material
Long-distance measures		Key		Key		
Instant measures			Key		Key	
Measures on very large parts				Key		Key
Deep penetration of material	Base	Base	Base	Base	Base	Base
No damage to material surface					Key	Key
Portable	Con-strained					

Figure 25.4 Completing the function/application matrix

dipping the parts into water. 'Not hydrolysing the material' is a constrained function (a defect that should be avoided) whilst 'detecting the flaws' is a use function that the clients actually buy for solving their problem.

To conclude on the issue of use functions we can distinguish between the 'key' functions that really make the difference for the client, for instance a unique or very important function and the 'base' function that the client will find in a range of products. From here you can build up a function/application matrix (Figure 25.4) which will give you an indication of the performance level required in every function.

When drawing up the list of required functions do not forget that upstream or downstream of your client other supply chain participants may have some compulsory requirements. For instance, if you sell a nuclear vat you must consider that it must be carried on a lorry, it must be an appropriate size so that it can be sensibly handled. If you sell plastic dashboards for cars then consider that the plastic must be capable of being recycled at some future stage.

DETERMINING THE ANALYTICAL LIST OF REQUIREMENTS

Using the function list previously discussed you can now develop another matrix in which you cross the functions with the components required to provide the product with those functions (Figure 25.5). This matrix is called the value analysis matrix. It enables you to obtain a good idea of the cost of the product if, for example, you need functions 1 and 4. By adding up the components required to provide this application you can

Functions / Components	Long-distance measures	Instant measures	Measures on very large parts	Penetrate the matter deeply	No damage to material surface	Portability
Input laser	★	★	★	★	Laser diode	Pocket-sized
Output laser	★	★	★	★	Laser diode	Pocket-sized
Optical guide	★	★	★			Pocket-sized
Interferometer	★	★	★			Pocket-sized
Software	Quick fix	Quick fix	Quick fix			★
Computer	★	★	★			Pocket-sized
Sweeping device	★		★			

Figure 25.5 Value analysis matrix

determine your analytical list of requirements. In this case to provide functions 1 and 4 we need components 2, 4, 5 and 6.

DETERMINING YOUR COMPETITIVE POSITION

The last step of the technical analysis is to determine your position compared to alternative technologies or products. For every application in order to do this build up a so-called technology application matrix in which you indicate the competing technologies for every application (Figure 25.6).

You can indicate which technology is best adapted to the problem by applying a series of ratings – the more asterisks the better. For instance, two asterisks means 'the best technology for the application' and one asterisk means 'this technology is in place but we can compete against'. This will enable you to make a judgement about how effectively you can compete against these technologies. To complete the matrix, in each relevant box give an indication of the performance level reached by the competing technologies for the different functions required.

One last tip to check if your product is properly designed

If you really want to know how good (or bad) your product is from the client viewpoint, buy the product your client makes in which your product is, or could be, incorporated or used and test it to see how it works. You may now understand why your clients are resistant to change or prefer to buy your competitor's product.

Applications / Competing technologies	Outdoor defect detection	Defect detection in hostile environment	Defect detection in parts when in continuous motion	Defect detection in large metal structures	Defect detection in composite material	Defect detection in composite material
Adhered EMA probe		★		★		
EMA probe in water pool		★			★	
Rubbing metal shoes			★★	★		
Gamma rays	★	★		★★	★	★
X-rays					★	★
Penetrant testing	★★					

Figure 25.6 Filling up the technology/application matrix

Marketing analysis   **26**

KEY POINTS

- *Marketing analysis is the means by which we describe and therefore understand the structure of the market.*
- *The market can be thought of as a chain of inter-linked buyers and suppliers.*
- *The process starts by identifying the players in the market and then describing the relationship and influences between them.*
- *By drawing a market map it is possible to identify the way that product flows through various routes to reach the end user.*
- *The final step is to identify where and how competitors participate in the market.*

MARKET STRUCTURE ANALYSIS

Market analysis supports segmentation from a marketing as opposed to a technical viewpoint. Marketing analysis consists of an examination of

- market structure
- clients and their behaviour
- competition.

As mentioned several times in this book, we can think about an industrial market in the sense of a chain. Your clients have their own clients and so on until we reach the consumer or end user. Indeed if the product is recycled we can identify further members of the chain (Figure 26.1).

But of course it is not quite as simple as that. There are those who can influence the volume and value of the product that passes through this chain. Therefore one of the main purposes of our market structure analysis is to identify

- influences that support or increase product sales
- influences that reduce product sales
- the 10 per cent of the participants who influence the 90 per cent of others

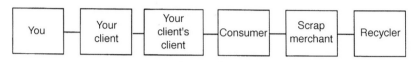

Figure 26.1 Defining the industrial chain

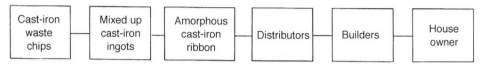

Figure 26.2 The amorphous cast-iron industrial chain

- which part of the chain we should influence
- the channels through which our products should flow.

Start this process by drawing a simple chain of how your product reaches the end user. Let us take the example of cast-iron waste illustrated in Figure 26.2. Taking into account your current business, the participants in the chain, your skills and abilities, product quality and routes to market, you can decide at which level in the chain you should apply your efforts. Would it be most appropriate for you to sell for example,

- cast-iron waste, chips and pellets
- cast-iron ingots containing waste chips and additional components
- amorphous cast-iron ribbon.

From this point you can now draw up a more comprehensive picture of your market and

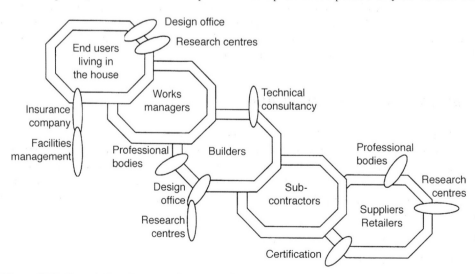

Figure 26.3 Completing the amorphous cast-iron industrial chain

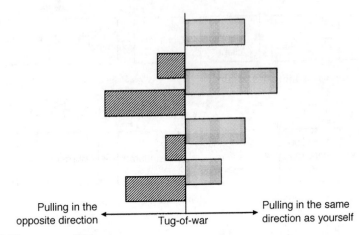

Pulling in the
opposite direction   Tug-of-war   Pulling in the same
                                                direction as yourself

Figure 26.4 The pros and the cons

add in the influencers who, whilst not directly participating in the market, will none the less affect the attitudes and propensity to purchase of those in the market (Figure 26.3). This will give you a good indication of those influencers who will add or reduce the value of your product. By colour coding them on the chart you can quickly identify the important players. The degree of influence could, for example, be indicated by the thickness of the line connecting the influencer with the influenced. Visual indications like this, sometimes called market maps, are extremely helpful in explaining how our market operates.

You can complete Figure 26.3 by a 'Tug-of-war' chart in which you show who is pulling in the same direction as yourself and who is pulling in the opposite direction (Figure 26.4).

The industrial chain can give you an excellent understanding of how products flow through markets. McDonald and Dunbar (1998) give a good example of how to use the industrial chain for this purpose. The example is one of fertiliser in the UK. Figure 26.5 shows the quantity of product flowing through the market channels and gives the market share of the product at every level in the chain.

CLIENTS AND THEIR BEHAVIOUR

Clients are influenced in their behaviour by two types of contrasting influences, perceived risk and motivation. Of course we should appreciate that companies as such are not motivated, but it is the individuals within the company on whom we should focus our attention. The way that we describe this when trying to analyse clients is in terms of the decision-making unit (DMU). For instance, if we are trying to sell complex machine tools members of the DMU could be:

- The Head of Operations Management
- Production Manager
- Purchasing Manager

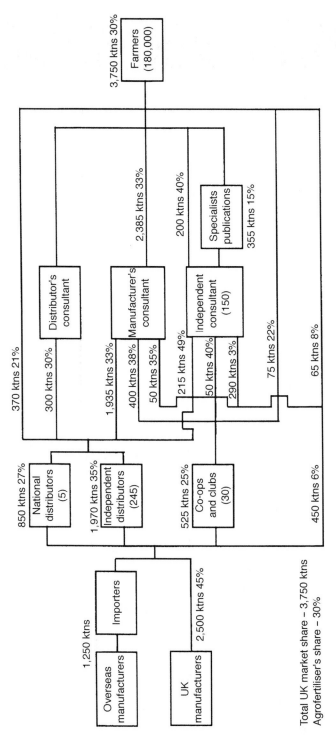

Figure 26.5 Quantifying the product flows along the industrial chain (Macdonald and Dunbar 1998 with permission from Macmillan Press Ltd)

Total UK market share – 3,750 ktns
Agrofertiliser's share – 30%

Risk or motivations	Level of actual risk	Level of perceived risk	Client's DMU		Likely client's behaviour	Your possible action
			Name	Job		
Risks						
Technical risk	Low	Low	Sharpe	Purchaser		
Risk related to the product use	Low	Medium	Scott	Maintenance		
Financial risk	Medium	High	Johns	Financial Director		
Motivations						
Differentiation	High	High	Asbery	Marketing Manager		
Environmental	High	High	Lee	'Mr Green'		

Figure 26.6 Client's behaviour analysis (adapted from Salle and Silvestre 1992)

- Finance Director
- The user.

If we can understand the issues of risk and motivation relating to each DMU member this can be helpful to us in understanding how we can sell a product. We can analyse this by drawing up a chart as demonstrated by Figure 26.6. The risks and motivations can then be listed as shown in Figure 26.7.

Risks	Motivations
• Technical	• Technical
• Product availability	• Industrial
• Ability to use the product	• Commercial
• Financial	• Competitive
• Dependency on supplier	• Strategic
• Supplier's commitment	• Social
	• Financial
	• Environmental
	• Regulation
	• Personal
	• Fashion

Figure 26.7 Risk and motivations

	Technical position		
	Material expert	Equipment specialist	Generalist
Real commercial strategy — Short delay price list	Specialised university laboratories		Overseas competitors trading worldwide
No real commercial strategy — Long delay			Small service companies
No real commercial strategy — Short delay	Large companies internal material laboratories	University laboratories	

(Commercial strategy shown along the left axis)

Figure 26.8 Segmenting the material measure supply market (from Millier 1999)

COMPETITOR ANALYSIS

You, together with your competitors, form a group that can be segmented exactly as in any other market. To be consistent with the segmentation process that we discussed in

		Technical position			
		Security kits		Built-in security	
		Hardware and software	Software only	For PC	For networks
Top quality	Direct sales			Big PC manufacturers	Network manufacturers
Top range	Distribution	Large electronic companies	Big brand software companies		
Low price	Sales				
Bottom Range	Distribution	Electronic stores	Small software companies	Clone manufacturers	

(Commercial strategy shown along the left axis)

Figure 26.9 Segmenting the computer security supply market

Chapter 24 we suggest that you use a two-dimensional matrix. In this matrix the columns are the different technologies used by your competitors and the rows the different strategies that your competitors adopt (see Figure 26.8). This supply-side segmentation could for instance be applied by a company selling computer security solutions, as illustrated in Figure 26.9.

This first matrix can give a good overview of the types of companies you are competing against and indicate your areas of market strength and weakness. Nevertheless this matrix is sometimes not enough, you may need to develop a more precise understanding of your position in each segment. If you need to do this then you can build up a final matrix (Figure 26.10) in which you cross-reference the segments and the groups of competitors. Let us come back to the previous example.

A methodical analysis of the market, customers and competitors will improve your understanding of the market as well as build your confidence in your own ability to conduct this work and take the subsequent strategy decisions. The analysis will also highlight further areas to explore and analyse. By regularly recording your analysis you will build an increasingly refined volume of information to serve as the basis of your marketing strategy. You are well on the way to becoming an expert as well as *the* expert in your company.

	Market segments			
	SMEs	Big companies	Banks	Army
Big PC manufacturers			★★	★
Network manufacturers			★★	★★
Large electronic companies		★★		
Electronic stores	★			
Big brand software companies		★★		★
Small software companies	★★			
Clone manufacturers	★			

(Competitors)

Figure 26.10 Combining the segmentations of both demand and supply markets

Diagnosing the marketing situation   **27**

KEY POINTS

- *The diagnosis is a means of assessing your current marketing position.*
- *Matrix tools commonly used for this purpose include the SWOT analysis and directional policy matrix.*
- *Through the analytical process the aim is to determine the optimum strategy based on a full understanding of the external, internal and competitive environment.*
- *A new product launch or other specific set of circumstances may require a more detailed analysis.*

BUILDING ON SEGMENTATION

After segmenting your market, you will then need to gain a relative understanding of the prospects in each segment, a diagnosis of the situation as you see it. There are several marketing tools that can be used for this diagnosis. In principle they take the form of a matrix, which can be developed in various ways to help you to understand strengths, weaknesses, opportunities, constraints, risk, etc.

We shall start by discussing the ubiquitous SWOT (strengths, weaknesses, opportunities, threats) matrix, and then develop this, building on the principle of the direction of policy matrix (DPM). This is essentially a sophistication of the SWOT matrix developed by Prof. Heinz Weih and originally used to link the external threats and opportunities to the company's strengths and weaknesses systematically to find out strategic opportunities (Cranfield Marketing Group 2000). We shall conclude with an explanation of how this type of diagnosis can be used when introducing, for example, a new technology. This represents one of the highest levels of uncertainty.

SWOT ANALYSIS

The SWOT matrix is a good basis to build an understanding of the principles of many diagnostic tools. It provides a chart in which you can locate your market segments as a way

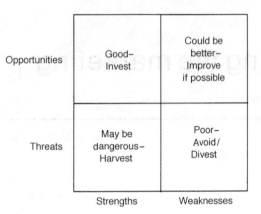

	Strengths	Weaknesses
Opportunities	Good– Invest	Could be better– Improve if possible
Threats	May be dangerous– Harvest	Poor– Avoid/ Divest

Figure 27.1 The SWOT analysis

of summarising and distilling your judgement. The X axis measures strengths and weaknesses, the Y axis opportunities and threats. From the example shown in Figure 27.1 we can conclude that we should concentrate our efforts in the top left-hand corner, work hard to improve prospects for segments in the top right-hand corner, either exit or avoid the bottom right-hand corner and perhaps consider a graceful exit from the bottom left-hand corner. The SWOT analysis can be made more substantial by the use of a list of criteria following the principles outlined in the next section discussing the directional policy matrix (DPM).

THE DIRECTIONAL POLICY MATRIX

The directional policy matrix (DPM) was a further development of the matrix tool technique. McKinsey, an international firm of management consultants, in conjunction with General Electric in the USA and Shell in Europe developed it (Cranfield Marketing Group 2000). It was originally introduced as a 3×3 matrix rather than the more conventional 2×2. It is now used in either format. However, this is not an essential difference, the major difference being in the way that the axes are constructed.

The DPM widens the scope of the axes and considers market attractiveness and business strengths. Each of these can incorporate a wide range of factors that may be important or specific to the circumstances. A range of factors can be included under each broad heading, for example:

Market attractiveness	Business strengths
Growth rate	Market share
New channels developing	Flexible production capacity
Premium pricing opportunity	Trained salesforce
Export opportunities	Technical service network
Weak competitors	Established distribution system
Increasing quality requirements	R&D skills
etc.	etc.

Once the list of criteria are decided they are then weighted in terms of importance and ranked in comparative terms against competitors or other products, for example. It is important to define the unit of analysis carefully before embarking on this exercise. This process can be demonstrated by selecting a few examples from the list of 'Business strengths' factors.

	Weight %	Ourselves Score (× weight)	Competitor A Score (× weight)
Market share	35	6 × 0.35 = 2.10	4 × 0.35 = 1.40
Flexible production capacity	25	8 × 0.25 = 2.00	7 × 0.25 = 1.75
Trained salesforce	25	4 × 0.25 = 1.00	8 × 0.25 = 2.00
Technical service network	15	9 × 0.15 = 1.35	3 × 0.15 = 0.45
Overall score		**6.45**	**5.60**

Criteria: A list of factors considered critical relative to the market and unit of analysis.

Weight: Based on allocation of 100 percentage points.

Score: An assessment on a 1–10 scale of performance against the criteria.

Overall score: Weight multiplied by score for each criteria, added to give the overall score on a 1–10 scale for the axis. This is then plotted on the matrix.

This principle of scoring, as demonstrated by the DPM, provides the scales that can be applied to the vertical and horizontal axes as demonstrated by the SWOT tool.

DIAGNOSIS FOR A NEW PRODUCT LAUNCH

Diagnosis is the operation whereby you judge your own situation in relation to each market segment. Diagnosis is used to measure risk. It guides you in your choice of segments and in building up your strategy. This requires a host of assessment criteria to help you estimate the risk entailed by your company on each particular segment. There are two distinct parts to it: technical diagnosis (technical risk assessment) and commercial diagnosis (or commercial assessment). Thereafter you can rank market segments in order of interest, and choose the targets on which to focus (Millier 1999).

Technical diagnosis

Technical diagnosis consists in evaluating two different dimensions of risk – technology-related risk and risks related to the technological environment. When you want to evaluate technology-related risks, you use the following criteria:

- the technology's performance levels in relation to the application
- the technology's enhancement potential
- the technology's image

- the company's proficiency levels when using technology
- coherence between project and company's technological strategy.

To evaluate risks related to the technological environment consider

- supplier's capacity to keep up with your growth
- risk of take-over
- enhancement potential of competing technologies
- general demand for this technology
- customer implementation.

Each of these criteria is assessed from 0 to 4 (or from − − to + +), by giving low marks to criteria that slow down product diffusion, and high marks to criteria that promote it. You use the same method and scale to evaluate risk and uncertainty variables affecting the criteria. For instance, you are in an uncertain situation if you do not know yet what performance the customer wants. Give a low mark to the performance criteria to avoid overestimating your position.

Once you have marked all the criteria, you calculate the average then transfer the risk score to a diagram called a technical risk chart. However, you need to be careful here as some criteria have more significance than others. These are called veto or hygiene criteria because they stop you penetrating a segment if their score is low, whatever the marks are for the other criteria. For example, very poor product performance is enough to cause failure. There is no point even in calculating the average because you know that maximum technology-related risk is involved (equal, therefore, to 1), whatever marks have been attributed to the other criteria. When you have assessed both dimensions of technical risk, you are in a position to plot your overall technical risk as shown in Figure 27.2.

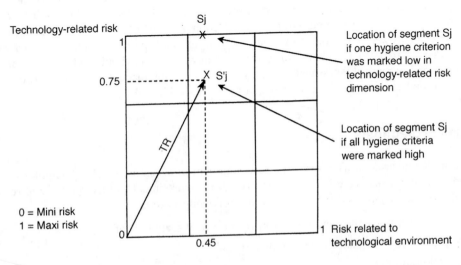

Figure 27.2 Technical risk chart

Commercial diagnosis

Commercial diagnosis consists in assessing two dimensions of the risk involved:

- Company advantages and shortcomings.
- Market appeal and constraints.

The following criteria are used to evaluate commercial risk using the dimension of company advantages and shortcomings:

- experience and adaptability of the sales function
- company adaptability
- capital
- degree of synergy
- business activities integrated downstream
- service
- company image
- consistent quality.

Using the dimension of market appeal and constraints the following criteria are used in evaluating commercial risk:

- market dynamics
- growth rate
- politico-economic risk
- intensity of competition
- customers seeking leading-edge technology
- price levels and returns on investment
- size and volume of market
- coherence between your strategy and the target market.

You assess commercial risk in the same way as technical risk, bearing in mind that veto or hygiene criteria exist here, too, and obtain the commercial risk chart shown in Figure 27.3.

PRESENTING THE RESULTS OF YOUR DIAGNOSIS

After assessing technical and commercial risk, next develop a strategic index chart. Your commercial risk index corresponds to the horizontal axis, your technical risk index to the vertical axis. Each segment is positioned accordingly on the chart, so you achieve an initial ranking for your segments. This operation is the basis for diagnosis (Figure 27.4). There are recommendations to follow about how to use the results.

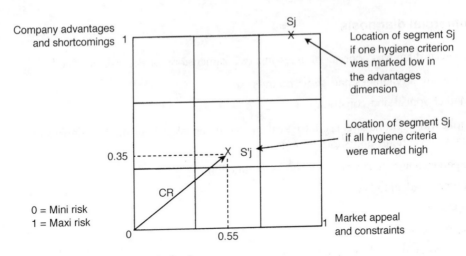

Figure 27.3 Commercial risk chart

USING THE DIAGNOSIS

Diagnosis gives you an initial idea of how to go about planning development, because it justifies the order in which you address the segments. Your first approach should be to develop the segments in the zone of least risk according to the strategic index (near the origin). Most of the time well-placed segments are soon dealt with. On the other hand, it is not unusual to meet groups of market segments with a similar structure to the example of non-destructive ultrasonic laser shown in Figure 27.5. On this strategy diagram you can see there are two small segments that are easily accessible in the short run without risk. On the other hand, segments with high stakes are very risky at the moment, that is to say currently inaccessible. It would be suicidal to launch into one of these high-risk segments today without trying to improve your situation first.

If you identify the criteria responsible for such high technical or commercial risk this will give you guidance on what action to take and what strings to pull. Very often, just one veto or hygiene criterion with a bad score is enough to explain an apparently

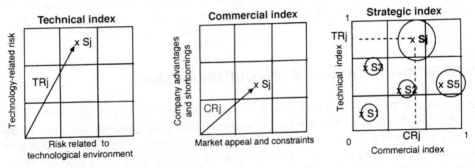

Figure 27.4 Schematic summary of diagnosis

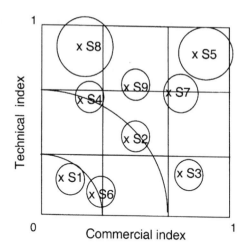

Figure 27.5 Diagnosis of the non-destructive laser control market

disastrous situation. Once these criteria have been identified, you need to ensure that it is economically and technically possible to reduce the risk entailed.

For example, with segment 4, they still could not manage to carry out non-destructive control on parts in a fast-travelling linear movement, but they did know what type of research to undertake for that purpose and they were practically sure they would soon master the problem. So they did a simulation to map the positive impact of removing the veto, and found S4 right in the middle of the most favourable zone for launching. This operation on product performance was momentous in itself as regards S4, because in fact the only reason for S4's bad position was the product's inadequate performance (Figure 27.6).

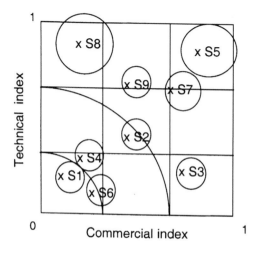

Figure 27.6 Evolution of the non-destructive laser control market

Your strategy now is to review all the criteria that constrain your segments by assessing lead-times in cost or risk reduction for each case. Then you can start to develop a general plan of action in line with your resources, priorities and collaborative potential (see Chapter 6). That is, you decide in what order you are going to penetrate segments and what obstacles need to be removed (i.e. what risks you must reduce on hygiene criteria) in order to do so.

Marketing planning templates **28**

In this chapter you will find some pro-forma tools that you can use as a basis for developing your own marketing planning documents. Adapt and amend these to meet your particular requirements and experiment with ideas of your own. You will find

- an overview of the ten-step marketing planning process
- the table of contents of a typical marketing plan document
- different tables summarising the main supporting data for your plan.

THE TEN-STEP MARKETING PLANNING PROCESS (FIGURE 28.1)

- This is a comprehensive overview of the planning process successfully used in many companies.
- Remember that this is not a linear process, there will be a need to iterate the steps before finally arriving at a conclusion.

MARKETING GOALS

1. To increase the turnover in 200_. to £_____ and in the next years realise an annual increase of at least _____%.
2. To further develop the brand recognition in the target area.
3. Increase the turnover in 200_ by _____% in relation to 200_.
4. Realise a market share of _____% in the next __ years.
5. To realise a prominent presence on the Internet and the World Wide Web.

- Marketing goals/objectives should be clearly stated in order that they can be measured.
- Use timescales and quantify wherever possible.

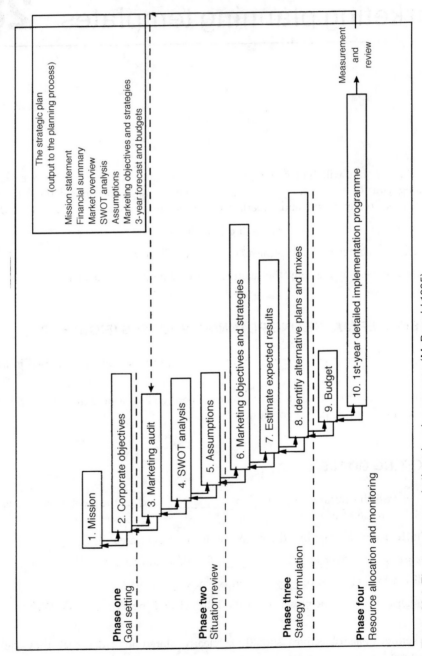

Figure 28.1 The ten-step marketing planning process (McDonald 1995)

- Consider breaking objectives down and assigning personal responsibility and accountability.

MARKETING PLAN, 200_ – HEADINGS

page

- executive summary
- the target markets
- marketing goals
- sales goals
- marketing strategies
- the pricing policy
- the distribution management
- the competition
- the suppliers
- the marketing personnel
- the human resource development programme
- the market research programme
- advertising and sales promotion
- sales projections
- the marketing budget
- the marketing timetable
- evaluation and progress monitor
- Adapt this as required for your own purposes.
- The best marketing plans tend to be the shorter ones, either summarise background information or keep it separate for reference purposes.

PLAN SUMMARY SHEET

- A simple planning sheet (Figure 28.2) serves as an overview summary of objectives/ strategy/and tactics.
- Use a sheet such as this as a shorthand reference. A one page summary can be easily kept in the briefcase for ease of reference, or photocopied as a handout or OHP slide, or presented on a laptop/desktop.

Market segment:-		Planning year:-			Last updated:-		
Objective	Strategy	Product	Price	Prom.	Place	Timing	Action
Quantified/ qualified commitments within a timescale	Activities to achieve objectives	Detailed elements of the marketing mix selected to fulfil the strategy				To be completed by	Named person or team
Example							
Increase market share by 5% in the next 12 months	Employ extra sales staff				Place recruit-ment advert	By end Month 1	HR dept
	Launch new product	Final field tests				By end Qtr. 1	R&D Manager
			5% premium over current product				
				New service fee schedule		By end Qtr. 1	Product Manager
					Brief distri-bution staff	Pre-launch	Sales Manager
				Prepare literature		By end Qtr. 2	Product Manager
				Organise trade show stand		By end June	Marketing Services Manager

Figure 28.2 Plan summary sheet

PLAN OVERVIEW (FIGURE 28.3)

- Inevitably a series of quantified measures will be required.

- Prepare a comprehensive summary sheet containing a series of financial and marketing metrics that link to objectives.

Plan overview	This year	200__	200_	200_
General information				
Number of employees				
Number marketing employees				
Number of sales staff				
Market size (currency)				
Market size (volume)				
Market growth in %				
Market share in %				
Number of customers				
Number of competitors				
Number of existing products				
Number of new products				
Number of eliminated products				
Financial data				
Sales total in volume				
Turnover total in £				
Sales volume product line 1				
Turnover in £ product line 1				
Sales volume product line 2				
Turnover in £ product line 2				
Sales volume product line 3				
Turnover in £ product line 3				
Sales volume product line 4				
Turnover in £ product line 4				
Total gross profit				
Total net profit				

Figure 28.3 The marketing plan overview

Marketing expenditures	First quarter		Second quarter		Third quarter		Fourth quarter	
	%	£	%	£	%	£	%	£
Advertising								
Newspaper								
Magazine								
Trade publications								
Radio/television								
Direct mail								
Point of sale								
Other								
Sales promotion								
Trade promotions								
Trade shows								
Other								
Administration								
Office								
Managers								
Secretarial								
Telephone								
Travel								
Necessities								
HR development								
Video/Audio								
In-house								
Seminars								
Other								
Sales staff								
Motivation programme								
Recruitment								
Salaries/bonuses								
Telephone								
Training programme								
Travel								
Other								
Market research								
Computer time								
Salaries/bonuses								
Necessities								
Travel								
TOTAL								

Figure 28.4 The marketing budget

- Develop and use tools such as these as a way of managing, monitoring and controlling marketing activity.
- Such tools when consistently applied are also valuable as a means of communication.

THE MARKETING BUDGET (FIGURE 28.4)

- Marketing is often regarded as a cost rather than an investment.
- Be prepared to be accountable and subject to scrutiny.
- Manage within the budget limits agreed and check again before committing to large expenditures.
- Budget phasing can be as important as overall levels. Take care to phase your spending and ensure that this is communicated.

GOALS FOR THE PLANNED DISTRIBUTION CHANNELS (FIGURE 28.5)

- Remember that the overall level of sales is composed of sales through each channel or route to market.
- The management of channels and distribution can be poor in industrial markets.

Distribution channel	Existing channels sales in £	Average sales p/month	New channels sales in £	Average sales p/month
Own internal sales staff				
Own external sales staff				
Sales by commission				
Own stores				
Independent stores				
Own distributors				
Independent distributors				
Other channels				

Figure 28.5 The distribution goals

NUMBER OF EMPLOYEES IN MARKETING (FIGURE 28.6)

- Marketing staff can represent a significant part of the overall budget.
- Sales staff productivity is a key issue for companies.

	Total next year	Region A	Region B	Region C
Managers under contract				
Sales staff under contract				
Sales staff by commission				
Admin. (secretarial)				
Other				
Total marketing personnel				

Figure 28.6 The marketing staff

MARKET RESEARCH PROJECTS NEXT YEAR (FIGURE 28.7)

- Marketing should be deeply involved in the new product development process.
- Information can be regarded as the raw material of the marketing process, so only obtain information that has high potential to add value.

Market research projects next year

Product research	Expenditures	Description
Existing product line 1 £	....	....
Existing product line 2 £	....	....
New products £	....	....
Advertising research £	....	....
Other research £	....	....

Figure 28.7 Market research yearly planning

Bibliography

REFERENCES AND FURTHER READING

Chapter 2

Peters T. (1989) *Thriving on Chaos*, London, Harper Collins.

Chapter 3

Palmer R. and Meldrum M. (1998) *The Future Of Marketing In Industrial And Technological Organisations*, Research Report, Cranfield School of Management, Cranfield University.

Chapter 4

McDonald M. (1995) *Marketing Plans. How to prepare them, how to use them*, 3rd edn, London, Butterworth Heinemann, p. 103.

Millier P. (1989) *Le marketing des produits high-tech – Outils d'analyse*, Paris, Editions d'Organisation, p. 228.

Millier P. (1999) *Marketing the Unknown*, London, J. Wiley & Sons, p. 198.

Roqueplo P. (1983) *Penser la technique. Pour une démocratie concrète*, Paris, Seuil.

Schultz D., Tannenbaum S.L. and Lauterborn R.F. (1993) *Integrated Marketing Communications*, NTC Business Books.

Senge P. (1990) *The Fifth Discipline*, London, Century Business.

Chapter 5

McDonald M. and Meldrum M. (1995) *Key Marketing Concepts*, London, Macmillan Press.

Michel D., Salle R. and Valla J-P. (1997) *Marketing Industriel*, Paris, Economica, Chap. 4.

Millier P. (1995) *Développer les Marchés Industriels. Principes de Segmentation*, Paris, Dunod, p. 129.

Millier P. (1999) *Marketing the Unknown*. London, J. Wiley & Sons, pp. 92–6.

Rangan K. and Isaacson B. (1994) 'What is Industrial Marketing?', Harvard Business School, 18 Sept.
Reicheld F. and Sasser W. Earl (1990) 'Zero Deflections: Quality comes to services', *Harvard Business Review*, Sept–Oct, pp. 301–7.
Salle R. (1985) 'Banalisation et stratégies concurrentielles en milieu industriel', *IRE*, June.
Salle R. and Silvestre H. (1992) *Vendre à l'industrie*, Paris, Editions de Liaison, p. 9.
Turnbull P. and Valla J.-P. (1986) *Strategies for International Industrial Marketing*, London, Croom Helm.
Webster F. (1974) *Industrial Marketing Strategy*, London, J. Wiley & Sons.
Williamson O. (1975) *Markets and Hierarchies: Analysis and Antitrust Implications*, New York, The Free Press.

Chapter 6

Millier P. (1999) *Marketing the Unknown*, London, J. Wiley & Sons.
Peters T. (1998) *Thriving on Chaos*, London, Harper Collins.

Chapter 7

Goleman D. (1998) *Working with Emotional Intelligence*, London, Bloomsbury Publishing.

Chapter 8

Bernoux P. (1985) *La sociologie des organisations*, Paris, Points Seuil.
Berry M. (1986) 'Logique de la connaissance et logique de l'action' in *La production des connaissances scientifiques de l'administration* edited by M. Audet and J.L. Malouin, Laval, Les presses de l'université, pp. 181–231.
Carnegie, Dale (1994) *How to Win Friends and Influence People*, Mass Market Paperback. Reissue Dorothy Carnegie and Arthur R. Pell (eds) January.
Goleman D. (1998) *Working with Emotional Intelligence*, London, Bloomsbury Publishing.
March J. and Simon H. (1958) *Organizations*, New York, J. Wiley & Sons.
Moriarty T. (1975) 'Crime, commitment and the responsive bystander: two field experiments', *Journal of Personality and Social Psychology*, 31, pp. 370–6.

Chapter 9

Buzan T. (1974) *Use your Head*, BBC Publications.
Malaval P. (1996) *Marketing Business to Business*, Paris, Publi-Union.
Michel D., Salle R. and Valla J.-P. (1997) *Marketing Industriel*, Paris, Economica.
Millier P. (1999) *Marketing the Unknown*, London, J. Wiley & Sons, p. 131.

Chapter 10

Majaro S. (1992) *Managing Ideas For Profit*, London, McGraw Hill.

Chapter 11

Black R. (1987) *Getting Things Done*, ed. Michael Joseph.
Gleeson K. (1994) *The Personal Efficiency Programme*, Chichester, J. Wiley & Sons.
Hobbs C. (1987) *Time Power The Revolutionary Time Management System That Can Change Your Professional and Personal Life*, New York, Harper & Row Publishers.

Chapter 12

McDonald M. (1995) *Marketing Plans. How to prepare them, how to use them*, London, Butterworth Heinemann, 3rd edn.
Millier P. (1999) *Marketing the Unknown*, London, J. Wiley & Sons, p. 198.
Webster F. (1974) *Industrial Marketing Strategy*, London, J.Wiley & Sons.

Chapter 13

Millier P. (1999a) *Cas SPYMAG*, Paris, CCMP. Sept.
Millier P. (1999b) *Marketing the Unknown*, London, J. Wiley & Sons, p. 209.

Chapter 14

Millier P. (1999) *Marketing the Unknown*, London, J. Wiley & Sons, p. 52.
Valla J.-P. (1985) Les décisions de la stratégie marketing en milieu industriel. Working paper, Lyon, IRE, Nov.

Chapter 15

Lilien G.L. (1981) 'Le rôle du gouvernement dans la diffusion des technologies nouvelles', *ISSEC Journées d'études*, 20 November.
McDonald M. (1995) *Marketing Plans. How to prepare them, how to use them*, London, Butterworth Heinemann, 3rd edn, pp. 133, 272.
Salle R. (1985) 'Banalisation et stratégies concurrentielles en milieu industriel', *IRE*, June.
Valla J.-P. (1985) Les décisions de la stratégie marketing en milieu industriel. Working paper, Lyon, IRE, Nov.

Chapter 16

Banting P. (1978) 'Unsuccessful innovation in the industrial markets', *Journal of Marketing*, January.

Buzzell R.D. and Gale B.T. (1987) *The PIMS Principles: Linking strategy to performance*, New York, The Free Press.

Miller G. (1956) 'The magical number, plus or minus two: some limits on our capacity for processing information', *Psychological Review*, vol. 63, no. 2, March.

Webster F. (1974) *Industrial Marketing Strategy*, London, J. Wiley & Sons.

Chapter 17

Dubois B. (1996) 'Marketing situationnel et consommateur Caméléon', *Revue Francaise de Gestion*, Sept–Oct.

Hakansson H. (ed) (1982) *Industrial Marketing and Purchasing of Industrial Goods. An interaction approach*, Chichester, J. Wiley & Sons.

Keiser T. (1989) 'Comment négocier avec un client qu'il ne faut pas perdre', *Harvard-Expansion*, Summer.

McDonald M. (1995) *Marketing Plans. How to prepare them, how to use them*, London, Butterworth Heinemann, 3rd edn.

Michel D., Salle R. and Valla J.-P. (1997) *Marketing Industriel*, Paris, Economica.

Salle R. (1989) 'Les méthodes et outils marketing développés par l'IRE En Milieu Industriel', *IRE*, Support de conférence, April.

Chapter 18

Michel D., Salle R. and Valla J.-P. (1997) *Marketing Industriel*, Paris, Economica.

PART VI Introduction

Morin P. (1980) 'Réponse au refus des produits nouveaux', *Revue Française de Gestion*, Jan.–Feb.

Chapter 19

Meldrum M. and Palmer R. (1998) 'The future of marketing in industrial and technological organisations', Research Report, Cranfield School of Management, Cranfield University.

Chapter 20

Allen T. (1977) *Managing the Flow of Technology*, Cambridge, Massachussetts, MIT Press, p. 239.

Millier P. (1999) *Marketing the Unknown*, London, J. Wiley & Sons, p. 27.

Chapter 21

Gupta A.K. and Rogers E.M. (1991) 'Internal marketing: integrating R&D and marketing within the organization', *The Journal of Consumer Marketing*, vol. 8, no. 3, Summer.

Gupta A.K. and Wilemon D. (1985) 'R&D and marketing dialogue in high tech firms', *Industrial Marketing Management*.

Gupta A.K. and Wilemon D. (1988) 'Why R&D resists using marketing information', *Research Technology Management*, vol. 31, no. 6, pp. 36–41, Nov.–Dec.

Millier P. (1989) *Le Marketing des Produits High-Tech – Outils d'Analyse*, Paris, Editions d'Organisation, p. 24.

von Hippel E. (1988) 'Trading Trade Secrets', *Technology Review*, Feb.–Mar.

PART VII Introduction

Millier P. (1989) *Le Marketing des Produits High-Tech – Outils d'Analyse*, Paris, Editions d'Organisation, p. 41.

Chapter 24

Millier P. (1995) *Développer les Marchés Industriels: Principes de segmentation*, Paris, Dunod.

Millier P. (1999) *Marketing the Unknown*, London, J. Wiley & Sons, chap. 4.

Chapter 25

Millier P. (1993) 'L'analyse des fonctions', Note technique, *IRE*, September.

Chapter 26

McDonald M. and Dunbar I. (1998) *Market Segmentation. How to do it, how to profit from it*, London, Macmillan Business, 2nd edn, p. 64.

Millier P. (1989) *Le Marketing des Produits High-Tech – Outils d'Analyse*, Paris, Editions d'Organisation, Ch. II.3.

Millier P. (1999) *Marketing the Unknown*, London, J. Wiley & Sons, pp. 92–96.

Salle R. and Silvestre H. (1992) *Vendre à l'Industrie*, Paris, Editions de Liaison.

Chapter 27

Cranfield Marketing Group (2000) *Marketing Management: A Relationship Marketing Perspective*, Basingstoke, Macmillan.

Millier P. (1999) *Marketing the Unknown*, London, J. Wiley & Sons, Ch. IV.

Chapter 28

McDonald M. (1995) *Marketing Plans. How to prepare them, how to use them*, London, Butterworth Heinemann, 3rd edn, p. 26.

Supplementary reading

Anderson J. and Narus J. (1999) *Business Market Management, Understanding, Creating and Delivering Customer Value*, Upper Saddle River, Prentice Hall.
Christopher M. (1997) *Marketing Logistics*, Oxford, Butterworth-Heinemann.
Cooper R. (1996) *Winning at New Products*, Wokingham, Addison-Wesley.
Ford D. (ed.), (1998) *Managing Business Relationships*, Chichester, John Wiley & Sons.
Gattorna J. and Walters D. (1996) *Managing the Supply Chain*, Basingstoke, Macmillan.
Kotler P., Armstrong G., Saunders J. and Wong V. (1996) *Principles of Marketing*, European Edition, London, Prentice Hall.
Murray J. and O'Driscoll A. (1996) *Strategy and Process in Marketing*, Hemel Hempstead, Prentice Hall.
Reichheld F. (1996) *The Loyalty Effect*, Boston MA, Harvard Business School Press.
Vandermerwe S. (1996) *The Eleventh Commandment. Transforming to Owning Customers*, Chichester, John Wiley & Sons.

Index